MW01092578

TREES of NEW ENGLAND

TREES of
NEW ENGLAND

A Natural History

Charles Fergus

Illustrations by Amelia Hansen

FALCONGUIDE®

GUILFORD, CONNECTICUT
HELENA, MONTANA

AN IMPRINT OF THE GLOBE PEQUOT PRESS

To buy books in quantity for corporate use
or incentives, call **(800) 962–0973, ext. 4551,**
or e-mail **premiums@GlobePequot.com.**

Copyright © 2005 by Charles Fergus

All rights reserved. No part of this book may be reproduced or transmitted in any form by any means, electronic or mechanical, including photocopying and recording, or by any information storage and retrieval system, except as may be expressly permitted by the 1976 Copyright Act or by the publisher. Requests for permission should be made in writing to The Globe Pequot Press, P.O. Box 480, Guilford, Connecticut 06437.

Falcon and FalconGuide are registered trademarks of Morris Book Publishing, LLC.

Illustrations by Amelia Hansen
Maps by Zach Parks © Morris Book Publishing, LLC.

Library of Congress Cataloging-in-Publication Data

Fergus, Charles.
  Trees of New England : a natural history / Charles Fergus ; illustrations by Amelia Hansen.
—1st ed.
    p. cm.
  Sumary: "Trees of New England is a natural history of the more than seventy tree species that grow in New England. The book includes detailed illustrations and range maps"—provided by the publisher.
  Includes bibliographical references and index.
  ISBN 0-7627-3795-6
  1. Trees—New England—Identification. 2. Trees—New England—Pictorial works. I. Hansen, Amelia. II. Title.
QK121.F47 2005
582.16'0974—dc22

Manufactured in the United States of America
First Edition/First Printing

The author and The Globe Pequot Press assume no liability for accidents happening to, or injuries sustained by, readers who engage in the activities described in this book.

To the memory of my father,
C. Leonard Fergus

Contents

Introduction

This book is not a field guide. Although the text gives information that can help a reader identify trees—and some of the illustrations and captions point out descriptive aspects of buds, leaves or needles, bark, and fruit—the purpose of *Trees of New England* is an altogether different one. The book is meant to take up where a field guide leaves off. It presents the natural history of the trees growing in New England: when and how they reproduce themselves; how their form or physical structure protects them from wind and snow, from cold or fire; how animals get food and shelter from trees; how people have used trees, both in the past and in modern times; and how diseases, insect pests, and environmental degradation are affecting trees today.

Trees have been and continue to be extremely important to the landscape, ecology, and economy of New England. The region was heavily forested when English Puritans first came ashore in 1620 at Plymouth Rock. They and subsequent settlers found a great forest interrupted by natural openings—bogs and fens, grasslands bordering rivers, and tracts denuded by lightning-sparked fires—as well as areas that Native Americans had cleared for agriculture and had burned off to provide forage for the animals they hunted, including deer. Over the next three centuries, English and European immigrants and their descendants cut down essentially all of the old-growth trees, using their wood and other products and clearing many acres of land to create farms.

As the twenty-first century opens, most of New England is again wooded. The trees cloaking the land are not necessarily tall, majestic specimens like those that greeted the settlers, but members of a younger forest, one that is in a state of flux, responding to influences of microscopic pathogens, introduced insect pests, pollution, rising global temperatures, and an expanding and ever more urbanized human population. Forest products make up a significant part of the region's economy. People spend many hours enjoying healthful outdoor recreation in woodlands: hiking, birding, hunting, snowshoeing, cross-country skiing. *Trees of New England* seeks to inform outdoor-oriented people about trees, with the goal of increasing their appreciation of our sylvan companions.

Trees, and the forests and copses and woodlots they form, serve many valuable functions. They limit soil erosion and protect watersheds by soaking up rainfall. They allow other organisms to live because they release oxygen as a by-product of photosynthesis. They help stabilize the earth's climate by absorbing carbon dioxide, a gas produced naturally and by humans burning fossil fuels. They yield wood, which we turn into a multitude of products, including fuel, paper, lumber for building our homes, and items as diverse as clothespins and fine furniture. They provide food: nuts and seeds for wildlife, maple syrup for humans.

All of the trees native to New England are described in this book, and range maps are included for almost seventy species. (The maps are drawn from the *Atlas of United States Trees,* by Elbert L. Little, published in book form by the USDA Forest Service and available in a digitized format on the World Wide Web: http://climchange.cr.usgs.gov/data/atlas/little.) The last chapter describes common introduced trees. Rather than placing the various species in a taxonomic order, as is usually done in field guides, they are arranged alphabetically, so that readers can more quickly find entries for specific trees. The indexes include other common or colloquial names by which people may know certain trees and scientific names.

Trees can be separated into two general categories: needle-leaved and broad-leaved. The needle-leaved trees, which number thirteen of the seventy-four species detailed in the text, are the older, less highly evolved group. They include balsam fir, eastern hemlock, the spruces, tamarack, the pines, and the cedars. Their needlelike foliage performs the same function as do the leaves of broad-leaved trees: They capture sunlight and then use it, in combination with water and nutrients picked up by the roots, to create carbohydrates, which fuel a tree's growth and reproduction. The needle-leaved trees are sometimes called conifers because they bear their seeds in cones or conelike structures. (Some of the broad-leaved species also present their seeds in cones.) People often call the needle-leaved trees evergreens, as they hold on to their verdant needles for more than one growing season—although one of the needle-bearing species, tamarack, sheds its needles each fall, right along with the broad-leaved trees.

The broad-leaved species evolved later than the needle-leaved trees. Instead of needles, broad-leaved trees possess leaves: flattened blades of different shapes and sizes, depending on the species and the individual tree. Photosynthesis takes place just below the leaf surface. Broad-leaved trees shed their foliage in autumn; if they did not, snow and ice would build up on the leaves, tearing them off and damaging the twigs and branches that bear them. Broad-leaved trees are also known as deciduous, referring to the periodic shedding or falling off of their foliage.

From the time I was a child, I have stood in awe of trees—not just the huge, impressive ones but also the scraggly types and sprawling sorts and gangly saplings, trees that branch low and trees that tower high. I find trees beautiful, intricate, and reassuring. They are plants, to be sure, but sometimes they seem to have minds of their own; clearly, they have strategies—embedded in their genes, if not the product of an intellect—to help them survive and prosper.

Trees are vibrantly alive. They cannot pick up their roots and wander, but they travel through the dispersal of their seeds. They move in the wind. Their branches sway. Their leaves clatter or whisper or rasp, their trunks groan and creak, their nuts thud the ground. They are steadfast, yet remarkably changeable. An exciting and rejuvenating aspect of trees is how different they appear at different times of the year. Trees are a key part of how I perceive nature and sense its ongoing cycles.

In spring the swollen buds promise that winter's austerity is nearing an end. Trees put forth flowers, including some that are quite beautiful, if rarely seen, high in the branches—flowers that develop into fruits and nuts of the utmost importance to many wild animals.

Summer's foliage covers up the frameworks of the deciduous trees, a forgivable event since the leaves are so young and soft-appearing and verdant, full of promise, perfect in shape and appearance. The leaves cast shade during the heat of high summer—shade that refreshes the woodland walker, shade that is essential for nesting birds, amphibians dwelling in moist nooks, trout finning in chill streams. By late summer the leaves have become tattered, pinholed, skeletonized, used by life; they remind us that time is limited and must come to an end for every living thing.

Most leaves change their color in autumn. Their energy-producing process, photosynthesis, shuts down when the days grow shorter and light becomes more limited. As their green chlorophyll breaks down, hidden pigments in the leaves are unmasked, and the forest becomes a kaleidoscope of bright colors set against the abiding green of the needle-leaved trees. The deciduous leaves come flurrying down. On the forest floor they deteriorate and release elements needed for plant and animal growth. Nuts fall, changing the behaviors and movement patterns of wildlife.

I think I like trees best of all in winter, when their shapes stand out boldly along city streets, on the edges of fields, and against the snowy forest floor. The forces and exigencies that affect a tree, and the lifestyle that it follows, can be seen in the shape and stature and soundness of its trunk and in its fruit, limbs, and twigs. Every tree, no matter how twisted or stunted, presents a fundamental and honest beauty.

— Charles Fergus
The Butternut Farm
East Burke, Vermont
January 2005

Alder

IF ONE FOLLOWS THE USDA Forest Service's definition of a tree—a woody plant attaining a height of 13 feet or more and having a single trunk at least 3 inches in diameter at breast height, or 4½ feet above the ground—then the alders do not qualify. Most of them are shrubs. But a book about New England trees that ignores these fascinating swamp dwellers is, to my way of thinking, incomplete.

Speckled Alder *(Alnus incana).* Speckled alder spans the continent from Labrador to the Yukon and extends south as far as West Virginia and Iowa; it is regionwide in New England. Other names include hoary alder and gray alder. (A superseded scientific name is *A. rugosa.*) Altogether, seven alder species occur in North America. Most are shrubby, although one—red alder, in the Pacific Northwest—attains the stature of a tree, sometimes standing 80 feet tall. The alders

are closely related to eastern hornbeam, ironwood, and the birches.

Alders grow best in wet but well-drained soils that are sandy or gravelly. They require full sunlight. Usually an alder arises as a composite plant consisting of several to many crooked, branching trunks, all springing from a central rootstock. The egg-shaped leaves are 2 to 5 inches long, with prominent veins and toothed edges. They feel thick and leathery to the touch and sometimes have a rippled or wrinkled aspect. In summer alder leaves are a deep glossy green, darker on top than on the bottom. In autumn they turn bronze-yellow or take on a brownish cast before falling.

Speckled alder is so named because the bark on twigs, stems, and trunk is heavily stippled with pale yellow speckles. The speckles are lenticels, pores that permit the exchange of gases between the plant's interior tissues and the surrounding air. Look for speckled alder on flats alongside streams, in swamps, in damp depressions, and in areas that flood in spring. Its leaves are the same size as those of smooth alder, but speckled alder leaves differ slightly: They have coarsely toothed edges (the edges of smooth alder leaves are more finely toothed), and they are not rippled or wavy.

In April, before an alder leafs out, its flowers open and expand into furry catkins. Male and female flowers may occur on the same twig. Wind carries pollen from the male to the female flowers. Over the summer the fertilized female flowers develop into conelike structures that open in autumn to release small, winged seeds. Empty cones may hang on the twigs until the following year. The cones—rounded, woody, and about ½ inch long—look like miniature pine cones.

Most alders stand no taller than 10 feet, although the occasional specimen will reach 20 or 25 feet. The trunks, or stems, are rarely larger than 4 inches in diameter. Eight, ten, even twenty stems issue from a clump. Often they curve outward before bending up, on account of heavy snow having flattened them when they were young. Thickets of young alders can be almost impenetrable.

Alders have shallow root systems. Like aspens and some other trees, alders can reproduce vegetatively: Their roots radiate out through the soil, then send up other stems several feet away from the parent plant. This underground root network with its attached, aboveground stems is called a clone. The roots of neighboring alder clones mesh with each other and sometimes even graft themselves together. Along a stream, interwoven alder roots help anchor the soil and prevent bank erosion.

The roots serve another function important to the ecology of bogs. They possess nodules, small bumps located just beneath the surface of the soil, in which nitrogen-fixing microorganisms live. The alders supply the microbes with organic food, and, in turn, the microbes give the alders nitrogen in a form that the trees can use. Such a mutually beneficial relationship is called symbiosis. The microbes also release nitrogen into the bog soil, a highly anaerobic and acidic environment where nitrogen, an element essential for plant growth, is scarce. Alder leaves are rich in nitrogen, and when the stems shed their leaves in fall and the leaves subsequently break down, more usable nitrogen enters the soil.

Beavers eat the buds and bark of alders and use the remaining woody parts for building or repairing their dams and lodges. Moose often feed on alder. White-tailed deer browse alder, although it is not a preferred item in their diet; some sources call it starvation food. Cottontail rabbits and

Alders carry their seeds in small cones. The developing fruits are borne farther out on the twigs than the previous year's cones.

snowshoe hares eat twigs and bark, and ruffed grouse take buds and catkins. In autumn, goldfinches, chickadees, redpolls, and pine siskins eat alder seeds.

Alders may be more important to wildlife as cover than as a food source. Woodcock often rest on the ground in alder stands, probing their bills into the soft soil in search of earthworms, a favorite food, while overhead the crowded, interwoven branches shield them from hawks and owls. Deer hide amid the dense growth; in October and November I find alder stems much scuffed and frayed by buck deer, which, seized by the rut, slash their antlers at the pliant trunks. In spring and summer many birds nest in alder thickets. The alder flycatcher gets its name from this favored habitat. Yellow-bellied flycatchers, yellow warblers, common yellowthroats, red-winged blackbirds, and swamp sparrows also nest in alders. Ducks rest on potholes and small streams that wander through alder areas.

"No commercial value," say the tree texts, since the trunks of alders are insufficiently straight and thick to yield marketable timber. Yet this plant offers much more.

Smooth Alder *(Alnus serrulata)*. Quite similar to speckled alder, smooth alder ranges from western Nova Scotia and southern New Brunswick south to Florida and Texas. It occurs in a swath from southern Maine across the middle of New England; it is absent from northern New Hampshire and Vermont. Smooth alder is sometimes called hazel alder, common alder, or tag alder. This wiry plant grows along streams, lake margins, and bogs.

Ash

BOTANISTS RECOGNIZE BETWEEN SIXTY AND seventy species of ash trees across the Northern Hemisphere. Sixteen species occur in North America, including three in New England. The ashes belong to family Oleaceae, the olives, and are closely related to the well-known shrubs forsythia, privet, and lilac.

Ash trees have strong links to legend and mythology. Early Germanic peoples believed that a giant ash, Yggdrasil, supported the universe. One of the tree's roots extended into the underworld, another into the land of the giants, and a third into the home of the gods; dew that dripped from the tree's leaves made flowers spring up all over the earth. Scholars suggest that this "world tree" concept is reflected in today's maypole and Christmas tree traditions. English and European settlers brought with them a sense of awe regarding the ash, and in America they found ash trees very similar to the ones they had known in the Old World. To some immigrants, a door framed with ash was a "witch door" that warded off evil spirits. Others placed ash leaves in their boots and leggings, believing that no snake would ever cross such a barrier. If bitten by a snake, they treated the wound with preparations made from the buds and bark of ash.

White Ash *(Fraxinus americana)*. The largest and most abundant ash species in the Northeast, and the most valuable one for lumber, is white ash. It is a medium to large tree that grows in forests and open upland habitats from Nova Scotia west across southern Canada to Michigan and Minnesota, and south to Florida and Texas. White ash is regionwide in New England. (At one time taxonomists recognized a separate species, Biltmore ash, whose twigs are velvety and hairier than those of white ash, but today Biltmore ash is considered to be a variety of white ash.)

A mature white ash will stand 70 to 80 feet tall, with a trunk 2 to 3 feet in diameter; old-growth trees can reach more than 120 feet tall, with a trunk diameter of 6 feet. An immense white ash has been located in the Mohawk Trail State Forest in western Massachusetts: It is 145 feet tall and has a girth of more than 9 feet. The trunk of white ash tends to be quite straight and, on a forest-grown tree, clear of branches and branch scars for a considerable distance from the ground up.

Ash trees are among the slowest trees to leaf out in spring. In northeastern Vermont, where I live, the leaves do not come out fully until the last days of May. The compound leaves stand opposite each other on stout, gray-brown twigs. A single leaf is 8 to 12 inches long and composed of five to nine leaflets. Each leaflet measures 3 to 5 inches long by about 1½ inches wide and stands off from the main stem on a short stalk. Leaflets may be slightly toothed along their margins or not toothed at all. Lance-shaped and tapering to a point, the leaflets are a lustrous dark green above and silver-white below. Often a tree's leaflets do not appear to be parts of a compound structure, but rather a collection of individual leaves. In general the foliage is thickest on the outer fringes of a white ash, and an observer leaning against the trunk usually can look up and see the sky through the rather sparse crown.

The columnar trunk of the white ash is clad with distinctive bark made up of long, narrow, diamond-shaped fissures running lengthwise with the trunk. Fine, tight, slightly flat-topped ridges intersect with one another and stand between the diamond fissures. From a distance, the pattern suggests the reticulated skin of a snake. Some field guides state that the bark of the white ash is dark, but most of the ashes I see have medium gray or pale gray-brown bark. It is believed that the tree's common name comes from the bark's color, which resembles wood ash. (This ancient name presumably was first used to describe the European ash, *F. excelsior.*)

White ash does best in rich, moist, well-drained soil. It thrives along streams and lakes and rarely grows in swamps. Ashes tend to come up singly or in small clusters rather than in extensive same-species stands. White ash is vulnerable to drought, especially in spring and early summer.

Individual trees are either male or female. Trees of both sexes send out flowers just before they leaf out or while they are putting forth their leaves. Usually more male than female trees flower. The male flowers hang in dense, reddish purple clusters; the female flowers are also clustered but are airier and not crowded together as tightly. The wind carries pollen from the male to the female blossoms. Over summer, the female reproductive structures grow and mature into samaras, or keys. An ash samara is 1 to 2 inches long and consists of a seed encased in a thin husk, with a papery wing. Its overall shape and rounded tip resemble the blade of a canoe paddle. Ash samaras dangle in drooping clusters of a dozen or more seeds; they are not paired like maple samaras. In November and December it is easy to tell female ash trees from the males, for it is the former whose crowns are thick with samaras. The samaras gradually fall off the twigs through the winter. Seeds can lie dormant in the leaf litter on the forest floor for up to seven years.

Mature trees produce good seed crops about every third year. The wind may carry the samaras 400 feet or farther. Wood ducks, bobwhite quail, purple finches, pine grosbeaks, and squirrels eat white ash seeds; no doubt other wild animals also feed on them. Rabbits, beavers, and porcupines eat the bark of young trees, and deer and moose browse on twigs, foliage, and seedlings.

Early in its life, white ash is remarkably tolerant of shade. A seedling growing in deep shade may rise only a foot in fifteen years. However, its root system becomes quite well developed, letting the seedling respond rapidly if a neighboring tree dies or falls, opening up a gap in the canopy toward which the ash can lift its crown. The young trees have few branches; to minimize snow and ice loading, the boughs reach upward in a candelabra shape. As trees grow older, they become less shade tolerant and structurally sturdier. White ash generally forms a taproot that splits into several downward-growing roots, with side roots branching off at intervals. Stumps cut low to the ground freely send up shoots that may develop into new trees.

Both the leafstalks and the leaflets of white ash are opposite. White ash is found in dry to moist woods.

In autumn white ash begins to change its leaf color earlier than almost any other tree. In a dry year the foliage may simply turn a dull bronze and fall off; in other years the leaves become a beautiful purplish blue or burgundy. In *A Natural History of Trees,* Donald Culross Peattie nominated ash as "the most versatile colorist of all our woods," supplying, as it does, "the bronze and mauve tints that are the rarest in our autumn displays." I have noticed that the ashes here on the Butternut Farm are the earliest trees to drop their leaves in autumn, with the exception of the butternut trees for which our home place is named. After ash leaves fall to the ground, they enrich the soil with high levels of sugars and nitrogen.

Ash has some of the toughest wood, pound for pound, of all the American trees. It weighs about forty-two pounds per cubic foot, which is lighter than white oak and sugar maple, about the same as red oak, and heavier than red maple. Ash wood is strong and flexible, able to withstand sudden shocks. Native Americans used it for snowshoe frames, canoe paddles, and sleds—products that are made from ash to this day. Recently I bought a pair of snowshoes from Rick and Marie Boutin of Williamsville, Vermont. The shoes' frames are made from local ash, which the Boutins bend into the shape they need after heating the wood and saturating it with steam. On each of my shoes, a single piece of 1-inch by 1-inch wood is bent all the way back on itself and riveted together for the last 6 inches to form the tail. Crosspieces are of ash, and the whole is strung with rawhide lacing.

Settlers built wagon frames from ash; they also fashioned butter tubs from it, since the wood is flavorless and odorless. Today ash gets turned into tool handles (especially long tools, such as rakes, shovels, hoes, and scythes), oars, skis, porch swings, polo mallets, hockey sticks, and baseball bats. The noted Louisville Slugger, used by most major league ballplayers, comes from white ash cut mainly in northern Pennsylvania and southern New York. Buyers select young trees 16 to 18 inches in trunk diameter; larger than that, and the wood becomes "brash," lacking in resilience. White ash is a handsome wood with a warm, blonde color. I laid it as flooring in our house and had a local cabinetmaker use ash for our kitchen cabinets.

White ash is an excellent firewood that splits easily and can be burned even in a green or unseasoned state. Some authorities credit this property to flammable sap; in fact, white ash simply has a lower natural moisture content than other woods. An old English poem goes: "Ash wet or ash dry, a king will warm his slippers by." Over the years I have burned a fair amount of ash in heating my house, and it seems to me that the wood yields more ash than almost any other species of tree; I guess that makes its name even more apt.

Joseph Illick, the state forester for Pennsylvania in the early twentieth century, ranked ash among the premier timber trees, in part because of its "immunity from the attack of fungous diseases and insects." Unfortunately, ashes are nowhere near so healthy today. A generalized malady known as ash decline or ash die-back appeared in the Northeast in the 1980s and has stricken many trees. Scientists are unsure of the cause or causes but believe that drought, fungi, air pollution, and viruses may combine to play a role. A microbe classified as a mycoplasma-like organism, or MLO, has been isolated from the phloem or food-conducting tissue of ash trees afflicted with ash yellows, a possibly related disease. Sick trees grow slowly, have patchy foliage and stunted leaves, and turn colors prematurely in autumn. Branches die back, cracks appear in the trunk, spindly shoots arise from the trunk's base, and some ashes eventually die from the condition.

What has changed between the early 1900s and today? An increase in air pollution has resulted in acid rain and snow. It would not surprise me if such ongoing environmental degradation lay behind the decline of this beautiful, useful tree.

Black Ash *(Fraxinus nigra).* Black ash is a smaller, slenderer tree than its better-known relative, the white ash. A mature black ash may stand 60 to 80 feet tall, with a trunk diameter of 1 to 2 feet, although most black ashes encountered in the woods will be considerably smaller than that. State record trees in Maine and Vermont stand 78 feet and 84 feet, respectively, and have crowns that spread only 22 feet and 33 feet. Several black ashes grow in a low, wet area between a cou-

ple of hills in our forest in northeastern Vermont. They are typical for the species: around 30 feet tall, their trunks crooked and leaning, the branches extending strongly upward.

The northernmost of the ashes, *F. nigra* prefers cool, damp habitats and often grows in bogs, along streams, and in poorly drained floodplains. It occurs from Newfoundland west to Manitoba and south to Delaware,

West Virginia, Illinois, and Iowa. In New England the species' range takes in Maine, most of New Hampshire except for the southern part of the state, Vermont, western Massachusetts, and western Connecticut. Black ash grows on peaty soils, and on sandy and loamy soils underlain by a limiting layer of clay that contributes to a high water table. Two trees often found growing with black ash are red maple and American elm, both of which grow more rapidly than *F. nigra*. Black ash also grows in mixed stands along with northern white-cedar, balsam fir, black spruce, white spruce, eastern hemlock, tamarack, yellow birch, and paper birch.

Distinguish black ash by its wedge-shaped leaflets, which attach directly to the compound leaf's central stem rather than standing off on short stalks as do the leaflets of white ash; the leaflets have toothed margins. In black ash the overall composite leaf is 12 to 16 inches long—somewhat longer than that of white ash. In autumn the leaves turn a rusty brown, with no particular color variation. The bark of black ash may be tight and furrowed or somewhat scaly. Corky ridges on the bark can be rubbed off fairly easily with the fingers. The buds are extremely dark, almost black.

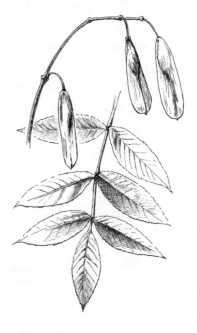

The seed-carrying samaras of black ash are almost rectangular in shape, and the leaflets of this wetlands tree attach directly to the stem.

Black ash flowers before it puts forth leaves in April or May. The fruit ripens in August or September, and the seeds let go between October and the following spring. The seeds are borne in samaras, which have blunt ends. (The samaras of white ash possess rounded ends.) Seeds may lie dormant on the ground for two to eight years before germinating. When a black ash is cut down, it sprouts readily from the stump. Deer browse young sprouts and seedlings heavily.

Two other names for this tree are hoop ash and basket ash. Craft workers will split a black ash billet into small sticks, then set a piece upright on a flat surface and, using a mallet, pound it on the end grain. The impact causes the wood to split into sheets along the annual growth rings. Cut into thin strips, or splints, and soaked in water for added pliancy, the splints can be woven into baskets and chair seats. People also use the tough, resilient wood for barrel hoops, oars, and furniture. Black ash probably gets its name from its dark heartwood. Its wood is neither as strong nor as hard as white ash.

Green Ash *(Fraxinus pennsylvanica)*. Green ash and red ash were once considered separate species (the latter has hairy twigs, the former doesn't), but now taxonomists merge the two under the generally accepted name of green ash. On a recent September day, I located several mature green ash trees at Button Bay State Park in Vermont, where they grew alongside large silver maples on the edge of a backwater of Lake Champlain. Green ash grows to a height of about 75 feet 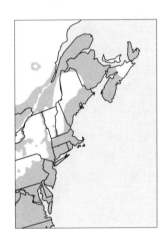 (50 to 60 feet is more usual, and some individuals can reach 100 feet) in wet habitats such as bottomland woods, stream banks, and moist fields. Green ash has shallow roots that spread wide, making it quite wind-firm. A study in North Dakota found that a green ash 38 feet tall had roots that had spread 48 feet laterally and penetrated 3.6 feet downward. Green ash tolerates soils that are even damper, and ones that remain flooded for longer periods of time, than does the closely related black ash.

Green ash grows from Atlantic Canada west to the Rocky Mountain states and south to Florida and Texas, the largest range of any North American ash. In New England it is found in northern and coastal Maine, the Champlain Valley in Vermont, parts of southern Vermont, southeastern New Hampshire, and throughout Massachusetts, Rhode Island, and Connecticut. Trees commonly growing along with green ash are box-elder, red maple, sycamore, eastern cottonwood, black willow, and American elm. On a lowland site, green ash may follow after and succeed eastern cottonwood, quaking aspen, or black willow. More rapidly growing species, such as red maple and American elm, ultimately outstrip green ash, so that the proportion of *F. pennsylvanica* in a mixed elm/ash/maple stand usually decreases as the years go by.

Green ash tends to be branchier and to have a more crooked trunk than white ash. The gray-brown bark is fairly tight and interrupted by closely spaced furrows and ridges. The composite leaves consist of leaflets on short stalks attached to a central stem. The leaflets number five to nine per leaf; some have toothed edges, and some do not. The twigs are either hairless or velvety. Overall, the leaves measure 10 to 12 inches long. I identified the green ashes growing along Lake Champlain by examining their bark and leaves. And since it was autumn, I was able to study their fruits, which are called samaras; the samaras of green ash are narrow and wedge-shaped, with a papery wing that stops short of its base. The seed, housed inside a thin skin, is plump and narrowly pointed at both ends. Green ash usually begins to produce fruits when it has gained a trunk diameter of 3 to 4 inches and become 20 feet tall.

Although green ash is found almost exclusively in lowlands, it will thrive when transplanted into moist upland soils. Green ash has been widely planted as a street tree, an ornamental, and a shelterbelt tree, particularly in the western states. In Pennsylvania and West Virginia, land managers have used groves of green ash to reforest lands disturbed by strip-mining.

The wood of *F. pennsylvanica* is heavy, at forty-four pounds per cubic foot, and it is hard, strong, and flexible. Generally loggers and lumber mills do not distinguish it from white ash, and it has been used for many of the same applications, including tool handles, wagon frames, and canoe paddles.

Aspen

IN THE LATE 1970S, THE owner of our land in northeastern Vermont sold off the timber in the hills to the west of the house. Chain saws whined, a log skidder growled, and where a forest of spruce, fir, maple, and birch had stood, tangles of branches and leafy treetops littered the ground. Within a year or two, blackberries would have pushed up between the stumps. And soon new trees would have been evident on the sunbathed slopes, among them bigtooth aspens, straight thin shoots lifting their apple-green leaves skyward.

Botanists regard aspens as pioneer species, able to quickly establish themselves on abandoned fields or lands where logging, avalanche, disease, or fire suddenly wipe out a stand of trees. In spring aspens produce millions of tiny seeds, each tufted with white plant down. The wind scatters the seeds over miles. If they land on bare ground, the seeds germinate quickly and begin turning disturbed lands back into forest.

Two closely related species of aspen grow throughout New England: big tooth aspen and quaking aspen. Quaking aspen prefers dry sites, especially sandy or gravelly soil. Bigtooth aspen colonizes dry, gravelly habitats, and it also thrives on rich, moist sites, including floodplains. In general it is slightly taller and longer-lived than its quaking cousin. Both species are known as "poplar" and "popple."

Bigtooth Aspen *(Populus grandidentata).* Bigtooth aspen ranges from Nova Scotia west across southern Canada to Minnesota, and south to North Carolina and Kentucky. It is found on suitable sites throughout New England.

Bigtooth aspen is a small- to medium-size tree. Most specimens top out at 30 to 40 feet, although on good growing sites they may achieve 80 or even 100 feet. At maturity, the trunk is 1 to 2 feet in diameter, straight and with little taper, and often clear of branches for more than two-thirds of its height. The crown is narrow, rounded, and open. In general bigtooth aspens are short-lived: Sixty years is reckoned a long life, although the root system, or clone, from which the trunk may have sprung is often very much older. (See the description of quaking aspen for an explanation of aspen clones and their potential antiquity.)

The bark of a young bigtooth aspen is pale olive green with a hint of gold. The bark is greenish because, like the leaves, it is living tissue, housing cells that contain the green pigment chlorophyll. During photosynthesis, chlorophyll captures the sun's energy and uses it to change water and carbon dioxide into energy-rich sugar for fueling the tree's life processes and growth. The life-giving gas oxygen is a by-product of photosynthesis. The dark, horizontal welts on the smooth bark of aspens and some other trees are lenticels, pores allowing the exchange of gases between the stem's internal tissues and the atmosphere. As an aspen ages, its bark thickens, becoming harder and rougher and taking on a dark gray-brown color, and sometimes turning almost black; this color change starts at the base of the trunk and proceeds upward. The upper trunk and the limbs keep their photosynthesis-capable bark with its distinctive green-gold color. A beautiful color it is, especially in winter when the low sun lights up the vertical gold stripes of a stand of aspens, often the only brightness in the woods.

As the tree's name suggests, bigtooth aspen has a leaf with large teeth along its outer margin. The quaking aspen leaf, by comparison, has many more, smaller teeth. The bigtooth's leaves are shaped like a heart, minus the deep notch. They are 3 to 4 inches long, deep green above and paler green below. The leafstalk, or petiole, is flattened and thin, like a ribbon, so that the least breeze sets the blade pivoting on its stalk. Bigtooth aspen is one of the first trees to leaf out in spring. According to J. H. White in *The Forest Trees of Ontario*, bigtooth aspen is "at once picked out in the forest when the leaves are unfolding in the spring by the downy appearance of the whole crown contrasted with the green of other species." In autumn the leaves turn a soft yellow, with a few trees turning orange or red.

In winter, when leaves are not present, one can tell bigtooth aspen from quaking aspen by examining the leaf buds, located on the twigs and containing the next year's foliage. On quaking aspen, the buds are shiny and less than ⅜ inch long; on bigtooth aspen the buds are dull and longer than ⅜ inch.

Wild animals dote on both aspen species. In March and April porcupines eat the drooping, fuzzy flower spikes, or catkins, some of the first new vegetation in the forest; in summer they nip off branch tips, where the most nutritious leaves grow. Black bears climb into aspens—or bend them down to the ground—to get at the new leaves in spring. Snowshoe hares and cottontail rabbits nibble the shoots and bark. White-tailed deer and moose browse twigs and foliage. Beavers prefer aspen to almost any other tree; the large rodents gnaw down aspens, eat the tender growing tissues and the bark on the branches and trunk, and use the leftover wood to build and maintain their dams and lodges.

The conservationist Aldo Leopold, a Wisconsinite, wrote of the aspen in *A Sand County Almanac*: "He glorifies October and he feeds my grouse in winter." Several times I have watched ruffed grouse eating aspen buds. In the day's last light, the birds alight in a winter-bare tree. Their feathers fluffed against the cold, they clamber about on the swaying branches, using their beaks to wrench off the energy-packed buds. They fill their crops quickly, in consideration of hawks and owls, and then take off in a thunder of wings and disappear into the gathering dusk. Aspen buds and catkins are favorite foods of the ruffed grouse throughout the bird's range, which largely coincides with the range of bigtooth and quaking aspen in North America.

Aspen is considered a "soft hardwood." The wood of bigtooth aspen is close-grained, brittle, weak, and fairly light at twenty-nine pounds per cubic foot, dry weight. The heartwood is pale brown, the sapwood greenish white. The wood goes for crates, pallets, excelsior, matchsticks, tongue depressors, ice cream spoons,

Both bigtooth and quaking aspens often grow as clones: interlinked stands of genetically identical trees sprouting from a common root system.

furniture parts, and interior house trim. Some aspens develop a rippling grain pattern, and such highly figured wood has been applied as a veneer on cabinetry and furniture. Aspen is often pulped, then turned into paper for magazines and books. Since the 1980s, aspen has increasingly been manufactured into building products such as oriented strand board (OSB) and I-beams, with chips or strands of the wood glued to form sheets and structural framing members.

Aspens belong to the willow family, Salicaceae, a group of species whose members contain the compound salicin in their bark. Salicin is the key ingredient in aspirin. In the past, Native Americans used aspen bark to treat fevers, coughs and colds, and menstrual pains.

When hiking or snowshoeing through our woods, I keep an eye on the aspens. The ones in the old fields north of the house are doing fine; often

I will flush a grouse from among them. In the hills that were logged in the seventies, some of the trees are already in decline, only a quarter of a century after they sprouted, now being shaded out by yellow birch and paper birch. Dried-out fruiting bodies of wood-decay fungi stud the trunks, and the boles of some of the trees have snapped off about halfway up. Woodpeckers have chiseled out nest cavities in rotting snags. The places where the aspens look healthiest are where the trees can still intercept plenty of sunlight: along the edges of old woods roads and log landings.

A process known as forest succession is taking place. The swift-growing aspens stabilized the soil on the logged slopes. They captured nutrients released by the rapid decay of branches and leaf litter, spurred by the increased temperature of the exposed forest floor. Enough sunlight had filtered down through their relatively open crowns to let the slower-growing birches, maples, and ashes thrive. The longer-lived hardwoods are now catching up with and outstripping the pioneering aspens.

Quaking Aspen *(Populus tremuloides)*. If even a faint breeze stirs the air, the leaves of the quaking aspen will dance and flutter, twisting on their pliant stems. The undersides of the leaves show silvery, then the green upper surfaces display their slick sheen, in a ceaseless, energetic, back-and-forth flashing that makes the observer wonder if the tree itself is generating light rather than simply reflecting it.

Small teeth rim the leaf's margin. The blade of a quaking aspen leaf—the main, sun-catching part—is round with a pointed tip. The leafstalk is flattened, thin, and longer than the blade. The stalk acts as a pivot, presenting one side of the leaf to the wind, then the other. Some scientists suggest that this near-constant motion helps the leaf get rid of excess moisture in much the same way that a handkerchief waving in the wind dries faster than one hanging in still air. The aspens belong to a group of trees known as the poplars, whose leaves all "quake" to some extent. Poplars grow rapidly, raising their crowns high and intercepting more sunlight than slower-growing, longer-lived trees. The poplars need to process a large volume of water to shoot up so quickly, and perhaps the quaking habit is a moisture-shedding strategy that keeps their growth systems operating at full throttle.

Quaking aspen (also called trembling aspen) has a larger natural range than any other North American tree. It grows from Newfoundland to Alaska, throughout New England and the Great Lakes states, and south in the Appalachian Mountains to Georgia and in the Rocky Mountains to northern Mexico. Aspens are extremely cold-hardy. They can survive temperatures as low as -80 degrees Fahrenheit. Forest ecologists suggest that aspens are genetically equipped to survive winters of a severity unknown since the last ice age.

Quaking aspens quickly reforest unstable or damaged habitats such as fire-charred woodlands, avalanche slides, gravel banks, and logged-over areas. They seed themselves onto abandoned fields. They prefer dry habitats but will sprout in most places and in almost all soil conditions except swamps. Aspens have a short life span—around sixty years—and are succeeded by hardwoods and conifers that grow more gradually in the partial shade cast by the aspens' relatively open foliage. Richly diverse shrub and herb communities often cover the ground beneath aspen stands.

Aspens are either male or female. Before leafing out in spring, trees of both sexes put forth dangling fuzzy flowers, called catkins. The wind blows pollen from the male to the female flowers. Later the wind scatters the downy seeds that have developed from the fertilized female flowers. The seeds are tiny and light (two to three million weigh one pound), so that the wind can disperse them; they do not carry much energy with them, in contrast to a nut such as an acorn, which is chock-full of carbohydrates to be used by the new plant as it seeks to establish itself. An aspen seed remains viable for only two to four weeks. The microscopic rootlets that the seed produces cannot penetrate through leaf litter; to survive, the seed must fall on bare ground.

An aspen seedling can stand 4 feet tall after only one year of growth. In its second year the sapling slows its upward growth while its roots spread out horizontally underground. In addition to reproducing sexually by means of seeds, aspens spread through vegetative reproduction, similar to the way a strawberry or a grass plant enlarges itself by sending forth runners, which themselves send down roots and give rise to stems. From an aspen's roots, new shoots or stems—botanists call them ramets—grow vertically. These new shoots develop into trees, complete with branches, leaves, and bark. A root may snake along for 100 feet before sending up a stem, and each new stem then sends out its own roots that sprout additional stems.

This unit of interlinked trees, all of them genetically identical, is called a clone. A typical clone may have a hundred stems and spread to a width of 80 or more feet. In the Wasatch Mountains in Utah, researchers in 1993 documented a quaking aspen clone that covered 106 acres and weighed an estimated thirteen million pounds, nearly three times heavier than the

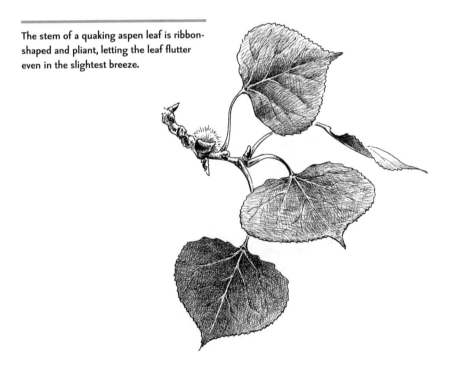

The stem of a quaking aspen leaf is ribbon-shaped and pliant, letting the leaf flutter even in the slightest breeze.

world's largest sequoia tree. The scientists gave the clone a name—Pando, a Latin word meaning "I spread"—and proclaimed it "the most massive living organism in the world." East of the Rocky Mountains, clones are believed to be smaller, usually no more than a few acres in extent.

A clone's extensive and intricate root network can shuttle water and nutrients from one part of the organism to another, a strategy that lets aspens thrive in a patchy environment. When fire or logging wipes out a clone's standing shoots, the root system immediately sends up thousands of new stems. In Pennsylvania a forester found 24,792 stems per acre of quaking aspen in a tract that had recently been lumbered. In the West, researchers have counted densities of 400,000 aspen stems per acre.

An individual aspen stem may live 200 years and achieve a height of 100 feet, although most do not live much beyond 60 or grow taller than 40 feet. But how old is the plant from which the tree may have arisen? A Minnesota clone has been aged at 8,000 years. Some researchers suggest that aspen clones may achieve an age of a million years or more. "In principal," writes botanist Michael Grant, one of the discoverers of Pando, "clones may even be essentially immortal, dying only from disease or the deterioration of the environment rather than from some internal clock."

Observant outdoor people can recognize clones and may be able to distinguish between the several clones that often merge to make up an aspen stand. The angle between individual branches and the main trunk tends to be a genetically determined trait: Branches on the trunks of one clone may angle off at 45 degrees, while those of another clone may form 60-degree angles. Different clones may leaf out at slightly different times in the spring. Autumn colors can vary from one clone to the next. Writes Grant, "Some clones turn a brilliant, shining yellow," while "others manifest a deep, rich gold, vibrating with many overtones. The leaves of still other aspens turn red; some show a barely perceptible tinge, others a rich scarlet." Here in northern Vermont the vast majority of quaking aspens turn a clear, rich yellow.

The wood of quaking aspen is very light: twenty-five pounds per cubic foot, dry weight. Soft, weak, and brittle, it is used for all of the products made from the bigtooth aspen. A neighbor of mine has a bedroom floor made of quaking aspen: The wood is generally considered too soft for flooring, but since a bedroom does not receive much foot traffic, it has worn adequately well, and its buttery-and-brown colors are quite lovely. Quaking aspen is the species most commonly logged for paper pulp, particularly in the Great Lakes states, with timber companies taking full advantage of the tree's ability to sprout prolifically after clear-cutting.

Wildlife feeds heavily on the buds, bark, and leaves of quaking aspen. Birds such as black-capped chickadees, white-breasted nuthatches, tufted titmice, and woodpeckers dig out nest cavities in decayed, standing aspen trunks. Forest tent caterpillars and gypsy moth caterpillars eat the leaves of aspens, sometimes defoliating thousands of acres. Entomologists have discovered that the aspens react chemically to an insect attack: Soon after the caterpillars start chewing, the trees' remaining leaves produce bitter-tasting phenol compounds to discourage further feeding.

Quaking aspen is an attention-grabbing tree year-round. In winter it shows off its attractive upright form and chalky white to pale yellow-green branches. In spring the fuzzy catkins and lime green new leaves give *P. tremuloides* a texture all its own in the forest tapestry. In summer the perpetual shimmering of the coinlike leaves dazzles the eye of the beholder. The sound generated by an aspen stand is akin to rushing water, ceaseless and ceaselessly changing, full of bright tones, pleasantly lulling. In fall the trees light up the hills like the flickering flames of a thousand candles.

Balsam Fir

Balsam Fir *(Abies balsamea)*. The word balsam comes from the ancient Greek *balsamon,* referring to a Middle Eastern shrub from which myrrh, an ingredient in perfume and incense, is obtained. A North American evergreen tree, balsam fir earns its name from the fragrance of its needles. In the overgrown fields on our farm in northern Vermont grow dozens of balsam fir seedlings. The knee- and waist-high trees are strongly cone-shaped. Branches circle each trunk, jut-

ting out laterally from the main stem at nearly right angles. The tiered boughs, regular and symmetrical, hold up gleaming, dark green needles. When hiking, I will often strip off a few of the needles and crush them between my fingers to smell their tangy citrus essence.

Balsam fir is the only fir species native to the Northeast. It grows from northern Labrador, Quebec, and Ontario south to the mountains of Virginia and West Virginia; westward, *A. balsamea* ranges to northern Alberta. In New England balsam fir is found in northern Maine and New Hampshire, throughout Vermont, and in western Massachusetts. It joins red spruce and white spruce as the three main species in the northeastern spruce-fir forest that cloaks some eleven million acres in New England and New York.

Balsam fir is a small- to medium-size tree. It generally reaches a height of 30 to 50 feet and occasionally achieves 75 feet. A short-lived species, it seldom persists longer than about eighty years. Its preferred habitat is moist woods. In New England and Canada balsam fir also grows on drier sites, along with white spruce, red spruce, quaking aspen, and paper birch. On high mountains, such as the spines of the Green Mountains of Vermont, balsam fir and black spruce mingle; as elevation increases, the trees gradually become smaller in stature until, reaching the limit of tree growth near the highest summits, both species grow as low shrubs.

Balsam fir needles are about ¾ inch long, flattened, and arranged in a pair of opposing rows that at first glance appear to fringe the twigs. In fact, the needles spiral around the twigs, a characteristic that can be discerned through a magnifying lens. You can tell balsam fir from the superficially similar hemlock by the fir's classic steeple shape and the whorled arrangement of its branches (hemlock is more irregular in shape and branch pattern); by the needles attached directly to the twig (hemlock needles stand off on small woody knobs known as sterigmata); and by the 2- to 4-inch cones carried upright in the fir's crown (hemlock's ¾-inch cones dangle at the ends of the branches). Fir needles are different than spruce needles: The undersides of fir needles bear two whitish lines that spruce needles lack.

As an evergreen, balsam fir holds on to its needles year-round and can con-

The bark of balsam fir is interrupted by resin-filled blisters. If a blister breaks, the resin flows out and evaporates on the trunk, leaving a pale residue.

duct photosynthesis whenever the sun shines. The balsam fir's thin needles, conical shape, and single trunk protect it against snow buildup and winter damage.

Each spring a balsam fir grows vertically from its uppermost leading bud. At the same time, side buds send out whorls of three to six branches, and branches already growing lower on the trunk expand and push farther outward. Count the tiers of branches, and you will know the tree's age. Its tapering shape helps a fir shed snow, much as an umbrella sheds rain. When snow starts to build up, the boughs sag downward, resting on those of the next layer below. The cone gradually collapses on itself like an umbrella being closed, with the strong, springy branches bending inward toward the trunk and offering less surface area to which snow can cling. Should the wind start to blow, the snow will cascade down and the branches will rise again.

Recently I sought out a mature balsam fir and, using a hand lens, studied its bark. The bark was light brown, relatively smooth, and stippled with tiny blisters. I punctured one of the blisters with a sharp twig and dabbed up a bit of the intensely fragrant resin. The Penobscot Indians of Maine applied this sticky substance as a plaster onto burns, cuts, and sores, and the loggers who worked in the Maine woods noticed and followed suit. Until recently, the resin found an application as a waterproof cement for mounting cover slips over thin-sectioned specimens on microscope slides and for cementing lenses into optical instruments.

Balsam firs put out male and female flowers on the same tree. The female flowers are slightly higher in the crown, where they are not as likely to be pollinated by the tree's own male flowers. Pollinated female flowers develop into seed cones possessing a fairly cylindrical shape. The immature cones have a violet or purplish tint. A tree produces cones annually, with a large crop arriving every two to four years. Small winged seeds fall from the cones in autumn, winter, and the following spring; they germinate from late May to early July. Balsam fir seedlings are shade tolerant and can grow in the forest understory beneath mature trees. The root system forms a shallow, spreading mat.

Aphids, midge larvae, and caterpillars feed on balsam fir. A major pest is the spruce budworm, a caterpillar that eats the needles of spruces and firs. In some areas it has killed many trees. It strikes mature and overmature trees, feeding mainly on fir and spruce and occasionally on tamarack, hemlock, and pine. Despite its name, the spruce budworm prefers balsam fir to spruces. When major budworm outbreaks first occurred in the 1800s, balsam fir was considered a weed tree because its value as a pulpwood species had not yet been discovered; spruce being more valuable to lumbermen, the budworm's name was linked to that economically important group of species.

At twenty-six pounds per cubic foot, the wood of balsam fir is extremely light. It is pale, limber, and soft; in contact with the ground, it rots rapidly. People use it for paneling, boxes for transporting foods such as fish (the wood does not impart a taste or odor), crates, barrels, and other products that do not require much structural strength. Balsam fir goes into paper pulp, although it yields less pulp per cord than denser softwoods such as spruce.

Porcupines, snowshoe hares, moose, and deer nibble on various parts of the balsam fir. Small rodents and songbirds eat the seeds. Yellow-bellied sapsuckers chisel feeding wells in the bark and drink the sap that fills the wells. Grouse, especially spruce grouse, nip off and eat the needles. Solitary vireos, yellow-rumped warblers, and evening grosbeaks frequently nest in balsam firs.

The same conical shape that helps a fir resist snow and ice also gladdens the human heart. Balsam fir is a popular Christmas tree: pretty, fragrant, and inclined to hold on to its needles longer than spruce. In the past, loggers and woodsmen stuffed their pillows with sprays of clean-smelling balsam and cut balsam boughs to make soft, springy mattresses.

Balsam Poplar

Balsam Poplar *(Populus balsamifera).* When we moved to northern Vermont, only 40 miles south of Canada, I encountered several new tree species on our wooded acres. Northern white-cedar, in the beaver flow north of the house, was easy to identify, thanks to its filigreed evergreen foliage. White spruce was more difficult; at first I took it for red spruce, until a combination of the tree's full, dense silhouette and its hairless twigs persuaded me otherwise. Then

I met with a small hardwood sapling coming up in an old field. The pale bark and upright growing habit suggested an aspen. But the tree had long-tipped, heart-shaped leaves larger than the rounded leaves of quaking aspen or bigtooth aspen. And its next-year's buds, long and pointed, were sticky to the touch and had a pleasantly sweet smell.

The stickiness and the resinous fragrance got me on track, and my field guide informed me that I had found balsam poplar. This tree is also known as balm, balm-of-Gilead, bam (probably a shortened form of balsam), tacamahac, hackmatack, cottonwood, and black poplar. The balsam and balm-of-Gilead names derive from the tree's aromatic qualities and hearken back to a desert shrub found in the Middle East and referred to in the Bible. Many plants, including the unrelated balsam fir, bear the "balsam" title.

In North America, in the company of white spruce, jack pine, balsam fir, and tamarack, balsam poplar marches north to the limit of tree growth, where it becomes the northernmost of the hardwoods, extending beyond even those boreal stalwarts the quaking aspen and paper birch. From Labrador the range of balsam poplar heads broadly west across Canada to Alaska's Arctic Slope. Its southern boundary takes in New England, northern New York, and the Great Lakes states, and scattered outposts of *P. balsamifera* crop up as far south as Pennsylvania, Ohio, Indiana, Iowa, and Colorado. In New England balsam poplar grows throughout Maine except for the southwest corner, in northern New Hampshire and Vermont, and in northwestern Connecticut.

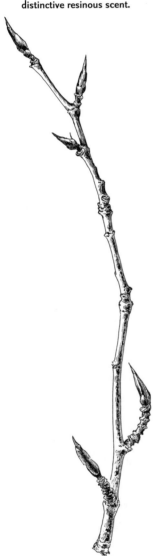

In balsam poplar the large, pointed leaf buds are sticky and have a distinctive resinous scent.

When mature, a typical specimen is 50 to 60 feet tall, with a trunk 1 to 2 feet in diameter at breast height. In river valleys north of the Canadian prairies, balsam poplar may soar to 100 feet tall and have a trunk 3 to 7 feet in diameter. In New England the largest trees approach 80 feet in height. The shape is like that of the closely related aspen: a long, straight, cylindrical trunk holding up a narrow, relatively open crown formed by several stout, generally ascending branches.

Older trees are often clear of limbs for 30 to 50 feet from the ground up.

The leaves are sharp-pointed, finely toothed, and 3 to 6 inches long by 1½ to 3 inches wide. They are a shiny dark green above and a pale silvery green below, often with rust-red veins on the lower surface. The slender leafstalks are round, as opposed to the flattened or ribbonlike leafstalks of the aspens. The leaves of balsam poplar flash as they turn and twist in the wind, although not as dramatically as do aspens' leaves. The bark is smooth and greenish to reddish brown on a young tree. It darkens and grays as the tree ages, developing thick ridges and deep furrows.

Balsam poplar often springs up along rivers, streams, lakes, and ponds; it seldom colonizes dry, exposed sites. The species makes its best growth in bottomland areas with deep sandy or gravelly soil and plenty of subsurface moisture. It invades old fields that are slowly returning to forest. Sometimes *P. balsamifera* takes root on swampy land that has a thin layer of organic soil, but it does not grow on peat. Balsam poplars occur as individuals or as clones, small clusters of genetically identical trees linked under the ground by a shared root system. Clones are either male or female. In New England balsam poplar usually does not form pure stands (as it does in the western and northern parts of its range) but grows in mixed stands along with tamarack, spruces, balsam fir, white pine, aspens, sugar maple, red maple, box-elder, basswood, paper birch, yellow birch, northern red oak, white ash, and other conifers and hardwoods.

Balsam poplar leafs out late in spring. Here in northern Vermont, June is well along before the balsams' leaves have completely unfurled; in northern Canada and Alaska, leaf-out may not be finished until July. Before the leaves emerge, in April and May the trees put forth flowers: Male trees produce small, inconspicuous flowers, and female trees set out lustrous green catkins that dangle down 4 to 6 inches, the longest of all the *Populus* species. Wind takes care of pollination. By May or June—when the trees' leaves are about two-thirds expanded—the female flowers have ripened to become a string of tan, ¼-inch-long capsules. The capsules are oval, with a pointed end. They split into two sections and release many tiny seeds, each one attached to a plume of silky plant down. The wind blows the seeds over great distances. The period of seed dispersal lasts for two weeks or longer.

Some seeds fall onto moving water and are carried along by rivers, later to be washed out onto floodplains. Seeds germinate quickly on flood-deposited sediments; on bare, moist mineral soil; on recently burned-over land; and in old fields. Seeds can remain viable for four to five weeks before sprouting. Seedlings are delicate and need ample water to survive. A balsam poplar can flower and produce seeds when as young as eight to ten years. In most years, trees produce good seed crops. *P. balsamifera* invades new habitats through its seeds, but more often individual trees reproduce themselves vegetatively. They send up shoots from their shallow root system or, if the tree has been cut down or killed by fire, from the stump or the base of the trunk. If a tree on a floodplain is buried by successive layers of silt, the section of the trunk that becomes covered will send out lateral roots, which in turn may give rise to sprouts. Root systems damaged or ripped apart by logging equipment will vigorously produce shoots. Balsam poplar can be readily propagated from root and stem cuttings.

Balsam poplar rapidly increases in height during its first four or five decades, and then its upward growth slows. Balsam poplar lives longer than quaking aspen; trees up to 200 years old have been reported from the Rocky Mountains and Alaska. Often it is succeeded on a site by white spruce. At first, the poplars produce a light shade that provides a perfect level of light for seedling spruces. Over the years, the spruces grow taller than the poplars. The dense evergreen foliage of the spruces casts a chilling shade on the soil. The balsam poplars cannot collect enough sunlight to photosynthesize efficiently, and their seedlings do not germinate in the shade. Ultimately, the poplars die out and the spruces dominate the forest stand. Other longer-living trees that also outgrow and replace balsam poplar include balsam fir, northern white-cedar, and American elm. Foresters consider *P. balsamifera* to be very intolerant of shade, much like quaking aspen and paper birch.

Because young balsam poplars have thin bark, they are easily killed by fire. Mature trees, with their thicker bark, withstand high temperatures better, and crown fires are rare in areas heavily stocked with balsam poplar, perhaps because the ground beneath the trees does not accumulate large amounts of fuel in the form of fallen limbs. Should fire wipe out a grove of balsam poplars, the trees' roots will send up suckers, and the stand will usually reestablish itself. A balsam poplar stand that is logged repeatedly will keep coming up in balsam poplar and will not be superseded by spruces or other trees.

Volatile compounds in the foliage of balsam poplar seem to deter some insect pests, including beetles and caterpillars, which feed on other poplars more aggressively than on *P. balsamifera*. Although moose and deer generally do not eat the leaves, they browse on twigs and small branches; moose may break off stems 2 inches thick. Snowshoe hares avoid the buds but eat twigs, stems, and bark. When hares or small rodents girdle saplings, the saplings die above the debarked area, and dormant buds below the damaged zone usually send up new stems. Ruffed grouse eat balsam poplar buds in winter. Beavers cut down and feed on saplings and trees.

The wood of balsam poplar is grayish white to grayish brown. Timber cutters usually lump it together with both species of aspens and call it all "popple." Because it is fairly strong for its weight, balsam poplar is made into boxes and crates. It also becomes lumber, core stock for furniture, flake board, excelsior, and fuel. It is most valuable as pulp for paper. People have used the sticky aromatic gum that covers the winter buds for liniments and salves. The buds, heated in oil, produce a mist that relieves congestion.

Have you ever wondered how trees such as balsam poplar withstand damage from frost in climates where the temperature plummets scores of degrees below zero? Balsam poplar, jack pine, black and white spruce, tamarack, some of the birches, aspen, and certain willows and alders have evolved a biological process known as extracellular freezing. Liquids inside the trees' cells migrate out into the tiny spaces between the cells, where they freeze; the resulting ice crystals do not damage the cells' structure.

Basswood

American Basswood *(Tilia americana)*.
Put yourself in the shoes of a settler in North
America in the 1600s, in the Massachusetts
Bay Colony, established by Puritans from
England. Walking in the woods, you chance
upon a tree—with a face carved into it.
Bulging eyes, thick and twisted lips set in a
sneer, a grotesque, startling image as white as
bone. The tree is a basswood, a species whose
pale outer sapwood is so soft that it can easily be carved with a knife. The Iroquois

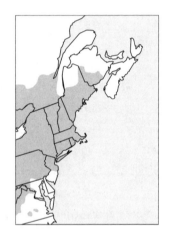

made masks in this way, working on the living trunk, then splitting off the
finished false face and hollowing it out from behind. The Iroquois were at
home in the eastern woods and used trees to make all manner of objects,
from baskets to bandages to ceremonial masks. The English, on the other
hand, feared the forest and saw it as a savage, hostile wilderness—although
they, too, learned to use the diverse products it so generously supplied.

Basswood grows throughout much of eastern and central North America, from Maine to Minnesota and south to North Carolina and Arkansas,
including southern Canada and all of New England except for northern
Maine. Michigan, Indiana, and Ohio stand at the approximate geographic

center of the species' range. Basswood does best on rich, well-drained, loamy soils along streams, and it also occurs on dry, stony sites. At one time the species was found in nearly pure stands, most of which were cleared for farming; today it is scattered through the woods. Basswood grows in the company of red oak, white ash, American elm, sugar maple, red maple, American beech, tuliptree, yellow birch, and many other species. Its colloquial names include lime tree, whitewood, bee-tree, whistlewood, and American linden. Basswood is a close relative of the lindens of Europe, renowned as shade trees, and our species is often planted to cast its cool, deep shade on city streets.

Basswood often grows as a clump of trunks
sprouted from a single root system.

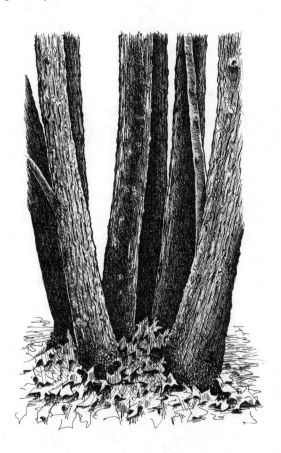

Basswood is fairly shade tolerant, and it grows faster than most other trees. On good sites, it can reach 120 feet, with a trunk diameter of more than 4 feet. A particularly large one has been located by big-tree enthusiast Bob Leverett in the Mohawk Trail State Forest in Massachusetts; it stands 111 feet tall and has a girth of 5½ feet. A basswood can live for 200 years, and some even achieve 300 years. Basswood often grows as a cluster of trunks developed from sprouts around an old, logged-off stump; lesser stems may surround a central, dominant one. The roots of basswood run deep and wide, making the tree quite wind-firm.

The leaves are 5 to 10 inches long. They are heart-shaped, with a lop-sided or uneven base. The leaf margin has distinct, sharp-looking teeth; the leaf tip is drawn out into an acute point; and the slender stem, or petiole, is several inches in length—about a third as long as the leaf blade. The leaves are a dark dull green above, with pale, shining undersides. Berry pickers used to cover berry-filled baskets with big basswood leaves to protect the fruit from the sun. The leaves turn a wan yellow in autumn, and when they fall, they enrich the soil with calcium, magnesium, nitrogen, phosphorus, and potassium.

The bark of young basswoods is thin, dark green, and shiny, while that of mature trees is grayish brown, with deep furrows running up and down the trunk, forming ridges that are themselves divided by transverse secondary furrows. The bark, although thick and firm, is easily cut. The inner bark possesses tough bast fibers that Native Americans wove into cordage and nets, and it's likely that the tree's common name evolved from "bast-wood." The inner bark also had medical applications: The Indians boiled it, then used the liquid to soothe burned skin.

Six to eight weeks after leafing out, basswood trees flower in late June and early July. The pretty, five-parted flowers are about ½ inch long and creamy yellow; it is hard to see them up among those expansive leaves. It's easier to detect them by smell: Their copious, powerfully sweet nectar tolls in bees, flies, butterflies, moths, and other nectar-feeding insects, which pollinate the flowers. Another clue to the presence of a flowering basswood is the loud buzzing of honeybees in its crown. (Basswood nectar makes a pale, strong-tasting honey prized by beekeepers and connoisseurs.) The flowers last for two to three weeks. Five to forty blossoms hang down in a cluster. The stem bearing the flowers connects to a green bract, a slender, winglike structure that, after the resulting fruits ripen and fall off the tree, acts as a communal parachute.

Basswoods begin producing seeds at about fifteen years of age. Most trees bear ample seed crops almost every year. On an August day, while hiking along on an old logging grade, my feet skidded on something round. Scattered all over the trail were little green spheres, about the size of peas, and ball-bearing hard. I trained my binoculars overhead: In the tops of tall basswood trees hung many more such fruits. Apparently, a crown-thrashing storm had passed through the hollow, knocking down thousands of the immature nutlets.

Under normal conditions, the fruits ripen and drop from the tree in autumn, sometimes hanging on until winter or early spring. Slowed down by their parachutes, the nutlike fruits drift within a distance of one to two tree heights from their point of origin. Each fruit contains one or two seeds, which have a tough coating and can lie dormant on the ground for up to four years before germinating. Basswood seeds form part of the mast crop of the eastern forest. Biologists report that bobwhite quail, chipmunks, squirrels, and mice eat the seeds. Alexander Martin, Herbert Zim, and Arnold Nelson write in *American Wildlife and Plants: A Guide to Wildlife Food Habits,* "The seeds are of practically no use to birds." Rabbits and white-tailed deer nip off basswood twigs and seedlings. Porcupines dine on the summer leaves and the bark.

The wood of *T. americana* is a pale tan color, the thick, creamy white sapwood merging gradually into the somewhat darker heartwood. It seasons quickly and weighs a mere twenty-eight pounds per cubic foot when dry. Native Americans hollowed canoes out of basswood logs. I used to keep bees, and in the spring my partner and I would place small frames made of thin basswood in our hives for the worker bees to fill with comb and honey. These days, round plastic sections are supplanting the traditional basswood frames for the production of comb honey.

Because the wood is light, odorless, and tasteless, people have used basswood for packaging food, including vegetables and berries, often weighing the negligible little boxes along with the produce they contain. According to Eric Sloane in *A Reverence for Wood,* in the 1800s strips of basswood were made into thin "scaleboards" and bent into all sorts of ingenious shapes, forming boxes with lids, some even made out of a single piece of wood. Basswood has been used as carriage stock, lightness being a virtue in a horse-drawn conveyance, as well as interior house trim, drawer sides, cores of furniture components (subsequently covered with veneers of more lustrous and expensive wood), excelsior, paper pulp, crates, yard-sticks, kitchenware, picture frames, models, and toys. Whistles can be made from the twigs. A knife easily cuts the soft wood across the grain, making it a favorite for whittling. Basswood blocks were a traditional choice for carving merry-go-round horses.

Beech

American Beech *(Fagus grandifolia).*
Beech is a fairly common tree in our woods.
And every beech that is large enough to produce nuts has graffiti on it: the claw marks of
hungry black bears.

American beech ranges across southern
Canada to Wisconsin and south to Florida
and Texas, including essentially all of the
eastern United States. It grows throughout
New England. Beeches prefer rich, moist
soils of both uplands and lowlands and
occur as scattered individuals or in small pure stands. In the middle latitudes of its range, beech shows up more abundantly on cool, moist, north-
facing slopes than on drier, south-facing aspects. In the southern
Appalachians the tree grows at elevations as high as 6,000 feet. Before the
ice ages, *F. grandifolia* grew as far west as California and probably flour-
ished over most of North America; today a subspecies, or race, survives in
the mountains of Mexico. Our American species is similar to *F. sylvatica,*
the European beech. The oaks and American chestnut are close relatives.

Mature beech trees typically stand 60 to 80 feet tall, with a trunk
diameter of 2 to 3 feet. Old-growth specimens can reach 120 feet. Forest-

grown individuals often show a different form than trees growing in the open. In the woods a beech tends to be tall and slender, free of branches for a long way up from the base of the trunk, yet with a deeper crown than many of its sylvan neighbors. Where it gets more sun, as in an old field, a beech will have a short, thick trunk with many long side limbs; the lowest branches will droop toward the ground, those in the middle will spread out horizontally, and the branches in the crown will extend upward, forming a dense, symmetrical crown. In our woods it is apparent that many small beech trees were spared when the property was logged by the previous own-

The smooth bark of a mature beech shows claw marks of bears that climbed into the tree to feed on beechnuts. A beech's leaves often remain attached to the twigs all winter.

ers in the late 1970s: They are open-grown, with branches extending out to the sides, even though they stand in what is now a fully regenerated forest well-stocked with birches and maples.

A beech's roots are shallow and wide-spreading; often they protrude above the ground for a few feet before angling down into the soil. Beech thrives in rich soil, and the species makes its best growth on limestone loam in the American Midwest. Early in our country's history, pioneers learned that beech trees signaled good soil, and settlers homed in on, and cleared for agriculture, the great beech forests that once blanketed parts of Ohio, Kentucky, Indiana, and central Michigan.

The most distinctive aspect of the beech is its bark. The thin, smooth, pale gray covering gleams in the shadowy woods. The bark of *F. grandifolia* must be unusually elastic because it never breaks up into plates and furrows like the bark of most other trees as they expand their girth with age. Beech bark gains character as it becomes blotched with lichens and scarred by animals' claws. The beeches on our land have numerous black linear scars made by bears and smaller scars left by other animals, probably raccoons and fishers. People also sometimes scratch their names or initials into the trees. The most famous inscription made on a beech is *D Boone cilled a bar on tree in year 1760,* carved into a tree along an old stage road in Tennessee. When the tree toppled in 1916—at an estimated age of 365 years—scars from Boone's message were still visible on its trunk.

The buds of beech are slender, spindle-shaped, sharp-pointed, many-scaled, and bronze in color. They're almost an inch long—five times as long as they are thick. In the spring, from these buds unfurl leaves that are 3 to 6 inches long and 1 to 3 inches wide. Beech leaves have a rather stiff, leathery texture. They are short-stemmed and ovate, with a central vein ending in a prominent point. The leaf edges are toothed. Leaves or leaf clusters (two or three leaves together) alternate along the twigs. There is a noticeable blue tint in the green upper surfaces of beech leaves, while the paler undersides are glossy and reflective. In autumn, beech leaves turn a clean, soft yellow. In winter some leaves will hang onto the tree for months, slowly fading to a pale tan like ancient parchment. Some trees keep hold of last year's leaves, even as the new leaves are emerging in spring.

Beeches flower in April and May, just before and during leaf emergence. Male and female flowers appear on the same tree. The yellow-green male flowers form a globe-shaped mass that hangs on a long stem. The paired female flowers are ¼ inch long, short-stemmed and urn-shaped, and bordered by reddish scales; wind brings about their pollination. Spring frosts can ruin the tender flowers.

The flowers develop into beechnuts that are protected by prickly husks. The nuts (those that aren't eaten in the treetops by foraging bears and raccoons) drop following frosts in September and October. They are triangular, shiny brown, and the size of a fingertip. The sweet meats make an excellent snack. If you find the nuts in quantity, you can make them into a flour. Mash the kernels, let the resulting paste dry, and grind it; substitute it for half of the flour in any muffin, biscuit, or bread recipe. Unless carefully dried, the fresh nuts keep for only a few weeks before turning rancid. The nuts contain about 22 percent protein and were a key food item in the diets of several woodland Indian tribes, including the Iroquois.

Beechnuts form a significant part of the main mast, or nut, crop in the northern hardwood biome, a forest type prominent in much of New England. The northern hardwood biome is composed largely of beech, birch, and maple trees, with northern red oak (also a mast producer) joining the species mix in some areas. Beech starts bearing substantial quantities of nuts when about forty years old and large quantities by age sixty. About every third year, a beech will produce nuts in abundance; in general, a heavy or a light nut crop will prevail throughout an entire region during a given year.

Many wild animals eat beechnuts. Squirrels climb into the trees' crowns and cut down the nuts in early autumn. Gray squirrels bury the nuts singly to store them; red squirrels fill middens—storage sites in hollow stumps, rock crevices, and voids inside brush piles—with caches of nuts; and chipmunks stockpile the nuts in their burrows. Bears often clamber into the trees, sit in branch crotches, and draw outer limbs in toward themselves while they feed, sometimes snapping the branch ends and leaving a messy tangle. Dead leaves remain clinging to bear-damaged branches after the bruins have moved on and the tree's other leaves have fallen; these conspicuous clusters of tan foliage and splintered limbs are sometimes called "bear nests." Indeed, bears sometimes will nest in those structures. A Pennsylvania biologist found a substantial nest, about 6 feet in diameter, almost 50 feet up in a beech; the nest had been built out of twenty-seven broken limbs and was sturdy enough that a bear slept in it for the first half of one winter.

Opossums, red and gray foxes, white-tailed deer, and mice consume beechnuts, as do wood ducks, ruffed and spruce grouse, bobwhite quail, wild turkeys, grosbeaks, and many other birds. Before humans drove them to extinction, passenger pigeons in their colossal flocks subsisted largely on beechnuts during autumn; the cutting of Midwestern beech forests to create farmland, along with unrestricted hunting, snuffed out that species during the early 1900s.

Blue jays are particularly fond of beechnuts and will flock to areas with nut-laden trees. The birds chip apart some of the nuts and eat them on the spot. A jay will collect surplus nuts, stuff them into its expandable throat and esophagus, and haul the food back to its home territory, which may be several miles away. A single bird may make hundreds of trips, carrying up to fourteen beechnuts per journey. Back home, the bird caches the nuts by pushing them into soft soil or covering them with plant debris; in winter and early spring, the bird seeks out the storage spots, digs up the nuts, and eats them. Jays do not remember all of the nuts they hide, and some individuals perish before they can retrieve their hoards. Since the birds are adept at selecting only sound, germinable nuts, they end up planting a lot of beech trees.

Scientists theorize that jays' nut-caching habits helped the beech and some oak species move rapidly northward following the last ice age, reforesting areas denuded by glaciers. Nut dispersal by jays remains ecologically important today, especially in places where humans' activities have fragmented forests, isolating patches of woods with grassland, farmland, and highways in between, forming barriers against the movements of small seed-dispersing mammals such as squirrels and mice. Jays help maintain genetic diversity in forests by transferring nuts between separate wooded tracts.

After falling from the tree or being buried by a squirrel or a jay, a beechnut remains dormant over winter. It germinates the following spring or early summer. Seedlings prosper in partial shade and protected openings; in direct sun the soil may dry out too much for them to survive. Seedlings can germinate beneath ferns and briars and gradually extend up through such cover. Beech is considered to be as shade tolerant as sugar maple. Beech seedlings grow slowly in deep, shady woods. In an old-growth hemlock and hardwood stand, foresters monitored the height of beech seedlings. The seedlings were 1 foot tall at age six, 2 feet at age ten, 5 feet at age twenty, and 7 feet at age twenty-five.

A beech requires twice as much water for transpiration and growth processes as some of the more drought-resistant trees, such as the oaks. Like an oak, a beech—especially a young one—will sprout from the stump if cut down. And like an aspen, a beech will also reproduce vegetatively by sending up sprouts, or suckers, from its root system, particularly on a marginal or a dry site. Forest scientists believe that more beech reproduction arises from sprouting than from seeds. Wherever beech limbs touch the ground, they send down roots, a process that is called layering. A tree's roots form a dense mat; most are shallow, but some roots may penetrate 5 feet into good soil. The root system of American beech is shallower than that of yellow birch and sugar maple, two species often found growing with *F. grandifolia.* Deer seldom feed on beech twigs or leaves if other trees are available. In overbrowsed areas beech may become dominant when deer suppress other tree species.

Beeches are very susceptible to death from flooding. Late spring frosts can severely damage the trees, and their thin bark makes them vulnerable to injury caused by fire, logging operations, insects (including, notably, a pest called the beech scale, about which more later), and humans wielding pocketknives. Once its trunk is breached, a beech may be invaded by fungi that cause bark disease and heart rot. As beeches age and their trunks thicken, wood-decay fungi often render them hollow. Such spaces provide habitats for cavity-nesting birds such as black-capped chickadees, tufted titmice, woodpeckers, and owls, and also porcupines, squirrels, opossums, raccoons, and, in really big, old trees, black bears.

Beech wood is a light reddish color. It is hard, strong, and tough. Difficult to season, it tends to warp and twist while drying. It weighs forty-three pounds per cubic foot. People have used it for pallets, flooring, butchers' blocks, veneer, containers, shoe lasts, clothespins, hangers, tool handles, and charcoal. When heated with steam, beech bends readily and later holds its shape, making it a favorite choice for bentwood furniture. Although tough to split, beech makes an excellent fuelwood, burning slowly and releasing ample heat. In Europe, beech bark gave early humans a ready-made drawing and writing surface. Our word *book* derives from the Anglo-Saxon *boc,* meaning a letter or a character, which in turn comes from an older wood, *beece,* for beech.

Like many trees in North America today, the beech is threatened by an accidentally introduced blight: the fungus *Nectria coccinea,* whose spores are carried from tree to tree by scale insects. Both the insects and the blight originated in Europe and were first detected on this continent in Nova Scotia in 1890. The scale insects are too small to be seen with the naked eye, and they are shifted about by the wind. Using their mouthparts, they pierce the bark of beech trees and feed on sap; in so doing, they may introduce *Nectria* spores. The fungus subsequently interrupts normal bark formation and causes pitting and cracking, which lead to infection by other fungi and invasion of the damaged trunk by carpenter ants. In turn, the ant colonies are excavated by pileated woodpeckers. All of these factors weaken beeches, and infected trees often snap off partway up the trunk.

Beech bark scale disease reached central New England in the 1940s and today is killing trees as far west as western New York and northern Pennsylvania. The disease affects mainly younger trees whose bark is thin enough for the scale insects' mouthparts to penetrate. After their trunks sustain damage, dying trees often respond by sending up root sprouts, which themselves are likely to become infected over time. Writes ecologist Tom Wessels in *Reading the Forested Landscape,* "If beeches are reduced to understory trees and produce few nuts, what will be the impact on turkey, squirrel, and bear? Bear rely heavily on beechnuts in central and northern New England to produce winter fat for hibernation, and with their numbers already in decline from habitat loss, the beech blight is not good news."

Birch

Paper Birch *(Betula papyrifera).* A cold, rainy morning on the shore of a Maine lake. The canoeists rise, emerge from their tent, and cast about for tinder to start the morning fire. No better way to ignite it than with a curl of bark from a fallen paper birch. Despite the dampness, orange flames leap from the bark as soon as the match touches it. Black smoke ascends in small clouds; the bark fizzles and sputters as the fire consumes it. The concentrated heat dries kindling  twigs and sticks, which also come ablaze—and the first steps have been taken toward a cup of coffee and a hot breakfast.

Paper birch spans the continent from Labrador to Alaska. From near the northern limit of tree growth, it extends southward in the East to New York, Pennsylvania, and high-altitude outposts in the Appalachians as far as North Carolina. It grows in a variety of soils and topographies and seems to do best in areas where average summer temperatures stay below 70 degrees Fahrenheit. In New England paper birch can be found across Maine, New Hampshire, Vermont, and Massachusetts, and in northern and western Connecticut. It grows on the borders of lakes, streams, and swamps; on rich forested slopes; in rocky woods with cool soils; in cutover areas; and in fields reverting to woods. Most paper birches become medium-size trees 50 to 75 feet tall, with a few trees achieving 85 feet; typical trunk diameters are 1 to 2 feet. Some paper birches in the original virgin forests towered to 120 feet. The largest paper birch currently registered with the American Forestry Association stands in Michigan; it is 107 feet tall.

With its white bark, paper birch is one of our handsomest trees, known through paintings and photographs to many people who have never seen it in nature. In young paper birches, the bark is reddish brown; it begins to turn white after about ten years. The white bark builds up in papery layers marked with narrow horizontal lenticels, which are portals between the interior wood tissue and the outside air. The outer bark scales off in lines going around the trunk, not up and down it. Beneath the loose paper, the tree's inner bark shows through in a creamy to pinkish or orangish white color. (A note to prospective fire-starters: Never peel the bark from a living birch, since the white layer will not be replaced and the trunk will bear ugly dark scars for the rest of the tree's life. Take instead the wrapper from a fallen log. Although the wood may be damp and rotten, the bark that encases it will retain its volatile oils.)

On the white trunks of paper birch, dark triangular markings, called chevrons, show where branches have died and fallen off. The closely related gray birch, *B. populifolia,* has whitish bark as well, but its bark is tight and nonpeeling and usually displays a greater number of large black chevrons at the bases of the self-pruned branches. Plant physiologists believe that these two cold-climate trees evolved their white coverings to reflect radiation throughout the entire light spectrum. This reflective property keeps the trunks from warming up prematurely on sunny winter days, then freezing during the cold nights that follow, leading to rapid contraction of the bark, causing cracks that would later invite the entry of pathogens.

The leaves of paper birch are 2 to 5 inches long, 1 to 3 inches wide, and roughly oval in shape. Their edges are double-toothed, and the tips taper to a point. Five to nine veins branch off on each side of a central rib. The leaves are dark green and smooth above, paler below, with tiny patches of hair, visible through a magnifying lens, where the veins join the rib. The leaves turn yellow in autumn. After falling, they break down quickly, enriching the soil by releasing calcium, nitrogen, phosphorus, magnesium, and potassium.

Although the root system of paper birch is shallow, high winds and ice buildup are more apt to shatter or bend the branches or trunk rather than uproot the whole tree. Since the bark is thin and highly flammable, even a large tree may be torched by a moderate groundfire. Although *B. papyrifera* does not clone itself from its root system, a young and vigorous tree will send up stems from the stump if the trunk is severely injured, cut down, or burned. Compared with trees that grew from seeds, the sprouts tend to mature earlier, after about fifty or sixty years, and deteriorate sooner, after seventy to ninety years. Paper birches rarely live beyond 140 years.

Flowers, borne on catkins, appear in April or May, before the leaves emerge. The male flowers stand on long drooping catkins near the twig tip, and the greenish female flowers blossom on short upright catkins farther back on the same twig. The wind shifts grains of pollen from the male to the female reproductive structures. Plant geneticists have learned that hybridization between the birches is common. Paper birch hybridizes with almost every other species in its genus. Hybridization causes a blending of outward traits and physical characteristics and is the reason why paper birches can be quite hard to tell apart from gray birches.

In paper birch the female flowers become narrowly cylindrical cones 1½ to 2 inches long. Their small winged seeds ripen in late summer and early autumn. Most seeds disperse on the wind from September through November. Some may lie dormant on the forest floor for a year or longer, but those that end up on bare soil, humus, or rotting wood will germinate the following spring. They grow better in partial shade than in the glare of full sun. After a year, seedlings rooted in humus may be 4 to 16 inches tall. A tree may begin to flower and produce seeds when fifteen years old. Optimum seed-bearing ages are forty to seventy.

Ruffed grouse eat the seeds and buds of paper birch. The seeds also feed black-capped chickadees, redpolls, pine siskins, and fox sparrows. White-tailed deer, moose, snowshoe hares, cottontail rabbits, beavers, and porcupines all eat the twigs or bark. Yellow-bellied sapsuckers chip holes into the bark and return to feed on the sweet sap that pools in the excavations; red squirrels gnaw similar wells to gain access to the sap. Hal Harrison, in *A Field Guide to Birds' Nests,* notes that black-throated green warblers often incorporate strips of white birch bark into their nests, which, he speculates, make the nests "easier to find in dark coniferous forests."

Native Americans boiled the sap of paper birch to make a sweet syrup. Perhaps no other eastern tree gave the continent's original inhabitants so many products. Different tribes used birch wood for showshoe frames and fuel; the sturdy, waterproof bark they fashioned into shelter coverings, boxes, cups, snow goggles, and horns for calling in bull moose during the

The white bark of paper birch is marked with black chevrons showing where branches have died and fallen off.

autumn rut. Their sophisticated technology included the making of birch-bark canoes, among the most beautiful boats ever crafted by human hands. Light, pliant, and strong, bark canoes were used in heavy rapids and on the ocean. Canoe makers peeled large sheets of bark away from tall, straight trees and wrapped them around a wooden frame fashioned out of cedar, birch, or maple. The split roots of black spruce or white pine were used to sew the sheets together; the stitching holes were then caulked with spruce gum. Notes John McPhee in *The Survival of the Bark Canoe*, "The bark of a birch-bark canoe is always inside out. The side that touched the wood of the tree is the side that touches the river." Another name for *B. papyrifera* is canoe birch.

The wood, weighing thirty-seven pounds per cubic foot, is softer and not as strong as that of yellow birch and black birch. People have used it for tongue depressors, toothpicks, clothespins, spools, broom handles, toys, and paper pulp. Here on the Butternut Farm, our woods were logged off by the previous owners in the late 1970s, and paper birches came in thickly in many areas. In thinning out our hardwood stands, I cut a number of paper birches for stovewood; although not as long-lasting as hard maple, the wood produces a reasonable amount of heat.

Foresters rank *B. papyrifera* as a shade-intolerant species. Among its usual associates in New England, only the aspens, pin cherry, and gray birch are considered less tolerant of shade. On regenerating logged land or in old fields that are becoming forest again, trees such as black cherry, sugar maple, yellow birch, oaks, and hickories will overtop paper birches, shading them out and causing their eventual demise.

Paper birches are susceptible to two major insect pests. A native beetle called the bronze birch borer lays its eggs in cracks in the bark. When the eggs hatch, the resulting grubs feed on the tree's cambium, or inner bark, creating long channels that can girdle and kill limbs; an early sign of damage is a dead area in the tree's crown. A second serious insect attacker is the birch leaf miner, a sawfly that originated in the Old World and was first noticed in Connecticut in the 1920s. The leaf miner lays its eggs on the trees' leaves; after hatching, the grubs eat the leaf tissues, causing the leaves to become papery and brown. The loss of too many of its leaves weakens a tree, making it more likely to die from other causes, including the bronze birch borer.

Gray Birch *(Betula populifolia).* People often loosely refer to both paper birch and gray birch as white birch. Gray birch is a smaller, bushier tree, usually 15 to 30 feet tall, with a trunk diameter of 9 to 18 inches. The bark, dull silvery gray to chalky white, does not peel or separate into layers as readily as that of paper birch. A greater number of black chevrons—inverted V-shaped markings at the bases of living and sloughed-off branches—adorn the trunk of the gray  birch. In many gray birch specimens, the base of the trunk is sheathed with furrowed bark that is dark gray to almost black; as the tree matures, this dark zone reaches farther up the trunk.

The leaves of gray birch and paper birch differ as well: Those of gray birch are more triangular and have longer, sharper-pointed tips, while the leaves of paper birch are more nearly oval in shape. Because the two species hybridize, intermediate leaf forms often can be found. Gray birch leaves have slender stems, and, like aspen leaves, they tremble and shimmer in the wind. The scientific name *B. populifolia* means "birch with poplarlike leaves," referring to the leaves' resemblance to those of the poplars, the group of species to which the aspens belong.

Gray birch ranges from Nova Scotia and southern Ontario south in the Appalachians to North Carolina. It can be found throughout New England with the exception of northern Maine. It grows on abandoned fields, hillsides, rocky slopes, and burned areas, often on dry, infertile soils. Other names for the species include wire birch, poverty birch, old-field birch, and poplar-leaved birch. Gray birch grows rapidly. During its brief life, it may function as a nurse tree, casting a partial shade that protects seedlings of other species from direct, desiccating sun. Some of the species that may flourish beneath gray birch are white ash, yellow birch, and white pine; ultimately, they will overtop and succeed gray birch on a given site.

Male and female flowers emerge on the same tree. The female flowers develop into cones 1 to 2 inches long. The seeds of *B. populifolia* are small, oval, and winged. The wind can carry them over great distances. Trees of this species can originate both from seeds and from the root systems of established trees. Gray birch sometimes grows as a clump of leaning trees emerging from an old stump. In gray birch, trunks and limbs are fairly flexible; when wet snow builds up on them, they bend all the way to the ground, only to spring up again unharmed when relieved of the snow load.

Donald Culross Peattie, in *A Natural History of Trees,* calls gray birch "a stunted sister" of the more graceful paper birch, and otherwise gives it short shrift. Many loggers regard gray birch as no more than a "weed tree." Hal Borland, in *A Countryman's Woods,* recognizing the role gray birch plays in forest succession, rightly notes that the gray birches so common in the reverting fields of his native New England "are of slight importance in man's economy, but nature's economy needs them."

Sweet Birch *(Betula lenta).* Sweet birch, also known as black birch and cherry birch, grows in a variety of habitats from rich, moist lowlands to dry, rock-strewn ridgetops. The species ranges from Maine to Ohio and south in the Appalachian Mountains to Georgia and Alabama. In New England it occurs in southwestern Maine, southern New Hampshire, northern and southern Vermont, and throughout Massachusetts, Connecticut, and Rhode Island.

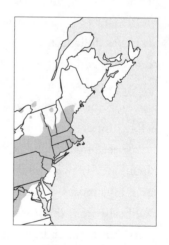

The bark of sweet birch is dark brown to purplish black, smooth and shiny when young and becoming rough and plated with age; it does not peel off in papery layers like the bark of other birches, although sometimes thick flanges of it stand off from the trunk. The bark shows prominent horizontally oriented lenticels, pores through which interior wood tissues exchange gases with the atmosphere. It looks much like the bark of black cherry, with which sweet birch often shares the same habitat. The two are distinguishable by the simple expedient of snapping off a twig; if the broken wood smells acrid or doesn't have much of an odor, it's cherry, but if it fills your nose with the clean fragrance of wintergreen, sweet birch it is.

Sweet birch generally grows 50 to 80 feet tall, with a trunk 1½ to 2 feet in diameter. Most of the tallest ones known in New England are in the 80- to 90-foot range. Tree-measuring enthusiasts report a massive specimen from Mohawk Trail State Forest in western Massachusetts, which towers up 102 feet and has a girth exceeding 7 feet. Another large sweet birch, in New Boston, New Hampshire, was 78 feet high and had a trunk diameter of almost 5 feet when last measured in 1989.

The leaves of sweet birch, extending from short spur branches, are alternate, sometimes in pairs. Their length varies from 2 to 6 inches. The shape is elliptical, pointed at the tip and often with a slight notch at the base; the edges are finely toothed with sharp-tipped projections. Nine to a dozen or more veins branch out prominently from each side of a central midrib (turn the leaf over to see this veining pattern in detail). The leaves are a dark dull green above and a lighter yellow-green below. Dappled light comes streaming through the partial canopy of wind-flickering birch leaves; I can spend many minutes in a stand of sweet birches, face upraised, watching the ever-changing spectacle. In autumn the leaves turn yellow before dropping.

Sweet birch seedlings can be hard to tell apart from those of yellow birch, but the sweet birch ones will have a more pronounced wintergreen taste. Like most birches, a sweet birch that has been cut down will sprout prolifically from the stump. Ground fires damage sweet birch, on account of its thin bark, and even a light scorching at the base of the trunk may open the way for attack from disease organisms and insects.

The flowers emerge in spring, before the leaves come out. The male flowers are arrayed on drooping catkins 3 to 4 inches long, carried on the twig tips; the shorter female catkins are about an inch long and sit higher on the twig. Writes ecologist Bernd Heinrich in *The Trees in My Forest*, "Trees improve their odds of fertilization by dispersing astronomical numbers of pollen grains. More than five million are released by a single birch flower or catkin, and each tree has hundreds of thousands of flowers." The pistils of the female flowers possess enlarged sticky areas to snag pollen grains out of the air. There is only a brief period when the sexual union can occur. "If flowers waited until after the leaves unfurled," notes Heinrich, "then they would be partially shielded from the wind and there would be less chance for the successful transfer of pollen between flowers."

The female catkins of sweet birch develop into brown, barrel-shaped seed packets that stand erect on the twig. The seeds mature in autumn. The catkins shed the tiny, lightweight, two-winged seeds. In winter the wind blows the seeds along on top of the snow, helping them to disperse over

As sweet birch ages, its bark thickens and breaks up into scaly blocks and plates.

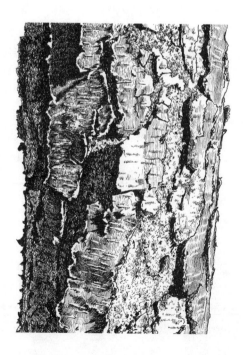

long distances. Trees begin producing seeds when about forty years old; they yield bountiful crops every year or two.

In spring birch seeds germinate in moist mineral soil, in humus, and on rotting logs. According to Tom Wessels in *Reading the Forested Landscape,* sweet birch does best in central New England on "moderate sites" which "lie in the middle of the continua for moisture, temperature, pH, and nutrient levels." Sweet birches may seed themselves heavily in a woods where trees have been blown down by hurricane winds or killed by fire. Seedlings need some shade for two or three months during their first summer; they grow best in succeeding years when side shade or partial overhead shade blunts the sun. Sweet birch ultimately is a shade-intolerant species, and as a tree it must become part of the forest canopy to survive.

Oil of wintergreen is a potent aromatic extract originally gotten by distilling the vegetation of a creeping forest plant called wintergreen. The oil has been used in small quantities to flavor medicines and candies, and to provide fragrance for disinfectants. People discovered that sweet birch yields the same substance in much greater volumes than the smaller plant. It takes approximately a hundred saplings to distill a quart of wintergreen oil; at one time, sweet birch was considered endangered because so many were being cut and chipped for distillation. As late as the 1950s in Pennsylvania, wood-fired birch stills dotted the forest. The average production of oil was about two quarts per cord (a cord of wood is a volume measuring 4 feet by 4 feet by 8 feet), with the best yield coming in early spring after the sap had started to run. The concentrated liquid is said to cause death if taken internally. Today, manufacturers produce oil of wintergreen through a different process, using wood alcohol and salicylic acid. Sweet birch sap can be turned into a syrup that is not as sweet or as thick as maple syrup, and it can also be fermented into birch beer.

The wood is fairly heavy, at forty-seven pounds per cubic foot; it is hard and dark brown with thin, yellowish sapwood. The properties and appearance of the wood are similar to those of yellow birch, and often the two woods are not separated at the sawmill. Sweet birch polishes to an attractive sheen. It is used for furniture, cabinets, and millwork.

Yellow Birch *(Betula alleghaniensis).* Fencerow trees cast sharp shadows in the moonlight. Beneath my snowshoes the snow groaned, and when I kicked a ball of ice, it made a hollow tinkling as it rolled along on top of the crust. I crossed our hay field, then climbed through a brushy pasture to where a logging road led into the woods.

Trunks of maple and ash etched dark vertical lines against the snow. I was brought to a halt by another tree that presented a different aspect. Its bark was pale and burnished. Thin, ragged strips of bark curled away from the trunk, catching the moon's glow. Moonlight bathed the tree from above and reflected up from the snow-covered ground below. The tree stood like a great, glimmering ice sculpture displayed on a field of pure white.

It was a yellow birch, also called silver birch and curly birch. Yellow birch is found mainly in cool, moist uplands, but it also grows in dry habitats. On our land in the hill country of northeastern Vermont, yellow birch is abundant on east- and north-facing slopes and in low areas fringing swampland dominated by northern white-cedars and balsam firs. Growing in the forest, yellow birch develops a tall, straight trunk with little taper, supporting a short and rather narrow crown. In a more open setting, the crown broadens and, with its drooping lower branches, takes on a rounded shape. The trunk may divide close to the ground, sending up three or more stems.

Unlike paper birch, which is found throughout the boreal region of the Northern Hemisphere, yellow birch is limited to eastern North America. It ranges farther north than three other *Betula* species native to New England—gray birch, river birch, and sweet birch—and it can survive temperatures as low as -50 degrees Fahrenheit. Yellow birch occurs from Newfoundland across southern Canada to Manitoba and Minnesota, and south to Iowa in the west and to Tennessee and Georgia in the east. It grows throughout New England, with the exception of Cape Cod, Martha's Vineyard, and Nantucket Island. Yellow birch does best on moist, rich, well-drained soil. The tree achieves its largest size in northern New England and in neighboring Canada and New York.

In the early 1800s the French botanist and explorer François André Michaux chose for yellow birch the scientific name *Betula lutea,* which literally means "yellow birch," in reference to the tree's golden-yellow bark. In the 1950s *B. lutea* was changed to *B. alleghaniensis,* "the birch from the Allegheny Mountains," citing a range within the Appalachian chain, centered on Pennsylvania, Maryland, and the Virginias, where yellow birch is abundant.

Yellow birch often keeps company with paper birch, sweet birch, eastern hemlock, sugar maple, red maple, beech, and basswood. It's easy to confuse yellow birch and sweet birch seedlings because they have similar leaves and both give off a pleasant wintergreen odor when their foliage and twigs are crushed; however, the scent in yellow birch is not quite as strong as it is in sweet birch. As the trees grow larger, they become easy to distinguish. Know yellow birch by its lustrous silvery-gray to yellow-bronze bark (the color is most pronounced when the tree is young), which is marked with narrow, horizontal dark lines, called lenticels; and by the small, shreddy bark curls that stand off all over the trunk. On very old trees, the bark may darken to brown or almost black while thickening and breaking up into flat plates.

Yellow birch is the largest of our native birches. Mature trees regularly grow 60 to 80 feet tall and have a trunk 2 to 3 feet in diameter. An occasional specimen tops 100 feet, with a trunk 4 to 5 feet in diameter. The largest yellow birch currently recognized nationwide by the American Forestry Association grows on Deer Isle, Maine; although the tree is only 76 feet tall, its trunk is massive at 252 inches, or 21 feet, in circumference.

In *B. alleghaniensis* the root system goes moderately deep and consists of several sturdy, wide-spreading laterals. The leaves are typical for the birches: 3 to 4 inches long by 2½ inches wide, elliptical in shape, ending in a sharp point, and distinctly and doubly saw-toothed, having teeth of two sizes around the margins. The leaves alternate along the twigs, sprouting singly or in pairs. In summer they are a dull green on their upper surfaces and a pale yellow-green below; in autumn they turn a vivid yellow.

Yellow birch puts forth flowers in April, before its leaves emerge. The flowers are borne in male and female catkins that appear on the same branch. The male catkins, which formed during the previous growing season, expand to a length of about 3 inches; they droop from their stems. The greenish female catkins are ⅔ inch long; they stand erect, farther back on the twig. Wind carries pollen from the male to the female flowers. During summer, the fertilized female catkins develop into egg-shaped cones ¾ inch to 1¼ inches long, covered with hairy scales protecting tiny winged seeds shaped like hearts and tridents. In autumn the scales expand, releasing the seeds. Yellow birches gradually shed their seeds throughout winter; the seeds are tiny and light, and the wind can send them skittering for miles on top of crusted snow.

Compared to an acorn, a birch seed is minuscule. It carries very little energy, and to survive it must quickly sink rootlets into the earth. Yellow birch seeds germinate readily on bare soil, especially on earth exposed by a forest fire; abandoned fields and logged-over tracts are also hospitable sites. Yellow birch can tolerate more shade and thrive in a wider variety of soil types than can its close relative, the paper birch. Yellow birch grows beneath gaps in the forest canopy caused by mature trees dying and falling over, or toppling in storm winds. Often the seedlings sprout on hummocks created by the heaved-up root masses of fallen trees.

Seeds and seedlings of yellow birch usually do not survive on thick leaf litter because they lack the energy reserves sufficient to root downward through such detritus. Sometimes they catch hold in strange places: a scrap of moss on a rock or the rotting summit of a stump left after logging. If a seedling finds enough nourishment and sunlight on such a perch, it gradually sends its roots to the ground—roots that are tough and able to withstand exposure to the air. Some yellow birches have roots that look like great, gnarled hands fingering down over a moldering stump; when the stump finally rots away, the tree is left standing on bark-covered stilts.

Yellow birches begin producing seeds when they reach around forty years of age. They bear large crops approximately every third year. A stand of mature trees can shower down more than a million seeds per acre. Usually some of the seed cones remain on the trees through winter, attracting resident birds, including ruffed grouse, as well as winter migrants such as redpolls and pine siskins. Grouse also eat yellow birch catkins and the long, spindle-shaped leaf buds; red squirrels and other rodents consume the seeds. In spring yellow birches provide sweet sap for yellow-bellied sapsuckers. Moose and white-tailed deer browse on the seedlings, saplings, and twigs.

Yellow birch is sometimes called hard birch, as its wood is harder than that of the other birches. In bygone times, people fashioned ox yokes and sledge frames from the relatively light but strong wood. Because it remains stable after it has cured, yellow birch was the top choice for wagon-wheel hubs; it kept a tight grip on the spokes so they did not work loose. People made brooms by splintering the ends of short lengths of trunk gotten from saplings. Perhaps surprisingly, a root-beer–like beverage was concocted from the sap.

A yellow birch seed may sprout on the top of a stump. After the stump rots away, the tree remains standing on stiltlike roots.

Today yellow birch is the most important hardwood lumber tree in eastern Canada and the most valuable of all the birches. The heartwood is a ruddy golden brown and the sapwood white. The wood weighs around forty-one pounds per cubic foot, dry weight. Most birch furniture is made from yellow birch; sometimes the wood is stained to resemble mahogany or cherry. Other uses for the wood include flooring, paneling, structural parts of furniture, plywood, and veneer. Some people craft rustic chairs out of the slender trunks and branches of young yellow birches, leaving the eye-catching bark in place. My friend Dave Brown, of Craftsbury, Vermont, is an inveterate snowshoer who often goes winter camping, both in the Green Mountain State and in northern Quebec. He loads his gear and supplies in a toboggan, which he pulls along behind him. He built his toboggan out of long, thin slats of yellow birch; after treating the wood with steam, Dave bent it back upon itself, forming a recurved prow that lets his toboggan skim over the snow rather than digging down into it.

Utilitarian items like clothespins, closet clothes poles, brush backs, kitchen utensils, handles for knives and brooms, popsicle sticks, and toothpicks all may come from yellow birch. I burn a lot of yellow birch in my woodstoves. It can be a difficult wood to split, so rather than attacking the center of a billet, I often use my maul to strike off the edges; this technique leaves a sizeable block of wood that, relieved of its moisture-imprisoning bark, dries out nicely and makes for good overnight burning.

As with other birches, the bark of the yellow birch is a near-impervious moisture barrier, and once a tree has perished, its wood rots quickly. Often a standing dead tree becomes little more than a cylinder of bark wrapped around a core of rotten punkwood. Native Americans dried this decayed cellulose and carried it with them for use as tinder in which to start a fire by friction.

Modern travelers in wilderness settings can start their own fires through the agency of yellow birch. Like that of paper birch, the bark contains combustible oils. Take several curls from a dead-and-down tree, build a tepee of twigs over them, and hold a match to the bark. Even if your kindling is damp, the intense heat from the flaming bark will soon dry it and set it blazing.

River Birch *(Betula nigra)*. This small to medium-size tree has collected many names. The one most widely used, river birch, describes the species' usual habitat: sandbars, banks, and silty islands of rivers and streams. River birch also grows in floodplains, wet woods, swamps, and along lake and pond margins. Another name, water birch, points out this riparian, or water's-edge, preference as well. The name red birch comes from the dark red color of the branchlets, and cinna-

mon birch from the pinkish brown bark of the young trees. Older specimens display evidence for another common name, black birch: Over the years, the bark on these mature trees darkens to a deep gray color that approaches black.

River birch is the most southerly of North America's birches. It grows from southern New England, along rivers in Massachusetts and Connecticut, west across New York to Minnesota, and south to northern Florida and eastern Texas. It is most abundant in the hot, humid Southeast.

In the South, particularly the Gulf states, river birch may grow to 90 feet or taller and have a 5-foot-diameter trunk. The tree rarely gets taller than 30 feet in the Northeast, with a trunk diameter of 1 to 2 feet. An exceptionally large specimen reported from Southington, Connecticut, is 72 feet tall; it has a trunk circumference of 11 feet and a crown spread of more than 95 feet. The classic mature form of *B. nigra* is a short trunk dividing, around 15 to 20 feet up, into three or four spreading, divergent limbs, which arch upward to create a narrow, oblong, irregular crown.

The leaves of river birch are alternate (never across from each other). They occur singly or in pairs. A typical leaf is 3 to 4 inches long and 1 to 2 inches wide, with six to ten pairs of lateral veins. The leaf margins are coarsely double-toothed: broken up into sawtooth projections, each of which is further divided into smaller points. The leaves are a shiny dark green above and show a pale yellowish green to almost white below. The undersides are usually hairy or velvety, as are the leafstalks, twigs, and buds. The twigs, when broken, do not yield a wintergreen scent, as do the twigs of sweet birch and yellow birch. Not a brilliant fall tree, river birch displays dull yellow foliage in October and November.

Probably the most handsome aspect of the river birch is its bark, papery, scaly flakes that peel back to expose inner layers showing rich reddish colors: pink-brown, pale mahogany, orange, salmon. The inner bark possesses a lustrous sheen that reflects the sunlight almost as brilliantly as does the surface of the rivers along which wild-grown river birches stand.

River birches flower in April and May. The male flowers are arranged on a yellowish catkin about 3 inches long that droops from near the twig tip. Farther back on the twig, and standing upright on a short stalk, is the greenish female flower, which appears at about the same time as the tree's leaves. The wind carries pollen from male to female blossoms. The female catkins develop during spring and summer, becoming brownish, roughly cylindrical, 1- to 1½-inch cones that remain erect on their stems. Botanists call these cones strobiles, a name that describes their overlapping scales.

The strobiles release small, hairy, winged nutlets in late spring or early summer; river birch is the only North American birch that releases its seeds prior to autumn. Trees produce good seed crops almost every year. Seeds that are not eaten by wild turkeys, ruffed grouse, songbirds, and rodents are transported by wind and water. If they end up on moist alluvial soil, they germinate rapidly. A pioneering species, river birch requires full sunlight and grows vigorously when it gets it.

Dense streamside thickets of river birch help prevent bank erosion. Floods and floating ice can damage or scour away young stands of this species. River birch often grows alongside sycamores, red maples, silver maples, and black willows. Mature specimens develop cavities that provide nesting space and shelter for wood ducks, woodpeckers, black-capped chickadees, white-breasted nuthatches, squirrels, and other wildlife. River birch has no serious insect pests. *B. nigra* can tolerate acidic conditions: In southern Ohio, researchers found it growing thickly on stream bottom areas that coal-mine drainage had rendered too acidic for other trees. Foresters sometimes plant river birch to help reclaim soils turned topsy-turvy by mining.

The wood is thirty-six to forty pounds per cubic foot, dry weight. It is soft but strong. The heartwood is light brown and the sapwood pale. The wood is used for furniture, barrels, basket hoops, woodenware, and paper pulp; in bygone days it was fashioned into ox yokes and peoples' shoes.

In the 1860s Prince Maximilian of Austria judged river birch the most beautiful of all the trees he viewed while touring in North America before he was installed as emperor of Mexico by Napoleon III. Today, cultivars of river birch are widely used as ornamental shade trees in parks, residential areas, and public grounds and along city streets. The trees are easily transplanted, grow rapidly, resist drought, and are rarely damaged by wind or ice. Because the trees cast a light shade, grass readily grows beneath them.

Black-Gum

Black-Gum *(Nyssa sylvatica)*. Some trees have cross-grained wood, and black-gum is one of them. Its lumber is twisted and contorted, the grain spiraling irregularly up the trunk. This arrangement differs from that in most other trees, whose annual growth rings run straight and vertical, like a series of progressively larger cylinders. Whether heavy or light in weight, cross-grained wood is tough, almost impossible to split lengthwise, even if you use a maul and wedges. In bygone days, if a person was contrary, hard to deal with, he or she was said to be cross-grained. Because of its cross-grained aspect, black-gum was largely shunned by our wood-using pioneer ancestors. But it is an important tree for wildlife and a species that is increasing in abundance in parts of the eastern forest today.

Black-gum ranges from New England west to Michigan and Wisconsin; southward, it reaches Florida's Lake Okeechobee, eastern Texas, and northern Mexico. The species is abundant on the Atlantic coastal plain and in the Ohio River valley. In New England it is found in southwestern Maine, southern New Hampshire, central and southern Vermont, and in Massachusetts, Rhode Island, and Connecticut. Black-gum grows in a variety of settings, including damp soil along streams, burned-over areas, logged-off woods, abandoned fields, dry mountain slopes, rocky ridges, and the edges of bogs and swamps.

At maturity a typical black-gum is 40 to 60 feet tall, with a trunk 1 to 2 feet in diameter. Exceptionally large individuals can be 125 feet tall and 5 feet in diameter. The trunk is fairly straight. But because black-gum is susceptible to ice damage, many individuals lose their leading stem and end up with an unsightly crown of scraggly sprouts and dead wood. (Such a tree is said to be "stag-headed" because the dead wood and numerous upright branches look like a deer's antlers.) In an undamaged state, the crown is dense and conical, sometimes flat-topped. The tree has crooked branches that gently zigzag back and forth. High branches usually ascend, while low branches droop toward the ground, and branches in the middle of the tree extend outward horizontally, yielding an intriguing winter silhouette.

Large black-gums are often hollow, providing nesting and escape habitats for wildlife.

Young trees—which particularly show the horizontal side-branching habit—are clad in grayish bark. As a tree ages, its bark darkens to almost black and breaks up into thick, scaly, squarish or many-sided blocks; some call this checkered pattern "alligator bark" for its resemblance to the reptiles' rough, ridged skin. The leaves of black-gum look tropical: glossy green and simple in outline, suggesting the evergreen leaves that many southern hardwoods hold onto year-round. A black-gum leaf is a smooth oval, lacking marginal teeth or lobes. Leaves are 2 to 5 inches long and end in a pointed tip. They have a firm, leathery texture. The leaves grow crowded on short twigs that project from the sides of the branches.

In autumn black-gums change color early, when the leaves of most other trees remain green. Guidebooks usually describe the fall foliage as scarlet; in fact, black-gum sets forth a range of attention-grabbing colors: yellow, peach, mustard, orange, orange-red, maroon, scarlet. In many leaves, the colors burn brightly along the central stalk and radiating ribs, while the rest of the blade remains a lush green. The bright colors draw resident and migrating birds, which eat the trees' fruit.

In May black-gums put out dense, many-flowered ½-inch-broad heads that support the male flowers, and few-flowered, slightly larger clusters of female blossoms. Male and female flowers are usually borne on separate trees. In some cases, black-gums bear flowers that possess both male and female parts; such bisexual flowers are termed "perfect." The flowers, greenish white, are less colorful than the bright red buds from which the young leaves unfurl. Insects, including honeybees, pollinate the female flowers; the tree is a major honey source, especially in the South, where black-gum is common and often becomes a very large tree.

Over summer, the female flowers develop into fruits, called drupes, that stand in twos and threes at the ends of long stems. The drupes are blue-black, oval, and pea-size, consisting of a thin pulp surrounding a slightly ridged stone. When I first tasted a black-gum fruit many years ago, I spat out the bitter thing immediately; yet many birds and some mammals relish them. In *Shake Them 'Simmons Down,* the naturalist Janet Lembke reports on a large black-gum, growing near her home in coastal North Carolina, whose fruit attracted mockingbirds, blue jays, brown thrashers, robins, cardinals, summer and scarlet tanagers, grackles, four species of woodpeckers, starlings, rose-breasted grosbeaks, Baltimore orioles, and veeries. Warblers and vireos flitted among the tree's boughs, taking flying insects attracted by the ripe and overripe drupes.

According to one study, black-gum fruits have a fat content of more than 14 percent, which is comparable to the fat-rich fruits of flowering dogwood (16.7 percent). Fall fruits of other trees are lower in fat and are less attractive to migratory birds: American holly (8 percent), mountain-ash (4.6 percent), and hackberry (4.4 percent). Fats provide almost twice as much energy as carbohydrates, making them ideal for birds that must burn huge amounts of energy during extended flight but cannot afford to load themselves down by gorging on bulky foodstuffs. The payoff to the plant comes after the seeds pass through the birds' digestive tracts and are defecated onto the ground, often hundreds of yards and sometimes several miles away from their place of origin.

On bitter winter days, I have watched small flocks of eastern bluebirds descend on black-gums and clean up all of the shriveled fruits remaining on the twigs. Pileated woodpeckers swing up and down on the supple branches, snapping up black-gum drupes with their big bills. Ruffed grouse, ring-necked pheasants, wild turkeys, gray squirrels, red and gray foxes, opossums, and raccoons also consume the fruits. In autumn black bears climb into mature black-gums and gorge on the fruits, whose seeds become packed by the hundreds in the bears' droppings. White-tailed deer browse the twigs and foliage of black-gum, especially the young sprouts.

Seeds that overwinter on cool, damp soil usually germinate the following spring. Seedlings and young trees grow best in nearly full sunlight but can survive overtopping by other trees. A small black-gum in the forest understory may spread out its crown in a single plane, like the palm of a hand, directed upward to catch any sunlight filtering down through the crowns of taller trees. *N. sylvatica* usually grows in mixed stands, where it is often a medium-size tree, taller than the dogwoods, which are even more shade tolerant, but not as lofty as the shade-intolerant species, such as hickories and most oaks. As oaks become fewer in some regions, on account of the devastation wrought by the gypsy moth, the numbers of several other trees, including black-gum, are rising. The current decline of flowering dogwood may also be contributing to an increase in black-gums in certain areas.

In wetlands black-gums grow along with yellow birch, white pine, eastern hemlock, swamp oak, pin oak, black ash, red maple, alders, and dogwood. Black-gums can tolerate brief springtime flooding, and they tend to become quite large on damp sites, such as the New Gloucester Black Gum Stand National Natural Landmark, in Cumberland County, Maine, one of the northernmost outposts for *N. sylvatica.* In drier habitats black-gum stands alongside sweet birch, sassafras, red maple, chestnut oak, black oak, and northern red oak. On dry sites with shallow soils, the trunk of a mature black-gum may only be forearm-thick.

Old black-gums usually die from the top down, so the trees become shorter as they age. Wounds caused by fires or broken branches let wood-decay fungi enter the trunk. Trees 2 or more feet in diameter are often hollow, their trunks still alive, even though their walls are only a few inches thick. Woodpeckers, wood ducks, hooded mergansers, squirrels, and raccoons nest in hollow black-gums. Owls roost in them by day. Black bears hibernate in large ones during winter. Because black-gum is not a valuable lumber tree, loggers generally leave black-gums standing, a practice that often preserves cavities in stands where heavy cutting may remove most of the larger cavity-containing trees.

Settlers sawed hollow black-gum trunks into various lengths and used them as hives for honeybees (called "bee-gums"), storage bins ("corn-gums"), and box traps ("rabbit-gums"). They rejected the wood for fencing, since it rotted quickly in contact with the soil and refused to be split into rails. Its moderate weight, about thirty-eight pounds per cubic foot when dry, and interlocking grain made it a good choice for wagon-wheel hubs.

The heartwood is yellowish white, and the thick sapwood is the color of old ivory. Because of its enduring strength, black-gum has been fashioned into maul heads, plowshares, rollers for cables in mine shafts, scaffolding, tool handles, pallets, boxes, ironing boards, rolling pins, chopping blocks, and flooring for factories. I have made a few walking sticks out of the lightweight, tough wood. If air-dried, black-gum shrinks and warps radically; lumbermen used to say that a freshly sawn black-gum board, when the sun shone on it, would curl up and crawl out of the lumberyard as fast as a blacksnake. Kiln-dried, the wood becomes more stable. It has an attractive ribbon figure when quarter-sawn; sometimes it is sliced as a veneer and stained dark to imitate mahogany.

Black-gum is also known as sour-gum because of its bad-tasting fruit. Some call it pepperidge, an obscure name that may derive from an Old English word for the shrub we now know as barberry. In the South, *N. sylvatica* is called tupelo, from a Creek Indian name, *ito opilwa,* meaning swamp tree. It's hard to figure out how it came to be called a gum, because, as the writer Donald Culross Peattie observes in *A Natural History of Trees,* "Nowhere on the American continent has anyone ever expressed from this dry and disobliging vegetable one fluid ounce of any sort of gum." The taxonomic name is both descriptive and poetic: *Nyssa* denotes a water nymph in classical Greek mythology, and *sylvatica* means "of the forest."

Butternut

Butternut *(Juglans cinerea)*. Three old butternut trees stand in a row just south of our farmhouse nestled in the rolling hills of northeastern Vermont. To the north, on Burke and Kirby Mountains—outliers of the White Mountain chain, which juts up more dramatically in New Hampshire than it does here—the soil is thin, stony, and acidic. But here on the Butternut Farm, as our place is known, the soil is deep and limestone-sweet: a perfect growing medium for butternut.

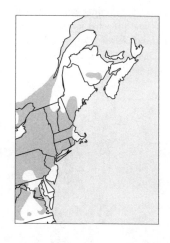

More resistant to cold than black walnut, butternut grows from southern New Brunswick and Quebec west to Minnesota; throughout central and southern New England (the nature writer Hal Borland called the butternut "New England's black walnut"); the Mid-Atlantic states; in the Appalachians as far south as northern Georgia; and west to Missouri and Arkansas. Unfortunately, the tree is dwindling rapidly across its range, the victim of a canker-causing fungus that some scientists believe could wipe out the species altogether.

Butternuts grow on well-drained sites including lowland woods, rich hillside pastures where the soil is enriched by underlying limestone, and along streams and road edges. The trees occur singly or in small groups, never in pure stands. They mix with basswood, white ash, sugar maple, American elm, northern red oak, and other hardwoods. *J. cinerea* grows best in sunny places and dies if it is shaded from above. A fast-growing tree, it usually does not live beyond seventy-five years.

A mature butternut is low and broad, its short, thick trunk branching into many stocky limbs; the overall form has sometimes been compared to that of an apple tree. The crown on a healthy specimen is broad, deep, round-topped, and somewhat asymmetrical, and looks rather sparse and open. The outermost branches may appear dark, almost black. Most butternuts stand 30 to 40 feet tall and have a trunk 1 to 2 feet in diameter. The occasional individual reaches 80 feet and has a 3- to 4-foot trunk. The largest butternut known today grows in Chester, Connecticut. It is 80 feet tall, has a crown spread of 86 feet, and is 265 inches (a bit more than 22 feet) around the trunk.

In fall and winter, butternut stems show distinctive leaf scars where shed leaves formerly attached to the twigs. Some observers say the scars look like camels' faces.

Butternut sends down a long central taproot, plus a set of deeply extending lateral roots. Windstorms rarely knock the trees down, even though butternuts usually grow in open sites rather than in dense forest stands, where massed sylvan companions blunt the force of gales. Wind-firm they may be, but butternuts often lose their stiff, brittle branches to storms and ice.

Pale grayish bark covers the young trunks and branches. As a tree ages, dark fissures develop between smooth, light gray bark ridges. Like black walnut and the hickories, butternut has alternate compound leaves. Each leaf, 15 to 30 inches long, consists of a central stem, called a rachis, which is studded with leaflets standing opposite each other, usually with a single leaflet at the rachis tip. The leaflets are 3 to 5 inches long, have toothed margins and pointed tips, and number eleven to seventeen per leaf. In general, the leaves of the butternut have longer stems and fewer leaflets than those of the black walnut, leading to the butternut's feathery, sparse-appearing foliage. The overall color of the leaves is yellowish green. The leaflets are slightly hairy above and paler and cloaked with soft hairs on their undersurfaces. They emerge quite late in the spring (not until late May here in northern Vermont), become tattered and dingy by midsummer, and, after turning yellowish brown, fall off in early autumn.

The greenish flowers blossom in May, when the leaves are partly developed. Separate male and female flowers occur on the same tree, usually on the same branch. The male flowers crowd together in furry catkins 3 to 5 inches long. The female flowers, positioned near the twig ends, develop from shoots of the current season; the male flowers, farther back on the branchlets, derive from the previous year's growth.

Wind pollinates the female flowers. Over summer, the fruits expand and lengthen, assuming the shape of a small lemon. Often three to five nuts hang in one drooping cluster. Green at first, the husk of a butternut turns brown as it ripens. It is furred with sticky, rust-colored hairs that will stain a person's hands brown. The husk conceals a rough, flinty shell 1½ to 2 inches long, studded with ridges and knobs and having a sharp point at one end. Inside the thick-walled shell lies the sweet, oily, edible kernel, which earns for the butternut the folk name oilnut. Nuts missed by squirrels and human foragers, plus those buried by the rodents and then forgotten, germinate the following spring. Butternuts begin producing nuts at around age twenty; trees thirty to sixty years old yield the greatest numbers of nuts. Good nut crops occur every two or three years.

The nuts of *J. cinerea* are delicious, like a mild black walnut with a hint of banana; they're particularly good in muffins and banana bread. Often they are mixed with maple sugar to make candy. You can free the kernels by hammering the nuts on their points. An old trick calls for half filling a burlap bag with butternuts, soaking it in hot water for half an hour, and hanging it up to cool; the treatment is supposed to make the nuts easier to crack and to keep the meats in larger pieces. The nutmeats tend to become rancid and need to be used promptly after harvesting. Some foragers pickle butternuts, gathering the green immature fruits in June or July and preserving them in vinegar.

Native Americans ate butternuts raw, cooked, and ground into a meal for baking cakes or thickening porridge. The Iroquois extracted the seed oil, cooked with it, and used it to dress their hair. Butternut sap can be boiled down and concentrated to make a sweet syrup; compared with sugar maple sap, it takes four times as much butternut sap to make a given volume of syrup. At the outset of the Civil War, secessionist soldiers boiled butternut twigs, leaves, buds, and fruits to make a dye that imparted a tan color to their clothes. Those troops, as well as Southern civilians and Confederate sympathizers in the North, henceforth were known as "butternuts."

The outer sapwood is narrow, rarely more than an inch in depth. The heartwood is brown, often a rich chestnut color, and sometimes with an intricate grain pattern, especially in boards sawn from branch crooks. The wood is lighter in color than black walnut, which is why butternut is sometimes called white walnut. Soft and rather weak, the wood weighs a mere twenty-five pounds per cubic foot. Carvers and woodworkers find it easy to shape the wood and finish it to a high luster. The wood is stable and rarely warps or cracks, and it darkens with exposure to the atmosphere. Butternut has been made into furniture, cabinets, paneling, the interiors of carriages and sumptuous private railroad cars, and carved church altars.

In 1928 Joseph Illick wrote in *Pennsylvania Trees* concerning butternut that "the old trees are very susceptible to the attack of wood-destroying fungi." Since Illick's era, a new and deadlier menace has arrived. It's not known whether this canker-causing fungus of genus *Sirococcus* is a recent accidental import or a native species that has mutated into its current lethal form. In the last thirty years, it has swept through the butternuts of North America, leaving few trees unaffected.

Scientists believe that storms blow spore-laden moisture droplets far and wide. The microscopic fungal spores enter young twigs through leaf scars and lenticels, and get into older stems through wounds and cracks in the bark. As an infection progresses, rain splashes the spores from lesions high in the tree onto branches lower down. Diseased wood becomes dark and mushy, with most of the damage hidden beneath the bark. As cankers girdle branches or trunk, they destroy the outer cambium layer and disrupt the flow of nutrients and water within the tree. The branches gradually die back, and after several years, most trees perish. Butternut canker fungus renders the nuts infertile and kills trees of all ages. At present, there is no known treatment for the disease.

The fungus was first reported from Wisconsin in 1967. An estimated 58 percent of Wisconsin's butternuts and 91 percent of Michigan's butternuts died over the next fifteen years. By 1986 approximately 77 percent of butternuts in North Carolina and Virginia had perished. Forest pathologists believe that more than 90 percent of butternuts in New Hampshire are affected. So many butternuts have died across the species' range that the U.S. Fish and Wildlife Service has added *J. cinerea* to the list of candidates for protection under the Endangered Species Act. Scientists are trying to locate trees that have natural resistance to the fungus; they hope to take grafts and preserve the trees' gene plasm. Mike Ostry, a forest pathologist with the U.S. Department of Agriculture and a leading researcher into butternut canker disease, has suggested that the butternut is more likely to become extinct than the beleaguered American chestnut.

Here on the Butternut Farm, our namesake trees are in bad shape. Most of the butternuts I come across in the woods are snags, or, if still clinging to life, they look unthrifty and ill, marred with cankers and dead branches. The three elderly trees standing to the south of the house—they provide a much-used habitat for a range of birds, from yellow-bellied sapsuckers to bluebirds to starlings—show clear signs of the plague. I'll miss them when they are gone.

Cedar

THE NAMES OF MANY AMERICAN trees have intriguing etymologies: European interpretations of Native American words; names commemorating historical events, botanical features, or traditional uses; and names that recalled for settlers the trees of their homelands, and even trees from biblical and other far-off places. The cedars belong in the last category. According to scientists, the true cedars are evergreen trees of the Old World genus *Cedrus,* which includes the famed cedars of Lebanon as well as certain trees in North Africa and the Himalayas. Our North American cedars are also evergreens, also fragrant and clean-smelling like the Eurasian trees. But they are not true cedars. The three species native to our region belong to Cupressaceae, the cypress family: eastern redcedar *(Juniperus virginiana),* found mainly in central and southern New England; Atlantic white-cedar *(Chamaecyparis thyoides),* growing in coastal swamps; and northern white-cedar *(Thuja occidentalist),* which occupies both dry sites and wetlands through much of the region.

Northern White-Cedar *(Thuja occidentalis).* Some authorities say that northern white-cedar's other and perhaps better-known name—arborvitae, Latin for "tree of life"—stems from its longevity: This slow-growing tree can live 300 to 400 years. More likely the name arises from an incident in Canada in the winter of 1535–36, when tea prepared by Native Americans from the foliage and bark of an unidentified conifer cured the French adventurer Jacques Cartier and his fellow explorers of scurvy, thereby saving their lives.

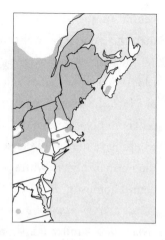

Northern white-cedar occurs in a broad band from Prince Edward Island and New Brunswick west across Canada to southeastern Manitoba. The species is found throughout much of northern New England and in suitable habitats across the southern half of the region. It grows in New York and in scattered locations as far south as North Carolina, Ohio, and Illinois. *T. occidentalis* has been planted and naturalized throughout the East, and horticulturists have bred more than fifty varieties for ornamental and landscape specimens. (After recovering from scurvy, thanks to the vitamin C contained in northern white-cedar, Cartier carried home seedlings of the curative tree, which were set out in Fontainebleau, the royal garden of the King of France: the first trees taken from the New World back to the Old.)

Northern white-cedar grows about 50 feet tall, with some exceptional individuals reaching 100 feet. (The tallest specimens known in New England top out at around 75 feet.) Trunk diameter of mature trees is 2 to 3 feet; the trunks of older trees may be swollen and buttressed at the base, in some cases dividing into two or more stems that lean and twist upward. If grown in the open, northern white-cedar takes on a symmetrical, conical shape. The bark of northern white-cedar is shreddy and fibrous, with many low ridges. The green, flattened, scalelike leaves are 1/16 to 1/8 inch long and arrayed in rows about the twigs, which overlap in fanlike sprays. The trees hold onto their leaves for two to five years. The fresh, pungent aroma of the foliage comes from tiny resin glands on the leaf scales.

In nature northern white-cedar occupies two major habitats: dry, calcium-rich uplands, including old fields and areas near limestone ledges; and rich fen peatlands, a type of swamp in which slow-moving water delivers a steady flow of nutrients. Botanists believe that the correct soil pH—

neutral or slightly alkaline—is more important to northern white-cedar than the amount of moisture in the soil.

At Vermont's Button Bay State Park, on the shore of Lake Champlain, I looked at some cedars standing among limestone formations that jutted out into the lake. A park naturalist told me that corings had shown the cedars to be 350 years old. Large and impressive trees, their growth rings would have been very dense—"often less than 1/16 inch wide, in contrast to the normal rings of white pine, which are up to 1/2 inch wide," write Elizabeth Thompson and Eric Sorenson in *Wetland, Woodland, Wildland: A Guide to the Natural Communities of Vermont,* concerning northern white-cedars in a similar lakeshore setting. At Button Bay the cedars mingled

Northern white-cedar has tight, scalelike foliage. The inset shows the opened seed cones.

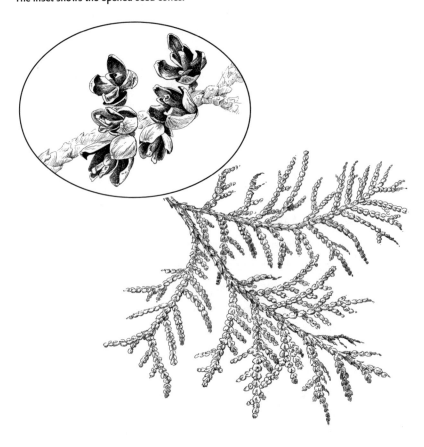

with large northern red oaks, white pines, and white oaks, forming an impressive and easily accessible old-growth stand.

Northern white-cedar grows slowly, adding an inch of trunk diameter every ten to twenty years. It thrives in deep shade. It fares poorly in or is absent from acidic swamps and bogs; there, black spruce usually becomes the dominant tree. In more alkaline wetlands, such as fen peatlands, northern white-cedar often exists in dense stands.

We have such a wetland on our property, fed by seeps and springs, just north of the house. Entering the swamp, I find myself in a different world. In summer it is a cool and moist realm. In winter the air is still, shielded from the cold wind by the dense vegetation but nevertheless frigid-feeling in its damp stillness. Low hummocks bump up the landscape. Water trickles and gurgles. Leaning trees, blowdowns, and the thick growth of cedars make travel difficult, so I usually stick to the network of deer trails that lace the swamp. In the canopy overhead, the crowns of balsam fir, tamarack, and, in the drier spots, yellow birch mingle with those of the cedars. Beneath the trees few shrubs prosper in the dim light. The soil is dark and mucky. Sphagnum moss grows thick. I haven't found them in our swamp, but a number of rare orchids thrive in rich fens, including fairy-slipper, ram's head lady's slipper, small yellow lady's slipper, and showy lady's slipper.

In spring, cedar swamps ring with the calls of hermit thrushes, yellow-bellied flycatchers, winter wrens, and northern waterthrushes. Other birds breeding in northern white-cedar stands include Canada warbler, yellow-rumped warbler, white-throated sparrow, and northern parula. As cedar swamps often do, ours merges with an active beaver pond, where I see great blue herons and ducks of various species.

Deer and moose take shelter in white-cedar swamps. When winter's snows get deep, deer "yard up" in the thickets, not moving much and feeding on the cedars' evergreen foliage. Snowshoe hares nibble on low branches. Red squirrels insulate their winter nests with strips of cedar bark. Masked and short-tailed shrews, deer mice, and red-backed voles also live in cedar wetlands.

In a swamp or fen, northern white-cedar often spreads through layering, when rows of trees sprout from the trunk of a tree that has fallen over. White-cedar also reproduces through its seeds, which are borne in slim, oval, ½-inch-long cones. After they ripen, the winged seeds fall from the tan-colored cones. Red squirrels eat the seeds, as do pine siskins.

Cedar wood is long-lasting in contact with soil and water: All of the fenceposts around our pastures are lengths of cedar. Other applications include cabin logs, shingles and shakes, railroad ties, utility poles, and rustic patio furniture. The wood is light, at twenty pounds per cubic foot, and is easily worked. Native Americans split short pieces of the wood lengthwise along its annual growth rings and used it to fashion the frames and ribs of their bark-sheathed canoes. Both Native Americans and modern herbalists have employed preparations from *T. occidentalis* to treat fevers, headaches, coughs, and rheumatism, and to ease menstrual cramps.

Atlantic White-Cedar *(Chamaecyparis thyoides)*. Of the three "cedars" native to New England, Atlantic white-cedar is the rarest. A small, spire-shaped tree, it grows in peat soils of freshwater swamps and bogs from Maine to Florida and west along the Gulf Coast to eastern Louisiana. It is also known as swamp cedar, post cedar, and arborvitae.

Atlantic white-cedar reaches its northern limit around Rockport, Maine. Vermont is the only New England state from which it is absent. In the region's five other states, *C. thyoides* occurs in widely scattered locales along the coast, an area where cutting, draining, and filling of wetlands have banished this tree from much of its former range. Atlantic white-cedar grows in only a few sites in eastern New Hampshire and southeastern Maine, but it becomes more abundant farther south.

Atlantic white-cedar looks much like its close relatives, northern white-cedar and eastern redcedar. It is an evergreen tree whose mature foliage is composed of closely overlapping scales, each about ¹⁄₁₆ to ⅛ inch long. The branchlets are flattened, forking sprays covered with green scales. On the outer shoots, the year's new growth is bright green, while the mature older foliage is a dull bluish green. When crushed, the foliage gives off a fresh, aromatic scent. The bark of the trunk is thin, gray to reddish brown, and has many narrow, shreddy ridges.

Atlantic white-cedar matures in fifty to seventy years. In New England the tallest trees generally stand 40 to 60 feet tall and have a trunk 1 to 2 feet in diameter. From Old Saybrook, Connecticut, in 2003 was reported a specimen 74 feet tall and with a trunk 75 inches in circumference (for a diameter of approximately 2 feet). *C. thyoides* makes its best growth in Virginia and North Carolina, where trees can become 120 feet tall and 5 feet in trunk diameter. Prehistoric trunks of white-cedar 6 feet across have emerged from the muck of wetlands, waterlogged but still sound; in the past, loggers "mined" such wood in New Jersey.

Atlantic white-cedar grows in wet depressions and swampy ground, sometimes on sandy soils but usually on muck (formerly called peat). Muck soils are usually acidic. Atlantic white-cedar is absent or uncommon on soils having large amounts of silt or clay. In New England other trees found growing with Atlantic white-cedar, in and along the edges of wetlands, include pitch pine, white pine, black-gum, red maple, yellow birch, gray birch, and eastern hemlock. In Connecticut peatlands the following shrubs and ferns may grow in the understory of white-cedar stands: spicebush, winterberry, poison sumac, mountain laurel, cinnamon fern, and arrowwood.

Atlantic white-cedar puts forth small cones that mature at the end of their first growing season. Initially, they are pale green covered with a bluish white bloom; in developing, they become a dark ruddy brown. When fully ripened, the cones are spherical and about ¼ inch across, and house five to fifteen winged seeds. In fall and winter the seeds are released. They are so small and light that they fall only 0.6 feet per second in still air. A 5-mile-per-hour wind can carry the seeds about 600 feet, although most of them land on the ground beneath or near the trees that shed them. Some seeds may disperse by floating away on the water. Atlantic white-cedars in open, sunny settings start bearing cones when four or five years old; trees in densely forested stands bear cones when ten to twenty years old. Atlantic white-cedars usually produce good seed crops each year.

Seedlings sprout in damp mineral soil, moist rotting wood, sphagnum moss, and muck. They usually do not germinate where pine needles or the leaves of shrubs or hardwood trees carpet the ground. Seedlings often come up in abandoned cranberry bogs and areas where mature trees have been clear-cut. In the northern part of the species' range, a seedling can be 10 feet tall after ten years. It then grows 1 to 1½ feet per year until it's about fifty years old, whereupon growth slows; by the time a tree is 100 years old, its upward growth has essentially stopped, although its trunk will continue to slowly increase in girth. When heavily browsed by white-tailed deer, Atlantic white-cedars may "layer," sending down roots where their branches touch the ground, with sprouts coming up from the new root systems. The roots of *C. thyoides* are confined mainly to the top foot or two of peat. Because of its shallow root system and its weak hold in the soggy ground, a mature Atlantic white-cedar is apt to blow over in a strong wind.

Atlantic white-cedar is more shade tolerant than gray birch and pitch pine, and much less shade-tolerant than red maple and black-gum. Crown fires kill white-cedars, and winds may knock over many trees in stands opened up by selective logging. Few fungi attack *C. thyoides,* whose heartwood is extremely resistant to decay. According to some sources, an individual Atlantic white-cedar may live as long as 1,000 years. However, trees rarely become more than 200 years old before fires, storms, or chain saws bring them down.

The wood is very lightweight: only twenty pounds per cubic foot when dry. It is straight-grained and aromatic. It shrinks and warps very little when seasoning, and it is easy to work with. Atlantic white-cedar was a highly valued wood during colonial times, when many cedar swamps were held in common and set aside for public use. Settlers made shingles, house siding, barrels, tubs, and small boats out of the durable wood. The trees were cut in winter, when the standing water froze in cedar swamps, letting men and horses enter those dense, miry places. Charcoal derived from swamp cedar was used for making gunpowder during the American Revolution. Colonists exported the wood in quantity to the West Indies. Later Atlantic white-cedar logs were bored out and used as water pipes in towns and cities. Atlantic white-cedar remains an important commercial species in parts of Virginia, North Carolina, South Carolina, and Florida.

In coastal New England, *C. thyoides* had become scarce as early as the mid-eighteenth century, when Benjamin Franklin, in the 1749 edition of *Poor Richard's Almanac,* urged Americans to start planting trees to replace the vanishing cedars. Writes Charles W. Johnson in *Bogs of the Northeast,* "Atlantic white-cedar peatlands, once common along the [Massachusetts] coast, have been repeatedly and extensively logged for their timber. Fortunately, a few have been preserved as natural areas." One such area is the White Cedar Swamp Walk in South Wellfleet on the Cape Cod National Seashore, where a boardwalk lets visitors explore raised hummocks forested with cedar. Notes Sheila Connor in *New England Natives,* the remaining white-cedar swamps of Massachusetts, Rhode Island, and Connecticut "may well represent the last vestiges of the awesome 'wilderness' that the colonists confronted and the Native Americans savored."

Eastern Redcedar *(Juniperus virginiana).*
This small- to medium-size tree is actually a juniper. It ranges from roughly the hundredth meridian—known as the Dry Line, running from South Dakota to Texas—east to the Atlantic coast, including all or part of thirty-six states from Maine to Florida, as well as southern Ontario. In New England eastern red cedar is found mainly in the central and southern parts of the region: southern Maine, southern New Hampshire, the
Connecticut Valley in Vermont, and throughout Massachusetts, Rhode Island, and Connecticut. The tree grows in old fields, in early successional woods, and on other dry to moist sites, although not generally in wetlands.

Redcedar is also called red juniper and Virginia juniper. Because of the color of its wood and bark, early French colonists named it *baton rouge,* or "red stick."

Redcedar can be a perplexing tree. It grows in two different forms and puts forth two different types of foliage.

A young redcedar looks like a green finger pointed heavenward. (Is that why people plant it so often in cemeteries: as an admonitory adornment?) The mature tree bears little resemblance to the upright, slender, youthful form, appearing conical but somewhat flattened at the top, wider and more hunkered-down around its short trunk.

The new, vigorously growing foliage consists of thin, sharp-pointed needles that resemble the tip of an awl. These awl-shaped needles are three-sided and up to ¼ inch long; often they bristle and flare out irregularly from the stems of seedlings that have been heavily browsed by deer. The mature leaves are dissimilar: about ⅟₁₆ inch long, each overlapping the next like a reptile's scales, and tightly pressed against the twigs, which branch out in dark green sprays. Often some of a redcedar's boughs will show a rusty tint

Redcedars often come up in old fields. Many songbirds nest in their dense foliage.

caused by old foliage that stays on the tree for several years after dying. To further complicate the situation, toward winter's end redcedar becomes an ill-looking brown and then greens up again in the spring.

The whiskery, reddish brown bark peels off, or exfoliates, in long, vertical strips. Extremely thin, redcedar bark offers little protection against fire; the green foliage of the tree, however, does not burn readily. The trunk of an old redcedar is often grooved, fluted, buttressed—anything but symmetrical and round.

Knee-high, waist-high, head-high, the young trees rise like columns from the soil of abandoned farms. Redcedars can grow 40 to 60 feet tall, up to 100 feet on an excellent site. The oldest age reported for the species is 300 years. Redcedars have been planted widely as ornamentals.

When Europeans arrived in North America, they found groves of tall, magnificent redcedars, and it was not long before they learned from the native inhabitants, and discovered through trial and usage, how to employ the wood. Redcedar is straight-grained, easy to split and plane, and long-lasting in contact with soil and water. Farmers used it for cabin logs and fences, craftsmen fashioned it into furniture, and shipwrights worked it into planking and parts for boats. Soft and uniform, redcedar makes a good carving wood. My maternal great-grandfather, Addison Osgood Foote, was a Union soldier during the Civil War; his Wisconsin regiment mainly did guard duty on railroads in occupied Arkansas, and chess was a favorite leisure-time game among the troops. I have a letter Add wrote in 1864 in which he describes whittling a set of chess pieces out of cedar wood.

For more than a century, pencils were made from redcedar: The wood is soft enough to be cut across the grain, which is how a mechanical pencil sharpener works, and light and fragrant in the bargain. In the early 1900s, as the supply of large redcedars waned, pencil manufacturers bought old cabins, barn floors, and fence rails that had stood exposed to the weather for decades, their interiors still sound—before finally turning to the incense cedar of the American West. Today redcedar is used mainly for fenceposts, with the largest quantities cut in Tennessee, Kentucky, Arkansas, and several other southern states. Because the aromatic wood repels clothes moths, it often goes into chests, wardrobes, and drawer and closet linings. Redcedar has creamy or yellowish sapwood and ruddy heartwood, and the two colors contrast dramatically.

In spring small, inconspicuous flowers open at the ends of minute twigs. Male and female flowers generally appear on separate trees. By autumn the pollinated female flowers have developed into round, berrylike fruits ¼ inch in diameter. Firm, sweet-tasting pulp encases a pair of seeds. The fruit is purplish blue, with a whitish powdery bloom; a tree well-set with fruit will have a noticeable bluish cast.

Anthonie Holthuijzen, a biologist working in Virginia, explored the ecology of redcedars for many years. In one study he documented yellow-rumped warblers, cedar waxwings, robins, starlings, bluebirds, mockingbirds, downy woodpeckers, and wood thrushes eating the fruit. The cedar waxwing was given its name because of its liking for redcedar berries; a flock of those social birds can pick a large tree clean in a few days. It takes twelve minutes for a cedar seed to pass through a waxwing's system, Holthuijzen determined, and the digestion process renders the seed three times more likely to germinate than a seed in a berry that has simply fallen on the ground.

Birds spread cedar seeds across the land, tending to concentrate their leavings beneath perching sites. When Holthuijzen scraped 356 bird droppings off a 317-yard-long fence, he found they contained 1,006 redcedar seeds. In some places, rows of bird-planted redcedars stand between old fields, having outlasted the wire or wood fences that at one time divided the plots. Rabbits, foxes, raccoons, skunks, and coyotes eat redcedar fruits, and the greenery helps feed deer in winter.

Many birds nest in the dense foliage, including sparrows, mockingbirds, cardinals, and robins. An even wider range of birds roost in redcedars, taking shelter from inclement weather and predators' eyes. Old foliage falling from cedars helps enrich depleted fields. Biologists have found that the soil beneath redcedars supports more earthworms than that beneath pine plantations.

People have reportedly used redcedar berries as flavorings for food. However, large quantities of the fruit are believed to irritate the urinary tract and kidneys. Native Americans of different tribes boiled the fruits and leaves to make elixirs for treating colds and coughs, and they drank an oil from the berries to relieve dysentery.

The related common or dwarf juniper, *J. communis,* grows in the northeastern United States and across Europe and northern Asia, usually as a shrub and rarely as a small tree. Its hard, pale blue berries are eaten by ruffed grouse, bobwhite quail, ring-necked pheasants, other birds, and mammals. People use the berries to spice stews and to give gin its distinctive tang. (The name *gin* comes from the French word for juniper, *genièvre.*)

Cherry

Black Cherry *(Prunus serotina).* Black cherry is the largest tree among the North American cherry species. It ranges from Nova Scotia to Florida in the east, and in the west from Minnesota through eastern Kansas to Texas, with a closely related race in Mexico and Central America. It is found throughout New England except for northern Maine.

Black cherry thrives on rich, moist soils of bottomlands and slopes. It also grows on dry, rocky sites that offer less in the way of nutrients. Forest-grown trees have narrow, irregular crowns. Often they are quite straight, with a long trunk clear of branches for half its length. A tree on a good site can top 100 feet in height, but demand for cherry wood is so great that few trees achieve such stature before they are cut. A typical mature specimen stands 60 to 75 feet tall, with a trunk diameter of 2 to 3 feet. In old-growth stands, black cherry can become more than 130 feet tall. A large black cherry reported from Monroe State Forest in Massachusetts stands 113 feet tall and has a 7.4-foot trunk girth.

The bark on young trees is smooth, glossy, and reddish brown, with whitish horizontal lenticels. As a tree ages, its bark thickens and becomes dark gray, breaking up into small, irregular plates with brittle edges that jut out from the trunk. The simple, alternate leaves are lance-shaped with small marginal teeth and pointed tips. They are 2 to 5 inches long. Their upper surfaces are a dark glossy green; the undersurfaces are light green, and small hairs may coat the midrib on the bottom side, especially near the leaf base. The leaves turn reddish or yellow in autumn.

In May or June, after the new leaves have pushed forth from their buds, multiple flowers bloom on a drooping stem, called a raceme, approximately the length of a human finger. The individual flowers are white, ¼ inch in diameter, and give off a fragrant smell. Insects pollinate them; many forest-dwelling solitary bee species visit black cherry for the flowers' nectar. Over summer the blossoms develop into pea-size cherries. The fruits are dark red, turning purple-black as they ripen during August and September. A cherry consists of a hard pit surrounded by a thin pulp. The pulp has a slightly bitter taste and is sour enough to make your mouth pucker. Most trees fruit

The bark of a mature black cherry breaks up into small, irregular plates with brittle edges. The illustration also shows leaves and fruit.

abundantly every third or fourth year. After the fruits fall to the ground, the seeds remain viable in the leaf litter for up to two years.

I know a logger who dons climbing spikes and ascends cherry trees to harvest the fruit, which he shakes down onto a tarp spread on the ground; he makes jelly out of the cherries. He has to pick quickly after he locates a fruit-laden tree because scores of bird species feed on black cherries, including ruffed grouse, wild turkeys, woodpeckers, thrushes, cedar waxwings, and grosbeaks. In autumn I have spotted robins flying haphazardly, gaining a perch with much awkward wing flapping, and sitting on branches or on the ground in a stupor, having intoxicated themselves by eating overripe, fermented cherries. Birds disperse cherry pits in their droppings or by regurgitating them. A pit that has gone through a bird's digestive system has an improved likelihood of germinating.

Black bears and raccoons claw their way into trees, sometimes breaking branches in their determination to get the fruit. Foxes, chipmunks, mice, rabbits, and squirrels eat cherries. Voles gnaw on cherry bark in winter, and cottontails nibble on the seedlings. Deer browse the leaves and twigs, even though they contain bitter-tasting cyanide compounds. Cherry foliage can poison domestic livestock.

Black cherry is often found along with oaks, maples, white ash, American elm, yellow birch, and basswood. Young cherry trees are fast-growing, and they thrive along the sunlit edges of forests and in small woodland openings where large trees have fallen. They also grow, albeit more slowly, in the shaded understory of mature woods. As cherry trees age, they become less tolerant of shade. Cherries have roots that spread wide rather than go deep, and strong winds sometimes fell the trees. Black cherries often lift their crowns above the general canopy in mixed-species stands, making them vulnerable to storm breakage. Damage from wildfires and logging stimulates trees to send up new shoots from the base of the trunk or from the stump. Black cherries can live 150 to 200 years, with some old-growth specimens exceeding 250 years.

Eastern tent caterpillars often build their weblike communal nests in the forks and crotches of black cherries; they represent one of more than

200 species of butterfly and moth caterpillars that feed primarily on the foliage of *P. serotina*. Tiger swallowtail caterpillars shelter in silk-spun nests inside folded-up cherry leaves. Cecropia moth larvae anchor their brown, bag-shaped cocoons to cherry twigs. Gypsy moths, which evolved in Eurasia, do not eat cherry foliage even when their populations peak and the caterpillars go starving.

Penobscot Indians made a cough remedy from the bark of black cherry. The tree's bark and leaves contain hydrocyanic acid, and extracts continue to be used in modern cough medicines. Early settlers mixed juice from black cherries with rum or brandy to make a drink known as cherry bounce.

The wood is considered weak—not recommended for structural framing members—and medium hard. It weighs thirty-five pounds per cubic foot. Cherry has been used for the casings of scientific instruments and spirit levels: The wood is stable, and once cured it is unlikely to warp. It has a fine, even texture, usually without much figure or obvious grain, but sometimes—as on a blanket chest and bed, which my wife and I had made from cherry wood—marked with a striking, colorful grain pattern. Cherry wood can also show a glowing quilted aspect, or bird's-eye speckles. The wood polishes to a fine luster. Black cherry is in high demand for use as interior trim, cabinetry, and furniture. In today's market, a large veneer-quality black cherry can fetch thousands of dollars.

Pin Cherry *(Prunus pensylvanica)*. Many pin cherry trees grow in our woods in northeastern Vermont. They are relics of heavy logging on the property in the late 1970s, a quarter-century before we came to own it. Now, these short-lived trees have reached full size and are starting to die off—no doubt having left behind seeds that would sprout should another round of cutting or insect devastation hit the forest.

Recently I checked on one of the better, healthier specimens. It stood about 30 feet tall and had a trunk diameter at breast height of 6 inches. The tree bore the slick, mahogany brown bark characteristic of the species, bark that shows to its best advantage in the low, angled light of winter, when it gleams like hammered bronze. As pin cherry matures, its bark may become gray and break up into scaly plates. Prominent lenticels—breathing pores that show up as horizontal marks—interrupt the bark of younger specimens.

Pin cherry is a small tree or a large shrub. At maturity, it generally stands no taller than 40 feet, with a typical maximum trunk diameter of 1 foot. Often the trunk divides into two or more stems. The branches are horizontal or ascending, usually forming a narrow crown, although on a good site the boughs may "elbow out a great deal of room for this swift-growing invader," writes Donald Culross Peattie in *A Natural History of Trees*. The leaves are 2 to 5 inches long, broadly lance-shaped, long-pointed, and finely saw-toothed along their margins. They are shiny green, with a smooth texture on both the upper and lower surfaces. The twigs are redder than the branches and have several buds clustered at their tips.

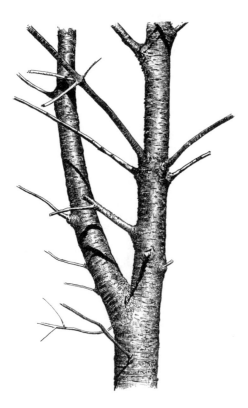

Pin cherry has slick, gleaming, mahogany brown bark. This small, short-lived tree often forks low to the ground.

Pin cherry ranges from Newfoundland to British Columbia and south in the Appalachian Mountains to Tennessee and Georgia. The species grows regionwide in New England. It is found at elevations up to 6,000 feet in the southern Appalachians, the region where it attains its greatest size. The currently recognized national champion is in Tennessee, in Great Smoky Mountains National Park, a 75-footer with a trunk 58 inches in circumference and a crown spread of 41 feet. The largest pin cherry known in Connecticut is 38 feet tall, has a trunk 21 inches in circumference, and has a 9½-foot crown spread.

Pin cherry grows on a variety of sites, from dry, sandy soil to wet loam. It crops up on logged land, clearings, roadsides, burned areas (another name for the tree is fire cherry), woodlands flattened by high winds, spoil banks left by mining, fencerows, and abandoned fields. In northern Pennsylvania, in the wake of widespread clear-cut logging in the early twentieth century, pin cherry often formed almost impenetrable thickets, with 3,000 to 5,000 saplings per acre.

When growing in a dense stand, pin cherry forms a closed canopy in three to seven years and reaches maturity in twenty to forty years. Often it stands alongside quaking and bigtooth aspens; paper and yellow birches; striped, red, and sugar maples; various oaks; and American mountain-ash. *P. pensylvanica* stabilizes newly exposed soil and prevents erosion while providing cover and light shade for the seedlings of other species destined to rise above the short-lived pin cherries and become the next generation of forest trees. Pin cherry requires direct sunlight and dies if it is shaded over—precisely what is taking place in our Vermont woodland, where maples, birches, and aspens are overtopping the pin cherries and causing them to fade from the scene.

In spring the leaves emerge in April and May. White flowers expand along with the foliage; the flowers are clustered together on umbels, structures in which a number of stalks emanate from a common point. (Black cherry, *P. serotina,* and chokecherry, *P. virginiana,* have their flowers on racemes, which are shared, elongated stems.) Pin cherry can fruit as early as two years after sprouting, although large quantities of fruits are not produced until the tree is four years of age or older. A West Virginia study found that a typical tree with a 4½-inch trunk diameter bore about two-thirds of a quart of cherries per year. Forest scientists have estimated that fifteen-year-old pin cherries growing in a pure stand can produce more than a million fruits per acre. In New Hampshire a scientist found from 140,000 to 450,000 viable pin cherry seeds per acre buried in forest soils.

The cherries ripen in late summer. They are red, rounded, and about ¼ inch in diameter, with a thin skin covering juicy, sour flesh and an oblong stone. Many birds and mammals eat pin cherries. Black bears usually pull the limbs toward their mouths, sometimes breaking them, and gobble down leaves, twigs, and fruits. A bruin may straddle a small tree and walk forward, riding the tree down and bringing its crown to mouth level. Beavers eat pin cherry bark, and deer and moose browse the twigs and foliage.

The droppings of bears, birds, and other wild animals spread pin cherry seeds throughout the landscape. Botanists believe the seeds can stay viable for 50 to 150 years, buried in the leaf duff that covers the forest floor. As the years pass, the seeds' tough coats become increasingly permeable to water and oxygen. If fire, logging, or some other event wipes out mature trees, the pin cherry seeds germinate, perhaps activated by a rise in soil temperature caused by the sudden abundance of sunlight.

Seedlings grow rapidly in full light. When a seedling reaches a height of about 3 feet, it begins sending out lateral roots. In West Virginia, foresters examined the root systems of wind-toppled twenty-five-year-old pin cherries and found that they were confined to the top 2 feet of soil. New shoots can arise from pieces of torn-off root left in the ground after a storm has knocked a tree over.

Many microorganisms may invade pin cherry during its short lifetime of about thirty-five years. They include molds, mildews, and rusts. The fungus *Fomes pomaceus* causes trunk rot in many northeastern pin cherries. A multitude of insects feed on the leaves, including the well-known eastern tent caterpillar and the graphically named uglynest caterpillar, a leaf-rolling species that constructs dense nests throughout a tree's foliage.

Fruit growers sometimes graft domestic sour cherry cuttings onto pin cherry rootstocks, one of the few uses that people have found for *P. pensylvanica*. The soft, weak wood is occasionally chip-harvested for fiber and fuel, and some trees go for paper pulp. I have burned pin cherry on occasion in my woodstove. I've made a number of pegs out of the smaller branch crooks taken from near the crown of the tree. I bandsaw them to leave a flat base and a short peg; finished with oil, they are a handsome golden color with ruddy highlights, and their rustic look seems just right in our remodeled farmhouse.

A close relative is chokecherry, *P. virginiana*. Chokecherry is mainly a shrub, although rarely—in rich, deep soil, particularly in the southern Appalachians—it becomes a scraggly tree. Growing in thickets, clearings, rocky woods, fencerows, abandoned fields, and roadside banks, it is regionwide in New England. Its name comes from the mouth-puckering astringency of its cherries, borne in long, drooping clusters. Many wild animals eat the fruits. A clear, claret-colored jelly can be made from chokecherries.

Chestnut

American Chestnut *(Castanea dentata)*.
At the opening of the twentieth century, the
American chestnut was the most abundant
large tree in the eastern forest, where it made
up almost 25 percent of all hardwoods. In
some areas, four of every ten trees were chestnuts. Scientists estimate that some four billion chestnuts grew from Maine to Georgia,
Alabama, and Mississippi, and from the
Atlantic coast west to the Appalachian
Mountains, where, foresters judged, *C. den-*

tata achieved its best development, in western North Carolina and eastern
Tennessee. In New England chestnuts occurred in southern Maine, in
southern and central New Hampshire and Vermont, and in much of Massachusetts, Rhode Island, and Connecticut. The species thrived in many different settings, from lowlands bordering rivers to mountain slopes and
ridgetops.

A mature chestnut stood 60 to 80 feet tall, with a straight trunk 3 to
4 feet in diameter. On an excellent site, this fast-growing species might soar
to 100 feet or higher with a trunk diameter greater than 6 feet. Today, in

the aftermath and the continued presence of an imported fungus disease, the American chestnut exists mainly as a shrub or a small tree.

The leaves of *C. dentata* are 5 to 9 inches long and 2 to 3 inches wide. Prominent side veins parallel one another, each ending in a small, forward-curving spike on the leaf margin. The leaves look somewhat like those of the American beech, but chestnut leaves are thicker, with a more leathery texture. Shiny yellow-green above, the leaves are paler below; they change to a rich yellow in autumn. The bark on young trees is smooth and greenish. On old trunks it becomes fibrous, with deep fissures divided by flat-topped ridges covered with dark brown scales. Its thick bark helps insulate the tree's cambium from groundfires, which are not uncommon on the dry sites that chestnut often colonizes.

Chestnuts flower in June or July, late enough that frosts rarely damage the blossoms. Flowers of both sexes occur on the same tree. Whitish or

In autumn the spiny husks of chestnuts open to reveal the ripe nuts.

yellow-green male flowers stand on upright, 6-inch catkins at the base of the leaf; the female flowers occupy shorter catkins. Wind takes care of pollination. The fertilized female flowers develop into fruits consisting of a burr 2 to 2½ inches in diameter, covered with ½-inch-long spines and containing two or three seeds. The seeds, known as chestnuts, are a shiny dark brown, flattened on one side and pointed at one end. The nuts are ½ to ¾ inch long. They have a rich, sweet taste.

Wayne Harpster, an elderly friend of mine, wrote about growing up in rural central Pennsylvania during the early twentieth century. Wayne reminisced about a family activity he called "nutting." To get chestnuts out of trees, Wayne's father would cut "a long, thin pole that had a limb at the large end. The limb would then be cut back to make a 7- or 8-inch hook that could be hooked over a higher limb on the tree. As our dad would climb, he would reach up and hook the pole above him. This would leave both hands free for climbing. As he got up to where the opened burrs were hanging, he would take the pole and switch or trim the limbs, causing the burrs and chestnuts to fall to the ground. ["Those things sure hurt if they hit you!" Wayne once told me.] When the tree was completely switched, father would climb down and we would all go under the tree to hunt the nuts." Wayne found the following entry in his father's diary for Monday, October 9, 1911: "Cool this morning. A grand day. The children and I picked 41 quarts of chestnuts."

During that era, people gathered chestnuts for their own use and sold any surplus. In cities, vendors roasted chestnuts on the street; passersby would purchase bags of the warm, delicious nuts. Deer, bears, squirrels, chipmunks, wild turkeys, bobwhite quail, and many other wild creatures, including the now-extinct passenger pigeon, ate chestnuts; farmers turned hogs loose in forests and woodlots to fatten on the nuts. Squirrels and chipmunks helped replant the trees by burying chestnuts.

The yellowish brown wood of American chestnut was even more valuable to humans than the nuts. Softer than oak, lighter (at twenty-eight pounds per cubic foot), and easier to work with, it was employed for general construction and for a range of products including wagon tongues, house trim, furniture, and shingles. People used the rot-resistant wood for fence posts and rails (chestnut can be split into rails easily), house and bridge sills, utility poles, and mine timbers. Chestnut was in demand from railroad companies for making ties to support the steel rails; some 2,500 ties were needed for each mile of new track, and more were required for maintaining the existing lines. Henry David Thoreau wrote in his journal in 1860, "It is well known that the chestnut timber of this vicinity has rapidly disappeared within fifteen years, having been used for railroad sleepers, for rails, and for planks, so that there is danger that this part of our forest will become extinct."

Many barns and outbuildings were built of chestnut. The bark supplied tannin used for tanning leather. Chestnut made an excellent fuelwood (the wood is said to give off sharp pops as it burns). Loggers were still harvesting lumber from long-lasting chestnut snags decades after the blight killed the trees. Chestnut stumps rot from the inside out. So tenacious is the wood that one can still find the stumps of second-growth trees sawed down in the early twentieth century; the pale, weathered stumps look like gravestones on the forest floor. Chestnuts logged even earlier—in the latter half of the nineteenth century—may still survive in the form of moss-covered mounds jutting up a foot or two from the ground.

The chestnut blight fungus, *Cryphonectria parasitica* (formerly called *Endothia parasitica*), is believed to have come to North America from China at the beginning of the twentieth century, hitchhiking on imported Asiatic chestnut seedlings. The blight was first noticed in 1904 on trees at the Bronx Zoo in New York. It was spread by the chestnut bark beetle, a native insect species. From 1911 to 1913, Congress appropriated $165,000 for research and control. States became involved in the struggle. Pennsylvania's legislature established a Chestnut Blight Commission in 1913 and spent $275,000—a huge sum at that time—for chemical spraying and for felling trees ahead of the blight. But the plague could not be stopped, and *C. dentata* showed no natural immunity to the foreign pathogen. Within ten years, trees across half of the species' range, including New England, had been destroyed. By the 1950s the chestnut had been virtually wiped out throughout its range in what some ecologists have termed "the greatest botanical disaster in history."

Scientists have since learned that the blight fungus produces two types of spores, which can be thought of as microscopic seeds: a dry disk carried by the wind and a smaller form that is washed down the trunk by rain and enters breaks in the bark—scrapes, branch stubs, woodpecker and insect holes—spreading the infection within the tree. The smaller spores are sticky; they cling to the feet of birds and may be transported for many miles. In attacking the inner bark, the fungal cankers split the wood and girdle the stem, killing the portion of the tree above the lesion. After a stand of chestnuts is infected, 95 percent of the trees die within ten years.

Periodically, the root systems of "dead" chestnuts send up sprouts, especially when they receive direct sunlight, after logging or storms remove tall neighboring trees that have been casting shade on the lingering chestnuts. One theory holds that most sprouts today come not from the stumps of tall forest trees, most of which were killed outright by the blight, but from old seedlings and former low-growing stems that had never become a part of the forest canopy. The root systems of those survivors have a limited life span, and many are now finally dying off. The trees they send forth rarely grow more than 30 feet tall and seldom produce nuts. Still, it is possible to find sizeable, nut-producing chestnut trees, particularly in southern New England. Look for nuts on the ground in autumn, and the telltale prickly husks in the leaf litter at other times of the year.

For decades, scientists have been working to create a blight-resistant American chestnut through cross-breeding, introducing genes from resistant Asian *Castanea* species. State forestry departments and private conservation groups, including the American Chestnut Foundation (with administrative offices in Bennington, Vermont, and a research farm in Virginia), are poised to begin planting hybrid variants in eastern forests. It's unlikely that chestnuts will ever again dominate the eastern woods, but they may be able to survive through human intervention.

The poet Robert Frost wrote these hopeful and perhaps prophetic lines about the American chestnut: "It keeps smoldering at the roots/And keeps sending up new shoots/Till another parasite/Shall come to end the blight."

Recently, a weakened, or hypovirulent, form of chestnut blight has emerged. It seems to infect the normal robust form of *Cryphonectria parasitica* with a virus, weakening it so that a tree can withstand its effects and wall off the invading fungus behind new bark tissue. Today researchers are studying methods of spreading the hypovirulent form in nature.

Cottonwood

Eastern Cottonwood *(Populus deltoides).* Eastern cottonwood ranges from southern New England and Canada west to the Plains states, where it intergrades with the plains cottonwood, *P. deltoides occidentalis,* a subspecies that continues west to the foothills of the Rocky Mountains. The eastern species grows in the Connecticut River valley and in western Massachusetts and Connecticut. It also occurs in parts of New York and Pennsylvania and on the shores of several of the 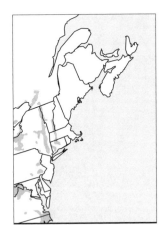 Great Lakes; it becomes more abundant starting in Ohio and heading west and south from there. The core of its range includes the humid lowlands of the Mississippi River drainage, where eastern cottonwood achieves its best growth.

Cottonwoods prosper in moist, rich soils of floodplains and river bottomlands. They also thrive along stream banks and lake borders and in swamps. Planted as a shade tree, a cottonwood will grow if its roots—shallow but wide-spreading—find a reliable source of the moisture that this tree requires in abundance.

P. deltoides has a handsome form, which becomes particularly visible in winter: an expansive, open crown of very thick, often slightly drooping branches. Most cottonwoods stand 50 to 75 feet tall. Some achieve 100 or more feet, and observers have reported heights of 175 to 190 feet. Three large cottonwoods recently reported from different counties in Vermont stand 121, 123, and 124 feet tall, respectively. Trunk diameters of 2 to 4 feet are typical, and large specimens can be 4 to more than 6 feet across the trunk. Often a cottonwood forks into two or more stems a few feet above ground level. Young cottonwoods on excellent sites may add 5 feet to their stature in a single growing season and 40 feet in ten years.

Deep vertical furrows mark the ashy gray bark of the mature tree. The leaf is triangular, with a long, pointed tip. The best way to distinguish a cottonwood from one of the many planted hybrid poplars is to look at the leaf. A hybrid will tend to have a more ovate leaf, or, if triangular, it will lack the truncate or straight-across base exhibited by the cottonwood. Cottonwood leaves are 3 to 5 inches long and rather thick, and they have rounded teeth along their margins. They are a deep, shiny green above and pale green below. The leaves alternate along the twigs. When crushed, both the leaves and buds release a sweet aroma. The stalks of cottonwood leaves are long and laterally flattened, like those of the aspens, causing the leaves to sway and flutter in the breeze. They make more of a rustle or a rattle, compared with the whisperings of the aspens' smaller leaves. In autumn cottonwood leaves turn yellow; they fall early, often leaving the branches bare in September.

Unlike quaking aspen and bigtooth aspen, eastern cottonwood does not clone itself by sending up genetically identical shoots from its root system. However, if cut down, a young tree will sprout vigorously from the stump, and cuttings planted in the ground will grow readily. Cottonwoods can be less-than-ideal neighbors in cities and towns, where their prolific, probing roots heave up sidewalks and clog sewers and drains. In rural areas they make effective windbreaks and are planted for erosion control along ditches, riverbanks, and the shores of lakes and ponds.

In spring, just before its leaves unfurl, the cottonwood sets out flowers. Male and female flowers appear on separate trees. The fuzzy male blossoms crowd together on drooping yellow catkins; the deep red female blossoms are larger and are displayed on drooping stems. Wind-blown pollen fertilizes the female flowers, which mature into elliptical capsules ⅜ inch long. The capsules split open around June, releasing many tiny seeds. Each seed has a tuft of downy fiber that acts as a parachute, carrying it several hundred feet or farther from the parent tree. I have visited Midwestern towns in late spring, when the cottonwood fluff blew down the streets and piled up in the gutters like snow. The tree gets its name from the cotton-tipped seeds.

Trees start producing seeds when five to ten years old. Scientists have estimated that a single mature tree can release as many as forty-eight million seeds in one year. Seeds often fall in the water, and spring floods deposit them on land. The seeds require abundant sunlight to germinate and grow. Cottonwoods often compete with willows to cover new sandbars and bare floodplains. When mature, they may stand among black ash, silver maple, American elm, hackberry, sycamore, box-elder, and other lowland dwellers.

The life span of *P. deltoides* is not long. Deterioration sets in as early as age seventy, with cracks and heart rot weakening and hollowing the trunk. Cavities in living cottonwoods are used for nesting and winter shelter by many animals, including wood ducks, woodpeckers, owls, opossums, and raccoons.

The heartwood of *P. deltoides* is dark brown, the sapwood white and wide. The soft but hard-to-split wood weighs a mere twenty-eight pounds per cubic foot—about the same as aspen. Loggers cut it for plywood, paper pulp, excelsior, boxes and crates, matches, and interior parts of furniture. The wood warps and checks badly as it cures. When my great-grandfather Addison Foote claimed a homestead on the Kansas plain in 1871, he put up a house quickly, believed to be the first frame dwelling (as opposed to a sod house) built in Mitchell County, Kansas. Add was said to be a good carpenter, but his material—the green or uncured wood of cottonwood, either the eastern or the plains variety—gave him trouble. Drafts were plenty in that humble abode. In later years, my great-grandmother, Sarah Gleason Foote, recalled that as a new bride she spent most of her first winter in Kansas with her feet in the oven of the kitchen stove.

Swamp Cottonwood *(Populus hetero-phylla).* Swamp cottonwood is a closely related species and an extremely rare tree in New England, where it occurs only in southern Connecticut. The species has a discontinuous range mainly in the Mid-Atlantic and southeastern states, and it is also found in parts of the Midwest and in the Mississippi River drainage. Swamp cottonwood grows on sites that are too wet for eastern cottonwoods: shallow swamps, lakeside

sloughs, and river bottoms where the soil stays wet during most of the year.

Dogwood

Flowering Dogwood *(Cornus florida)*. This small, well-known tree is adapted to live in partial shade. Mature dogwoods stand 10 to 40 feet tall and can have a trunk diameter of 12 to 18 inches; most specimens in New England top out at 25 feet tall or less. The trunk is short, quickly dividing into tiers of boughs that are generally horizontal and sometimes turned up at the ends. The species reaches its northernmost limit in New England, where it occurs in south- 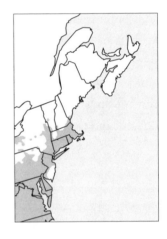 western Maine, southern New Hampshire, western Vermont, much of Massachusetts, and throughout Connecticut and Rhode Island. *C. florida* ranges west to Michigan and south to Florida and Texas. In much of the South, dogwood is—or was, until a disease epidemic swept through the eastern woods beginning in the 1980s—the most abundant species in the forest understory.

Flowering dogwood inhabits moist-to-dry woods, old fields, fencerows, and roadsides. It grows best in rich, well-drained soil and does not thrive in damp, mucky ground, terrain that is flooded frequently, or sandy soils that drain rapidly. A dogwood's roots are extensive but shallow. If the tree's trunk and crown are badly damaged or killed by logging or fire, the root system will send up shoots. Dogwood grows slowly, increasing the circumference of its trunk by adding annual rings no more than ⅟₁₆ to ⅛ inch wide. Individual trees may live 125 years.

Dogwood leaves conduct photosynthesis most efficiently in open shade where the light intensity is slightly less than one-third that of full sunlight. Where the shade is too deep, they either do not become established or they die off. *C. florida* seldom, if ever, grows in pure stands. In the Northeast, dogwoods are common in oak-hickory and in beech-birch-maple forests; they are uncommon in or are absent from coniferous woods.

The leaves are egg-shaped, 2 to 5 inches long by about half as wide, and marked by a prominent central vein with five or six curving lateral veins on each side roughly paralleling the leaf margin. Often they have wavy edges. They are a bright dark green above, paler green and covered with fine hairs beneath, and grow opposite each other on the twigs. The bark is rough, scaly, and broken up into small, squarish plates.

Dogwood flowers spangle the trees' branches in early spring. The four white "petals," opening to form a cross 2 to 4 inches wide, are in fact

The four white "petals" of flowering dogwood are actually bracts, coverings that protected the developing flowers, clustered where the bracts intersect.

bracts, coverings that protected the incipient, dormant flowers over winter. Most dogwoods have white bracts, although a few have pale salmon or pink ones. Insects pollinate the small, yellowish green florets clustered where the bracts intersect; the florets are the actual flowers, and each cluster has twenty to thirty of them. Dogwoods begin flowering at around age six and generally produce abundant seed crops every other year.

One to five or more of the central florets complete their development into fruit. The elliptical fruits are brilliant red, ½ inch long by ¼ inch wide, and borne at the ends of long stalks. (Near the fruits repose the next year's flower buds, ½ inch in diameter, silvery gray, and shaped like miniature turbans.) The fruit's pulp is thin and mealy; some sources say it is poisonous to humans, and in any case it is too bitter to be eaten. Hidden in the pulp is a hard, two-chambered, usually two-seeded stone. As the fruits ripen in September and October, the leaves of dogwoods become rose-colored or wine red, the undersides a paler pink. The bright colors attract birds, which alight and eat the fruits. Later, perhaps far from the parent tree, the birds void the seeds in their droppings. Dogwood seeds usually germinate in the spring after they have fallen.

More than thirty-six species of birds eat dogwood fruits: local residents, such as ruffed grouse, wild turkeys, and woodpeckers; short-range migrants, including wood ducks, yellow-shafted flickers, crows, cedar waxwings, robins, cardinals, and catbirds; and birds that travel long distances, including pine and evening grosbeaks as well as neotropical migrants such as red-eyed vireos and Swainson's and wood thrushes. The fruits, about 17 percent crude fat by weight, are loaded with energy, which the birds require for migrating.

The ecological value of dogwoods extends beyond feeding birds. The leaves of *C. florida* decompose quickly, freeing minerals for use by other plants. Dogwood leaves break down three times faster than hickory leaves; four times faster than the leaves of tuliptree, eastern redcedar, and white ash; and ten times faster than sycamore and oak leaves. They enrich the top layers of the soil with calcium, fluorine, potassium, phosphorus, magnesium, and other elements.

Native Americans made a scarlet dye from dogwood roots and treated diarrhea and fevers with a preparation made by boiling the inner bark. The pinkish wood is hard and very heavy, at fifty-one pounds per cubic foot. Fine-textured and homogeneous, it withstands abrasion and wears smooth under friction. People have used it for pulleys, knitting needles, sledge runners, hay forks, wheel hubs, rake teeth, splitting wedges, chisel handles, and the heads of mallets and golf clubs. In the nineteenth century great quantities of the wood went into the elongated, bullet-shaped shuttles used in the textile industry in New England, in other parts of the United States, and in England and Europe; many shuttles were manufactured in Massachusetts and Rhode Island. After World War II, plastic shuttles replaced the wooden variety in weaving machinery, and today looms operate without using shuttles.

I've often wondered if the name dogwood has a true canine connection. There is that old and apt mnemonic: "How can you tell a dogwood? By its bark." Most sources link the name to the Germanic word *dag*, meaning a skewer to hold meat together for cooking—and likely this hardwood would be up to the task. In *The Book of Forest and Thicket*, John Eastman suggests another explanation, based on his experiences cutting dogwood to clear survey lines: The name may come from the fetid smell of the freshly cut wood, which reminded Eastman of dog feces.

In the 1970s dogwoods in the Pacific Northwest began dying from a mysterious disease. Soon eastern dogwoods started showing the same symptoms: tan leaf spots that developed into large, purple-bordered blotches. Often the infection spread to twigs, branches, and trunk, with cankers girdling the main stem and killing the tree. The pathogen causing the epidemic turned out to be a fungus never before identified; it may have entered the continent on infected nursery stock, perhaps of *C. kousa*, an Asian dogwood that seems relatively resistant to the disease. Within a few years, the fungus, named *Discula destructiva*, spread throughout the East, affecting seedlings and adult trees and wild and ornamental specimens. Scientists speculate that birds feeding on dogwood fruits may carry fungal spores, spreading the infection.

Catoctin Mountain Park, in Maryland, lost 88 percent of its dogwoods between 1984 and 1988. On Pennsylvania's Allegheny Plateau, all of the dogwoods that researchers examined between 1995 and 1998 had either died of dogwood anthracnose, as the disease had come to be known, or were infected with it. Some scientists suggest that acid rain increases the incidence and severity of the plague. It is also possible that the fungus weakens dogwoods enough that drought or wood-boring insects cause the trees' death. Plant pathologist Victoria Smith, of the Connecticut Agricultural Experiment Station, monitored Connecticut dogwoods between 1990 and 1997. She found that both the severity and the incidence of anthracnose peaked in mid- to late June, about six weeks after leaf emergence. She did not observe severe dieback or decline in Connecticut dogwoods and suggests that powdery mildew, another fungal disease, is more apt to cause leaf damage or defoliation. She concluded that dogwood anthracnose "is not as devastating in Connecticut landscapes as in other areas."

Rangewide, some dogwoods seem able to survive the disease, particularly those growing away from damp habitats, in places where air circulation dries out the leaf surfaces and prevents the fungus from taking hold. It seems likely that not all dogwoods will perish—as forest pathologists once feared—but that the species will no longer be as numerous as it once was. The loss of so many dogwoods has changed the face and the ecology of the eastern woods, particularly in the South, where dogwood was formerly abundant. Without dogwood leaves continually restoring calcium to forest soils—many of which are calcium-poor in the first place—acid rain may leach the usable calcium out of the system. Soil invertebrates such as insects and arthropods need calcium for their exoskeletons; birds prey heavily on those invertebrates. Some scientists fear that the destruction of dogwoods has contributed to the decline in forest-nesting birds, which require calcium for their eggshells. Other animals that eat invertebrates, including salamanders and toads, may also be affected.

Studies conducted in Tennessee suggest that as dogwoods dwindle, two other bird-dispersed plants increase: black-gum and spicebush, both of which reproduce by offering high-fat fruits to wildlife in late summer and autumn.

A close relative to flowering dogwood—and one that so far has shown good resistance to dogwood anthracnose—is alternate-leaf dogwood *(C. alternifolia)*. Alternate-leaf dogwood ranges from Newfoundland to Alabama and west to Minnesota and Arkansas; it grows throughout New England. It is the only type of dogwood to have an alternating, rather than opposing, placement of leaves on the twigs. Alternate-leaf dogwood is also called pigeonberry, blue dogwood, or pagoda dogwood. More of a shrub than a tree—at most 30 feet tall and usually much shorter—it favors damp habitats such as wooded lowlands and shady ravines. Its small, cream-colored flowers bloom in clusters during late May and early June. By late summer, the flowers have developed into blue-black fruits that are eaten by many birds.

Elm

American Elm (*Ulmus americana*). Years ago, new to the technology of cutting wood and burning it in a heating stove, I chanced upon several dead, barkless trees in a grove on my landlord's farm. Most of the trees were about a foot in diameter. After getting permission to cut them for firewood, I chainsawed their trunks into billets 18 inches long. Then I picked up the splitting maul. Pound away as I might, I could not split the wood using the maul. After great  effort, I finally sundered one billet by driving a steel wedge through it with a sledgehammer. I ended up cutting the other pieces lengthwise with my saw.

The dead trees were American elms, whose wood knits together with spiraling, interlocking fibers. When I burned it, the dry, well-seasoned wood gave off heat—and a not-very-pleasant acrid smell. Later I learned that country folk, in consideration of how its wood smells, sometimes refer to *U. americana*—a stately and otherwise generally beloved tree—as "piss elm."

American elm grows from Nova Scotia to Saskatchewan and south to Florida and Texas; few other trees have such an extensive range. The species is regionwide in New England. Other vernacular names for the tree are white elm, gray elm, water elm, and soft elm.

U. americana prefers rich, moist, well-drained soil in bottomlands and floodplains and along the banks of streams and lakes. Elms do not occur in single-species stands but mingle with other hardwoods such as box-elder, eastern cottonwood, black ash, red maple, silver maple, hackberry, sycamore, and sweet-gum. In drier habitats—old fields, meadows, road-sides, hedgerows—elms grow alongside sugar maple, basswood, American beech, and numerous other species. On our wooded acres in Vermont, elms stand in abundance on both dry upland and damp lowland habitats. Fast-growing trees, elms colonize disturbed land, such as mined areas and abandoned city blocks. Because of the mature tree's pleasing shape, people have planted *U. americana* in parks, cemeteries, and farmyards and on campuses, streets, and lawns.

As is true with most trees, should an elm grow in a woods setting, it will exhibit one form, and should it flourish in full sunlight, it will take on a different form. A woods-grown elm, competing for light with neighbor-ing trees, sends up a long, straight trunk that divides into several equal-size branches 30 to 60 feet above the ground. If an elm grows in the open, its trunk usually divides 10 to 20 feet above ground level; each branch then subdivides again and again, with the outermost branches and twigs paral-leling the ground or bowing down toward it. In many open-country spec-imens, the crown is broader than it is tall. The overall shape, beautiful and unique among trees, suggests a vase or a flowing fountain. The eighteenth-century French botanic explorer André Michaux judged the American elm "the most magnificent vegetable of the temperate zone."

In *A Natural History of Trees,* Donald Culross Peattie describes the quality of shade found beneath an elm. "A big old specimen will have about a million leaves, or an acre of leaf surface, and will cast a pool of shadow 100 feet in diameter," he writes. "The leaves hang more or less all in one plane on the bough, and they make a pattern roughly like a lattice. Hence the dappling of shadow and light." The dappled shade pleases human sensibilities. Large elms seem to beckon people to gather beneath them—and, on occasion, to conduct momentous affairs there. An elm that stood on Boston Common in the 1800s was widely known as The Great Tree. Around the time of the Revolution, British soldiers camped beneath it, and their commanding officers ordered them to refrain from turning it into firewood. In Pennsylvania, beneath a stately elm in the Lenni-Lenape village of Sachamexing, William Penn signed a treaty in 1682 with the Native American tribe that was honored by both sides for many years, securing the future of Penn's New World colony.

A typical mature elm can be quite a large tree: 80 to 100 feet tall and with a trunk 2 to 5 feet in diameter. Some elms develop enlarged buttresses at the base of the trunk, giving them a diameter of 8 to 11 feet at breast height. Despite the ravages of a fungus that has killed many elms, some impressively large specimens remain, such as one in Yarmouth, Maine, which, when measured in 1997, stood 93 feet tall, had a trunk 20 feet in circumference, and a crown spread of 110 feet.

The leaves of American elm have saw-toothed edges. These leaves show the serpentine feeding trails of small insects known as leafminers.

Elm bark is gray-brown, with long, irregular furrows between broad, flat ridges. The leaves alternate along the stems. They are 4 to 6 inches long, oval to oblong, with saw-toothed margins and a long, tapering point at the tip. The base is rounded and asymmetrical: larger on one side of the stem than the other. Many straight side veins run parallel on the leaf surface. The blade is thin, dark bluish green, usually hairless on its upper surface, and paler and furred with soft hairs beneath. Elm leaves turn golden yellow in autumn. After the leaves have fallen, the massive trunks and limbs, ramifying into ever-smaller branches and zigzag twigs, stand etched against the sky, perhaps even more beautiful when bare than when clad with foliage. To my eye, elms are at their handsomest in May, when the tiny crisp new leaves unpleat from their buds while the still-green, unripe seeds remain bundled to the stems. The overall impression is of a luminous viridian haze through which the elbowing, curving, corkscrewing limbs stand out in their dark muscularity.

Elms flower in early spring, two to three weeks before the trees' leaves emerge. The small flowers, clustered on inch-long, drooping stalks, contain both male and female parts. The wind moves pollen from the male to the female structures. A rainy spring may hamper pollination because the pollen-bearing anthers do not open when the atmosphere is saturated.

Trees forty years old and older flower most abundantly and produce the greatest quantities of seeds. The disk-shaped fruit is a small samara about ½ inch across; it consists of a flat seed enclosed within a thin, papery envelope. The fruits ripen quickly, in April and May, before the leaves are fully expanded. The lightweight samaras detach from their stems, and the wind scatters them up to ¼ mile from the parent tree. Samaras that fall into moving water may be transported even farther.

Seeds landing on moist soil usually germinate within six to twelve days, although some lie dormant until the following spring. The seeds can send down rootlets into moist leaf litter, moss, and rotting logs and stumps. During their first year, seedlings grow best in partial shade—about one-third of full sunlight. Later, the young trees thrive in full sun. Elms can live a long time: 175 to 200 years, in some cases more than 300 years. In heavy, wet soil an elm's roots spread out and extend down only 3 or 4 feet; in drier soils they may penetrate 5 to 10 feet. Elms can withstand flooding during winter and early spring, but they usually die if inundated during the growing season, in late spring and early summer. After falling, elm leaves break down quickly, liberating large quantities of potassium and calcium.

Elm wood is variously cited as weighing thirty-five to forty-one pounds per cubic foot, dry weight. The heartwood is light brown; the sapwood is thick and paler in color. The interlocking grain that I found so difficult to split makes elm useful for high-strength items like hockey sticks, mine props, and barn flooring. While constructing stone walls, I have used elm billets as rollers for moving large stones. Since the wood tends to warp upon drying, elm finds few applications in finish carpentry or cabinetry. Screws grab hold of it more securely than almost any other wood. Iroquois Indians used elm bark to sheath their canoes, apparently because they had limited access to good-quality paper birch. Writes John McPhee in *The Survival of the Bark Canoe,* regarding Iroquois canoe builders: "If they wanted to get across a river, they might—in one day—build an elm-bark canoe, and then forget it, leave it in the woods." In later times, wheelwrights favored friction- and pressure-resistant elm for the hubs of heavy wagons. Men who drove the oxen yoked to those wagons might peel an elm's bark and braid its inner fibers into strong, supple whips. Other past and current uses include rope twisted from the bark fibers, ship parts, barrel hoops and staves, caskets, boxes, crates, and paneling.

Many wild animals eat elm seeds, including bobwhite quail, ruffed grouse, wood ducks, rose-breasted grosbeaks, purple finches, squirrels, and opossums. Gray squirrels nibble on the flower buds and flowers. Cottontail rabbits, snowshoe hares, and white-tailed deer eat the twigs and leaves. Butterfly and moth caterpillars—including those of the beautiful mourning cloak butterfly—relish elm foliage. Elms even attract human foragers: In May I look for morel mushrooms growing beneath dead elms. Elms, both living and dead, offer habitat to several wild species. Look for the pendulous, sack-shaped nests of Baltimore orioles in the dense foliage of outer branches. Red-headed woodpeckers chisel out nesting cavities in dead elms, of which all too many raise their barkless branches in the eastern woods these days.

In the 1920s elms in Holland began dying from a fungal disease of Asian origin. The fungus, *Ceratocystis ulmi,* arrived in the United States in the 1930s, its spores carried by European elm bark beetles that probably had hitchhiked on elm logs imported for the furniture industry. The beetles, scarcely bigger than a gnat, soon found their way to American elms, which had no resistance to the so-called Dutch elm disease.

Both the European beetle and a related native elm beetle breed in infected elms, then fly to healthy trees to feed. When I cut a dead elm for firewood, I sometimes find intricate channels like decorative engraving on the outer surface of the wood: brood galleries where the beetles laid their eggs. Evidence of such tunnels can also be seen on the inner bark that sloughs off from dead and dying elms. After the beetles introduce its spores to an elm, the fungus grows in the tree's sapwood, clogging it so that water and nutrients cannot make their way from the roots to the leaves. The leaves wilt and drop off, branches die, and eventually the tree succumbs. Death can occur within a single growing season.

Foresters believe that Dutch elm disease has wiped out more than half of our native elms. Trees in forest, countryside, and urban settings have perished. It is becoming increasingly rare to find elms old and large enough to exhibit the distinctive vase-shaped form. Writes ecologist Tom Wessels in *Reading the Forested Landscape,* "On certain riparian sites—floodplains and banks adjacent ro rivers or streams—in both central and northern New England, American elms dominated forest canopies and sometimes reached heights of over one hundred feet. The interlacing, arching branches of these giant elms must have created forests with the feel of living cathedrals. Not one of these dramatic floodplain forests remains in all of New England."

The American elm, however, seems not to be headed toward extinction. There are small elms cropping up all over our farm in northeastern Vermont. University of Vermont ecologist Bernd Heinrich has studied elms in western Vermont and reports his findings in *The Trees in My Forest.* Heinrich discovered that small, roadside elms are flowering at a very young age. Of 540 live trees he inspected, only 47 had trunk diameters greater than 6 inches, yet many had flowered and produced seed. Heinrich suggests that elms which reproduce early in life—before the fungus finds them—will be the ones to pass on their genes: The American elm of the future may be a small tree rather than a graceful, fountain-shaped giant.

Slippery Elm *(Ulmus rubra).* Two sorts of elms grow in New England: American elm and slippery elm. The latter is much less well-known than the American elm. It is also smaller, more ragged looking, and not as symmetrical in form, with stout limbs ascending to a crown that is often broad and flat-topped. Most slippery elms grow 60 to 70 feet tall, with a trunk diameter of 1 to 2½ feet. A few specimens exceed 100 feet in height. A huge slippery elm is reported from 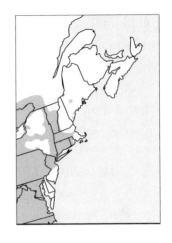 Vassalboro, Maine: 97 feet tall and with a trunk more than 200 inches in circumference as of 1995.

Slippery elm grows from Maine to Florida and west to the Dakotas and Texas, a range almost as extensive as that of American elm. It is most abundant in the southern Great Lakes states and in the Midwest. In New England it is found in limited areas in southern Maine, in much of Vermont and along the Connecticut River in New Hampshire, in western Massachusetts, and throughout Connecticut and Rhode Island. *U. rubra* prospers in moist, rich soils of lower slopes, stream banks, river terraces, and bottomlands. It also grows in fertile uplands, particularly those having limestone soil. Because it lives in such a broad range of climates and soil types, it is found with many other species of trees. A few of its sylvan associates are white oak, swamp oak, bur oak, American elm, black ash, sugar maple, yellow birch, butternut, black walnut, black cherry, aspens, eastern cottonwood, sycamore, black-gum, eastern hornbeam, and hemlock. Other names for *U. rubra* are red elm, gray elm, and soft elm.

The bark is thick, rough, dark brown, and deeply furrowed. The leaves are 5 to 7 inches long, somewhat larger than those of American elm. If an elm leaf feels smooth or only slightly rough, it belongs to an American elm; if it feels noticeably rough, it's a slippery elm—the opposite of what you'd expect from the slippery elm's name. The "slippery" appellation comes from the tree's inner bark, which is ⅛ to ¼ inch thick, mucilaginous and slimy, and with a licorice taste. (You can detect the slipperiness by chewing on a twig.) Native Americans chewed the tree's bark and roots to reduce the pain from sore throat. People have used the bark for wound dressings and poultices.

The flowers of slippery elm cluster on short stalks. They are inconspicuous, and they push forth in the spring before the leaves emerge. The resulting samaras look like those of American elm but are slightly larger. The fruits ripen during April, May, and June, depending on latitude and local weather conditions. It takes around 40,000 of the small seeds to make one pound. The wind disperses the samaras. The seeds can germinate in mineral soil and leaf litter and among grasses and other plants. Slippery elm sprouts readily from the stump, and its seedlings spread vegetatively, sending up shoots from their root systems.

U. rubra tolerates shade much better than does quaking aspen; it is judged only slightly less shade tolerant than sugar maple. Like American elm, slippery elm is vulnerable to Dutch elm disease, and it has been stricken with elm yellows, a disease caused by a mycoplasma-like organism, or MLO. According to John H. Cooley and J. W. Van Sambeek, in the chapter on slippery elm that they contributed to *Silvics of North America,* "These two diseases are so virulent and widespread that slippery elm seldom reaches commercial size and volume as a forest tree, and it is being replaced as a street tree in many localities."

The heavy, hard wood, in contrast with that of American elm, is easy to split. Slippery elm wood resists rotting in contact with the soil, leading to its occasional use for fenceposts and railroad ties. Early builders sometimes used it for framing covered bridges; a bridge spanning the Ottauquechee River in central Vermont was built with slippery elm posts, pine stringers, beech braces, and spruce siding. Other applications include furniture, paneling, and containers.

Hackberry

Northern Hackberry *(Celtis occidentalis)*.
The tree stood in a grassy yard along the
Connecticut River in central Vermont. I was
waiting for the man who was selling the old
hay elevator to fetch an electric cord and
power the device up, to show me it worked
before I laid down cash. I looked at the tree,
which stood between his house and barn. It
looked familiar, but I couldn't identify it.
Its crown, composed of slightly drooping
branches, held out an array of serrated leaves

that looked like those of American elm or slippery elm. I didn't think the
tree was an elm, even though its shape was rather vaselike. The bark was all
wrong: pale brownish gray, tight, and adorned with wandering corky ridges
and bumps.

In the end, I had to ask the landowner what kind of tree it was.

"Hackberry," he replied.

"Did you plant it?"

"No, it just showed up."

Northern hackberry belongs to the elm family. Central Vermont is as
far north as the species grows in New England; it also occurs in southern

New Hampshire, Massachusetts, Connecticut, and Rhode Island. On a continental scale, hackberry ranges north into Quebec, west to the Dakotas, and south to Oklahoma and Georgia; it tends to be larger in the southern part of its range. A related species, southern or lowland hackberry, *C. laevigata,* often called sugarberry, flourishes in the South; some botanists believe *C. occidentalis* and *C. laevigata* hybridize where the two overlap.

Hackberry does best in the rich, moist soil of floodplains, valleys, and river islands. It does not grow in swampy soil, but when mature, it can survive spring flooding in lowland sites. It ascends to bluffs, upland slopes, and limestone cliffs, usually growing as a single tree amid other hardwoods. Most hackberries are small- to medium-size: 20 to 70 feet tall, with large specimens soaring to 100 feet and taller. Under good conditions it springs up rapidly and can live for 200 years or longer. Growing in full sunlight, hackberry produces a vase-shaped crown similar to that of American elm.

Corky, wartlike projections stud the grayish brown bark of the hackberry.

Hackberry tolerates shade fairly well and can survive in the forest understory as a small tree. It sinks its roots deep—10 to 20 feet—letting it tap into groundwater during drought. With its thin bark, hackberry is badly damaged by fire, with any wounds opening the tree to wood decay organisms. After hackberries are logged off, sprouts shoot up from the stumps of smaller trees, although not usually from larger ones. Fire-damaged seedlings and saplings also send up sprouts.

The tree's common name is thought to be a corruption of the Scottish *hagberry,* which refers to a fruit-bearing cherry tree that grows in wetlands known as hags. Hackberry is also known as sugarberry, hoop ash, beaverwood, nettletree, and bastard elm—the last two names because its leaves resemble those of nettles, common herbaceous plants of genus *Urtica,* and American elm. Hackberry leaves are 2 to 5 inches long and 1½ to 2½ inches wide, ovate with a sharp, tapering point at the end, and with toothed margins. Some leaves feel sandpapery on their shiny green upper surfaces, and all possess three prominent primary veins and undersides that are a paler green than their top surfaces. Most of the leaves have an uneven or asymmetrical base, like the leaves of basswood. Hackberry leaves turn yellow in autumn.

In early May, about the time its leaves emerge, hackberry puts out small, greenish flowers at the ends of slender, drooping stalks. The inconspicuous blossoms are about ⅛ inch across. The male flowers cluster at the base of the annual twig growth, and the female flowers stand singly at the base of the upper leaves on the same shoot. Wind carries pollen from male to female flowers.

By September, the female flower has developed into a mature fruit, a ¼- to ½-inch spherical drupe, with purple skin and dry, sweet-tasting, orange-colored flesh. The flesh encloses a thick-walled nutlet with a single seed. Hackberries produce good food crops every few years and light crops in intervening years. Known as sugarberries, the fruits may hang on into winter, by which time they look like tiny, shriveled plums. Foragers report that they taste like dates.

Some seeds fall to the ground; others get carried by streams and rivers and are deposited on riverbanks and bottomlands. In a study conducted in Indiana, 34 percent of seeds germinated after being stored for a year in leaf litter, and another 20 percent germinated after being stored over two winters.

Many birds eat hackberry fruits: bobwhite quail, ring-necked pheasants, wild turkeys, woodpeckers, prairie chickens, crows, sapsuckers, flickers, robins, catbirds, brown thrashers, mockingbirds, cedar waxwings, and others. The birds scatter the seeds far and wide with their droppings. Squirrels, foxes, opossums, raccoons, and skunks have all been observed eating hackberries, and probably many small rodents consume the fruit and seeds as well.

A heavy wood, at forty-six pounds per cubic foot, hackberry is considered to be moderately hard. Some mills market it mixed in with ash or elm. The sapwood is pale yellow to greenish yellow, the heartwood slightly darker. Since it is tough and flexible, people have crafted hackberry into barrel hoops and tool handles. Boxes, crates, and plywood are also made from hackberry. Furniture makers use the wood for solid parts in furniture, then hide its plain face beneath veneers of walnut, cherry, or mahogany.

Hawthorn

HAWTHORNS, ALSO CALLED THORNAPPLES, ARE large shrubs that sometimes achieve the stature and spread of small trees. It's not certain how many species exist in North America. Some taxonomists recognize fewer than a hundred, while others cite a thousand or more. Hawthorns hybridize readily, blending their leaf shapes and flowering and fruiting characteristics, which makes the positive identification of many species impossible for amateur naturalists and very difficult even for professional botanists.

Key identification marks for the group are their long, slender, sharp-pointed thorns; their leaves, variable in shape but generally small, oval, saw-toothed, and often with distinct side lobes; the clusters of fingertip-size apples that are usually red but in some species ripen to become orange, yellow, or dark blue to almost black; and their preferred habitats of woods edges, old fields, and fencerows. People have also planted hawthorns as ornamentals and to create hedges.

The hawthorns are closely related to mountain-ash, shadbush, crab-apples, apples, cherries, and plums; all belong to the rose family, Rosaceae. The genus *Crataegus* has the center of its distribution in eastern North America. Some botanists theorize that the vast numbers of hawthorn species arose here after Europeans settled the continent, cutting down old-growth forests and converting the land to agriculture. Uncountable acres of new open habitat let hawthorns spread widely and hybridize freely.

As handsome as hawthorn fruits appear, they are not overly attractive to wildlife. Because their fat content is low (1 to 2 percent, by weight), they do not provide much caloric value. Ruffed grouse, cedar waxwings, fox sparrows, and some other birds eat the fruits. Hawthorns are of greater value to wildlife as cover: predator-proof habitats in which animals can breed and rest. Many songbirds build their nests in the crowns of the dense, thorny plants. Of course, hawthorns did not evolve their thorns to protect birds' nests: The plants grow clustered together, and their intermeshed branches form a phalanx of spiky armor that may deter mammals from eating the shrubs' foliage. Noting that deer can successfully browse hawthorns (they feed between the spines), ecologist Don Janzen theorized that hawthorn armament evolved to thwart larger mammals, such as ground sloths, that were present in North America up until the Pleistocene.

The names given to some of the hawthorn species are both descriptive and historical: Brainerd's hawthorn *(C. brainerdii)* honors its discoverer, Ezra Brainerd, a Vermont botanist and president of Middlebury College from 1885 to 1908. Fireberry hawthorn *(C. chrysocarpa)* puts forth striking, dark red fruit. Biltmore hawthorn *(C. intricata)* is named for an estate in North Carolina where early studies of hawthorns were conducted. Downy hawthorn *(C. mollis)* has leaves densely covered by white hairs; one of the largest hawthorns, occasionally reaching 40 feet in height, it was transplanted to Europe as early as the 1600s. Frosted hawthorn *(C. pruinosa)* produces fruit cloaked with a glaucous bloom, like that of plums.

Two treelike hawthorns of New England are cockspur hawthorn and red-fruited hawthorn.

Cockspur Hawthorn *(C. crus-galli)*. Both the common and the species name refer to the sharp spines bristling from this small tree. Cockspur hawthorn ranges from southern Canada to northern Florida and west to Iowa and Texas. It thrives on limestone soil and often grows in extensive thickets.

Cockspur hawthorn can become 25 to 30 feet tall, with a trunk diameter of 10 to 12 inches. The short trunk usually divides into several stout, spreading branches that form a dense, flattish crown whose width can equal or exceed the tree's height. The dark gray or brownish bark is stippled with small scales, and spines project from trunk and branches. The reddish brown spines are long, slender, and needle-sharp. The alternate, simple leaves are spoon-shaped or narrowly elliptical, broadening from a narrow base to become widest beyond their middle portion. They have saw-toothed margins, usually are not lobed, and are 1 to 3 inches long. Thick and leathery, they glint a shiny dark green above; their pale undersurfaces show conspicuous veins. In autumn the leaves turn orange or red.

Cockspur hawthorn flowers in late May or June, after its leaves have emerged. With their five white petals, the flowers look like miniature apple blossoms. They are about ⅔ inch in diameter and, like the flowers of all hawthorns, include both female and male reproductive structures. The

The thorns of the hawthorns deter animals from browsing on the trees' foliage. The fingertip-size apples are red, orange, yellow, or dark blue to almost black, depending on the species.

fruit ripens in August and September and often hangs on into winter. The tiny apples are about ¼ inch long, greenish to dark dull red, and grouped in drooping clusters. Each hard, dry fruit has a thin pulp and one or two nutlets.

C. crus-galli has been planted and pruned as a hedge since colonial days. The wood is hard and dense, weighing forty-five pounds per cubic foot. People have used it for fenceposts and tool handles and burned it as fuel. The long spines made pins for closing the mouths of sacks.

Red-Fruited Hawthorn *(C. coccinea)*. Although red-fruited hawthorn can grow to 30 feet in height, it rarely exceeds 20 feet. The maximum trunk diameter is around 12 inches. The short trunk gives way to spreading, crooked branches that support a broad, flat crown.

The species ranges from southern Canada south to North Carolina and west to Minnesota and Iowa. Red-fruited hawthorn grows in open woods and fields and along road edges and stream banks, particularly in rocky woods and old pastures with sandy or gravelly soil.

The bark is variously described as red-brown and scaly, and light brown to ashy gray; it is roughened by shallow fissures and small scales. The stiff, rounded twigs sprout wicked thorns about 2 inches long; the thorns are straight, whereas those of most other hawthorns are curved. The leaves are 1 to 5 inches in length, broadly oval in shape, with pointed tips and rounded bases. Their margins are deeply toothed. Four or five lobes often project on each side of the blade from midleaf outward. Around June, when the leaves are almost fully developed, the flowers open. They are white and between ½ and 1 inch in diameter. Their odor, said to be unpleasant to human sensibilities, does not put off insect pollinators. The brilliant red fruit is about ½ inch in diameter and elliptical in shape; dry and mealy at first, it becomes more succulent as it ripens from August through September.

Also known as scarlet hawthorn, *C. coccinea* was one of three North American hawthorns first described by Linnaeus in 1753, from specimens sent to Uppsala, the university where he taught in Sweden. The wood is heavier than that of cockspur hawthorn and has been made into canes, napkin rings, rulers, and engraving blocks.

Hemlock

Eastern Hemlock *(Tsuga canadensis).*
Eastern hemlock is sometimes called Canada
hemlock and, in a confusing mishmash of
names, spruce pine. It ranges from Nova
Scotia west across southern Quebec and
Ontario to Minnesota; throughout New
England and New York; and in high, cool
settings in the Appalachians as far south as
Georgia and Alabama. A close relative, the
Carolina hemlock *(T. caroliniana)* occurs in
the mountains from West Virginia to north-

ern Georgia. Botanists recognize four species of hemlocks in North America and about six in Asia. (The genus name, *Tsuga,* is the Japanese name
for the hemlock.) Hemlocks do not occur naturally in Europe today, but
fossils show that they once grew there.

Hemlocks thrive in cool, moist woodlands, in ravines and river gorges,
and along the banks of streams and creeks. Usually they grow singly or in
scattered local groupings rather than in extensive pure stands. They occur
more frequently on north-facing than on south-facing slopes. Recently I
climbed a mountain in the Berkshires of western Massachusetts. I followed
a trail up the mountain's south slope, through oaks undergrown with

mountain laurel; as I crested the ridge and started down the north-facing slope, the forest turned abruptly to hemlock, with few shrubs growing in the shaded understory beneath the trees.

Most hemlocks are roughly conical in shape. If a hemlock grows in the open, its crown will be full and dense, with layers of branches descending to within a few feet of the ground. In a crowded stand, an individual tree will have a trunk free of lateral branches for several to many feet, culminating in a crown that is short and narrow. In hemlock the uppermost growing tip, or leader, is slender and pliant, as are the outer branches, providing protection against breakage caused by snow, ice, and falling branches.

Hemlock needles are borne on tiny, thread-thin stems, which attach to short, woody, peglike structures, called sterigmata, studding the sides of the twigs. The needles are not pointed like those of a pine or spruce. Rather, they are blunt or round-ended, thin, flattened, and ⅓ to ⅔ inch long. At first glance, they appear to be arranged in twin sprays, one lining each side of the twig, but they actually spiral around the twig. An inconspicuous, often sparse third row of needles grows on top of the twig, angling forward toward the twig's tip. Seen from the side or above, hemlock foliage is a dark blue-green; viewed from below, it looks silvery. The needles account for this bicolored aspect: They are dark green on top and pale below. The pale aspect comes from a chalky white line on either side of the central rib. The line is a series of stomata, openings that allow gas exchange between the needle and the atmosphere. Each needle conducts photosynthesis for about three years before dying and falling off.

Hemlock bark is grayish brown to reddish brown, rough, and hard, with long, vertical furrows separating broad, scaly ridges. On a mature tree, the bark is almost an inch thick and may constitute up to 20 percent of the tree's total volume. The inner bark is a bright cinnamon red.

A hemlock has shallow, spreading roots; close to the trunk, the roots' upper surfaces, cloaked with ruddy bark, may emerge from the ground. The roots snake past or straddle rocks, then angle down into the earth. Shade-loving trees, hemlocks flourish in the deep woods. With their shallow root systems, they are less vulnerable to toppling during high winds when they stand ranked with other trees. Search about in a hemlock grove, and you may find "stilt-rooted" trees, which sprouted in the moss on top of a boulder or a stump, then sent their roots down around that perch to reach mineral soil. A stilt-rooted hemlock is particularly vulnerable to being pushed over in a storm.

In spring male and female flowers emerge on the same branch or on different branches in the same tree. The male flowers are about ¼ inch long, rounded, and yellow; the female flowers are twice that size, oblong, and pale green. Wind carries pollen from the male to the female flowers, and the latter develop into seed cones by autumn. The cones look like little footballs, dangling below the tips of the branchlets. Their overlapping scales readily absorb moisture from the air and dry out again just as rapidly. When the weather is dry and windy, the scales part, letting the breeze free the small, lightweight (roughly 187,000 per pound) seeds, two of which line each scale. A 20-mile-an-hour wind can carry the winged seeds more than 4,000 feet. Most seeds fall during autumn and winter. Stands of mature hemlocks yield good seed crops every two or three years, and an individual tree can continue producing cones for 450 years or more.

In winter porcupines nibble on twigs and branch sprays in hemlocks; after the cuttings fall to the ground, deer may feed on them.

The seeds fall to the ground and germinate. Seedlings take root in moist, well-decomposed litter; in moss-capped soil, wood, and rocks; and in rotted wood on top of a decomposing stump or a "nurse log," often that of a fallen hemlock. Several hemlocks growing in a straight line show where a nurse log once lay. Drought spells death for small hemlocks, and full, open sunlight can dry out the soil around the seedlings' roots, killing them; they do better in partial or full shade. Once established, a hemlock receiving ample sunlight may increase its height by 18 inches a year, whereas a seedling deeply shaded in the forest understory may take forty to sixty years to reach a height of 6 feet.

T. canadensis is the most shade tolerant of all eastern trees. When scientists studied hemlocks in an old-growth stand in Pennsylvania, they found saplings 2 to 3 inches in diameter at breast height that were 200 years old—waiting in the shade beneath ancient, but ultimately mortal, giants. A tree with a trunk diameter of just over 10 inches was 359 years old; nearby dominant trees were the same age but stood much taller and were 24 to 36 inches in diameter. (It can be difficult to determine the age of a hemlock because saplings under severe suppression in the understory may not form a growth ring each year.) When an opening occurs in a hemlock grove—as when a mature tree succumbs to insect pests, drought, root damage, or a combination of such factors—smaller trees respond by growing rapidly toward the light. Over time, formerly suppressed hemlocks can become dominant trees themselves, claiming their share of the forest canopy.

Hemlock seedlings in the understory beneath hardwood trees grow slowly. But if no serious disruption—fire, logging, insect plague—hits the stand, the hemlocks will eventually become taller than the broad-leaved trees, most of which will finally become shaded out. (One exception is the shade-tolerant American beech.) Ecologists say that such a stand has reached the "climax stage": an assemblage of trees that cannot be invaded or replaced by other species requiring more sunlight to establish themselves.

Most hemlocks live 150 to 200 years, although many become much older. The oldest recorded age is 988 years for a tree having a diameter of 7 feet and a height of 160 feet. The current national record hemlock grows in Great Smoky Mountains National Park in Tennessee; when last measured in 1998, it stood 165 feet tall, and its trunk had a 202-inch circumference. Bob Leverett is an inveterate big-tree hunter living in Massachusetts. He writes: "Hemlocks in southern New England can easily surpass 100 feet. Above 115, they quickly sort themselves out. Even on the most favorable sites, they seem to hit a wall at 120 to 125 feet." An exception to this generality is a hemlock growing at Ice Glen, on public land in the town of Stockbridge, Massachusetts. The tree, which stands 132 feet tall and has a girth of 10.2 feet, is the largest hemlock known in New England as of 2004. Farther north in the region, hemlock "tops out at 95 to about 105 feet," notes Leverett.

Needles, old cones, and fallen twigs carpet the ground beneath a stand of hemlocks. The soil is usually fairly dry and highly acidic from the accumulated litter. Few herbaceous plants survive on such an inhospitable substrate and in the dim light; among them are rattlesnake plantain, wood sorrel, wild sarsaparilla, Canada mayflower, teaberry, starflower, New York fern, and Indian cucumber-root. Hardwood trees mixing with hemlocks in their typical habitats include yellow birch, sweet birch, sugar maple, red maple, American beech, tuliptree, black-gum, and various oaks. White pines mingle their pale green needles with the hemlocks' darker foliage. Balsam fir and spruces may grow in concert with hemlocks. Underground fungi can be abundant, sending up their fruiting bodies—mushrooms— after periods of wet weather, particularly in late summer and early fall. Two common fungi in hemlock areas are the honey mushroom, *Armillaria mellea,* and *Ganoderma tsugae,* a tough, woody, shelflike conk, its upper surface a gleaming mahogany color. The species name *tsugae* emphasizes the fungus's frequent association with *Tsuga canadensis,* the eastern hemlock.

More than twenty-four types of insects feed on hemlocks, including moth caterpillars and wood-boring beetles. The hemlock wooly adelgid is a new and potentially devastating pest. It is about the size of one of the aphids that cluster on the stems of tomato plants. The insect appeared on the West Coast of North America in the early 1900s, perhaps brought in on trees or shrubs imported from Asia. Western hemlock species showed some resistance to the adelgid, but eastern hemlocks have not fared as well: The adelgids are destroying hemlocks, or acting in concert with other environmental factors to cause the death of hemlocks, from Virginia to New England. So far in New England, the pest has cropped up in Connecticut, Rhode Island, Massachusetts, New Hampshire, and Maine. Scientists believe it is spread by birds, deer, and human activities.

Adelgid nymphs protect themselves with a white waxy covering that looks like the artificial snow sprayed by some people on Christmas greens. The nymphs feed by sucking sap from hemlock twigs. Millions of nymphs can infest a single tree. Their feeding causes needles to die and fall off. When adelgids invade trees already stressed by drought, mortality can be high. Some trees seem able to hang on and survive an adelgid infestation, which may be relieved when winter temperatures freeze the insects or rains wash them away. Entomologists are searching in Asia and in the U.S. West for parasites and predators to fight the adelgid, but no one knows if these potential natural controls will halt the insect's spread.

The dense evergreen crowns of hemlocks provide nesting cover for many birds, including the veery, golden-crowned kinglet, several warbler species (the colorful Blackburnian warbler is also known as the hemlock warbler), dark-eyed junco, pine siskin, sharp-shinned hawk, and goshawk. Their deep shade keeps streams cool even on hot summer days; cold-water aquatic life, from insect larvae to trout, requires such chill waters. Other wild animals depend on the cool, shady habitats. One such creature is the eastern small-footed bat, a rare species that often hibernates in caves and mine shafts in hemlock forests.

Yellow-bellied sapsuckers drill rows of holes in hemlock bark and feed on the sap that oozes into the excavations. Red squirrels and other rodents consume large quantities of hemlock seeds, as do birds such as the black-capped chickadee, red crossbill, and white-winged crossbill. The pine siskin's long, thin bill is well adapted to fishing out the seeds from beneath the scales of hemlock cones. In winter hemlocks offer shelter to ruffed grouse, wild turkeys, and various perching birds. When snow is deep, deer may congregate in hemlock groves; the trees hold great loads of snow on their dense boughs, so that the snow on the ground is not nearly as deep as beneath pines or bare-branched hardwoods. The deer browse on hemlock foliage and any twigs within reach. Porcupines climb into the crowns of hemlocks and stay there for days, nipping off foliage and eating bark. I have found sprays of needles and branchlets lying beneath hemlocks; deer tracks in the snow showed where the whitetails had eaten the porcupines' leavings.

No one seems able to explain why the hemlock, a tall and stately tree, should bear the name of a poisonous Old World plant (Socrates was invited to cause his own death by drinking a draught of poison hemlock, a relative of parsley). Native Americans of several tribes prepared a drink from hemlock needles and inner bark to treat illnesses such as colds and diarrhea. They also ground up the inner bark and used it as flour.

Hemlock bark is rich in tannins, acidic compounds that a plant produces to protect itself from being eaten by insects. The bark is such an inhospitable surface that few mosses or lichens will grow on it. Its chemical makeup resists rotting, and a hemlock stump may remain intact for decades, becoming a ring of bark encircling a decayed and hollowed-out center. Because of its high tannin content, hemlock bark can be used to cure leather, to which it imparts a reddish hue. In the 1800s and early 1900s, loggers felled countless hemlocks, spudded off the bark—it came off in huge sheets in spring—and sold it to the leather-tanning industry. In many cases the dead, naked trunks, called "peelers," were left to rot.

Hemlock wood is coarse-grained and brittle, inferior to pine for most, although not all, building purposes. The hard knots can dull or chip saw blades. People have used hemlock lumber for beams, shingles, laths, railroad ties, crating, and paper pulp. The floorboards upstairs in our old house are hemlock, and some of those boards are 18 inches wide. Hemlock makes a better rough siding than pine: It holds nails more securely and lasts longer when exposed to the weather. Many barns wear hemlock siding.

Hickory

TAXONOMISTS PLACE THE HICKORIES in Juglandaceae, the walnut family, all of whose members reproduce themselves through nuts: large, energy-packed seeds protected inside hard shells and husks. Other trees in the group include black walnut, butternut, and pecan. The hickories have pinnately compound leaves, with an odd number of leaflets (five, seven, nine, or eleven, depending on the species) arranged in twin rows, each row opposing the other on either side of a central stalk called a rachis, with the "odd" leaflet extending from the rachis tip. The leaflets have many small teeth on their margins; they are shaped like lance heads and are broader than the leaflets of butternut and black walnut. The compound leaves of hickories alternate along the trees' branches. Next year's foliage and female flowers lie folded up inside large twig-end buds, which can help the amateur naturalist seeking to confirm a hickory's identity. Both the foliage and the four-part nut husks give off a spicy, nose-tickling smell when scratched or crushed.

Shagbark Hickory *(Carya ovata).* Shagbark hickory is a large tree often reaching a height of 50 to 75 feet, with a trunk 2 to 3 feet in diameter; very old specimens on excellent sites can be 120 feet tall with a 4-foot breadth. Shagbarks make their best growth on rich, moist soil in full sunlight. The species ranges from Quebec west to Minnesota and eastern Nebraska, and

south to Georgia and Texas; outlying populations exist as far west as northeastern Mexico.
In New England shagbark hickory grows in
southern sections of Maine, New Hampshire,
and Vermont and throughout Massachusetts,
Rhode Island, and Connecticut. It prospers
on loamy hillsides and in fertile valleys, along
streams and the borders of swamps, and in
dry woods. Shagbark hickories often grow in
association with different species of oaks, and
the eastern oak–hickory forest biome contains

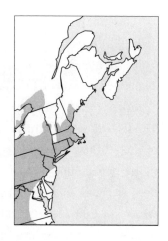

the largest area of any timber type in the United States.

As they mature, hickories send down long central roots into the soil;
these taproots anchor the trees against storm winds and help them take in
water during drought. Hickories grow slowly and may live for several hundred years. If young, vigorous trees are cut down, they usually sprout from
the stump.

The most noticeable aspect of the shagbark hickory is its shaggy, gray-
brown bark. As the tree expands its girth over the years, the bark shatters
into long, strap-shaped plates running up and down the trunk. The plates
can be 3 to 6 inches wide. Often they warp away from the trunk at both
ends while remaining attached in the middle. These strips cover the lower
trunk, giving it a decidedly whiskery appearance. The roughness often
extends to the main branches, while the bark of higher, thinner branches
remains smoother. Ecologists suggest that the rugged surface works as a
defense against creatures that lust after shagbark nuts. Perhaps it thwarts a
few raccoons and opossums, but judging from the number of squirrels I
have seen clipping nuts in the crowns of shagbarks, it's not a wholly effective deterrent. (Nor would a shagbark "want" to exclude squirrels from its
nuts, since the rodents help the tree reproduce itself by carrying off its nuts
and burying them in the ground.) Another theory holds that a shagbark's
thick bark acts as a defense against ground fires, preventing excessive heat
from damaging the tree's inner tissues.

The compound leaves of shagbark hickory are 8 to 14 inches long and divided into five, rarely seven, leaflets. The two leaflets at the base of the rachis are not as large or as long as the upper pair and the terminal leaflet. The leaves turn a bright candle-flame yellow in early autumn.

All of the hickories produce male and female flowers on the same tree. The male flowers are furry and 3 to 5 inches long. They dangle in groups of three from a common stalk; often several stalks cluster together. The shorter female flowers look like hairy spikes. Wind brings about pollination. Shagbark hickory puts forth its flowers in May, after the tree's leaves are almost fully unfurled. The female flowers develop into nuts that ripen by autumn. A thick husk gradually splits into four pieces, exposing the whitish nut, which has prominent ridges and a faint point. The nut is egg-shaped and about an inch long; a relatively thin shell surrounds the delectable kernel. A good way to shell a hickory nut is to hold the huskless nut on its side on a hard, unyielding surface (such as a vise or an anvil), position the nut so that the seam around its perimeter faces up, and tap the seam with a hammer. Use a nutpick to tease the meat out of the two matching, convoluted inner chambers.

As a shagbark hickory's girth expands, its bark shatters into long, strap-shaped plates running up and down the trunk.

Shagbarks begin bearing nuts when they are about twenty years old and produce good numbers of nuts from age forty onward. Bumper crops occur every second or third year, when two to three bushels of nuts can be gathered from beneath one good-size shagbark. Human foragers should plan to harvest in early October, after winds have shaken the nuts to the ground. The nutmeats of shagbark hickory are excellent in a white or yellow cake, or in a plain cookie, from which their subtle sweetness emerges; baking helps bring out the flavor. Many wild animals eat the nuts, including squirrels, chipmunks, mice, opossums, wild turkeys, and wood ducks. Often squirrels will strip all the nuts off a tree before the nuts ripen.

Yellow-bellied sapsuckers chisel feeding wells into thinner areas of the tree's bark and lap up the sap that oozes out. Some older trees have deep scars almost ringing their trunks, horizontal grooves left by the repeated drillings of sapsuckers. The brown creeper—a tiny, inconspicuous forest bird that hunts for insects and other invertebrates in tree bark—often chooses the shagbark for a nest site, hiding its elongated, hammocklike nest behind a curl of bark.

The word *hickory* comes from *pohickery*, an Algonquian Indian word. Native Americans pounded hickory nuts, boiled them, and strained the liquid, preserving the oily essence, which they added to other foods including cornmeal cakes and hominy. The early settlers put hickory wood to many uses. They fashioned tool handles and wagon hubs and carved hinges from the tough wood. They made mauls from hickory roots, further hardening the heads of those crude implements by holding them in the heat of a fire; the mauls were then used to pound in iron wedges and gluts for splitting chestnut logs into fence rails.

Some woods are stronger than hickory and a few are harder, but no other American species equals it in combined strength, hardness, and stiffness. Hickory is a third stronger than white oak and twice as shock resistant; the wood of the shagbark is reputed to be the strongest of all the hickories. People use it for tool handles, flooring, furniture, cross-country skis, charcoal making, and parts for musical instruments. Shagbark hickory wood weighs almost fifty-two pounds per cubic foot, dry weight. Its fuel value exceeds that of any other common American tree except black locust. One cord of hickory—a stack 4 feet wide by 4 feet deep by 8 feet long—releases as much heat when burned as a ton of anthracite coal or 175 gallons of fuel oil.

Pignut Hickory *(Carya glabra).* A medium-size tree, pignut hickory stands 50 to 80 feet tall and is 2 to 3 feet across the trunk at breast height. The maximum size is 120 feet tall and 4 feet in diameter. Most pignut hickories grow in mixed oak-hickory woods, and the crown of a forest-grown specimen tends to be oblong, tall, and narrow, with short, spreading branches; limbs lower down on the trunk may droop. Pignut hickories have five and occasionally seven leaflets per compound leaf, with an overall leaf length of 8 to 12 inches. The leaflets are hairless, dark glossy green above and paler below. Pignut hickories are some of the tardiest trees to set forth foliage in spring.

The bark is dark gray, with shallow fissures and tight, narrow ridges, hard and tough and about ⅔ inch thick. The bark rarely peels off from the trunk, or exfoliates, as botanists put it, and never as dramatically as in shagbark hickory, but on older pignut hickories it sometimes fragments—just enough that a white-breasted nuthatch can wedge one of the tree's own nuts between the plates and use them as a natural vise while hammering and picking away the shell to get at the nutmeat.

Hickories range across eastern North America and eastern Asia. Fossils show that they once grew in Greenland, Iceland, and Europe, but they died out in those places during the ice ages. In North America hickories and other trees gradually withdrew to the south, retreating ahead of the glaciers, and then extended their ranges northward again when the ice sheets began to melt. Scientists speculate that the north–south orientation of the Appalachian Mountain chain made such movements possible, as seed-carrying birds and mammals moved easily along valley corridors. In Europe the major mountain ranges lie on an east–west heading, which prevented plants with heavy, hard-to-transport nuts from shifting north again easily after the ice withdrew.

Today, pignut hickory occurs from southern New England west to Illinois, and south to Florida and Louisiana. *C. glabra* is the most common hickory in the forests of the Appalachians; many pignut hickories are harvested by loggers in Kentucky, West Virginia, and Tennessee, and in the hill country drained by the Ohio River. In New England pignut hickory is present in the southwestern corner of New Hampshire, in southern Vermont, and in Massachusetts, Connecticut, and Rhode Island. In the northern part of its range, the species grows mainly on dry ridges and hillsides and shows up less frequently in damp settings. Even in stony or compacted soils, pignut hickory sets down a long taproot; this central root has few laterals. On most upland sites, pignut hickory is less common than red maple and the red, black, white, chestnut, and scarlet oaks with which it mingles. Pignut and other hickories improve the soil because their leaves contain fairly high levels of calcium, released when the leaves decompose.

Pignut hickory has a compound leaf typical for the hickories. The inset shows the ripened nut with its thin husk withdrawing from the shell.

The male flowers are borne on catkins 3 to 7 inches long, and the female flowers appear in spikes ⅛ inch long, with both sexes on the same tree. Over the summer, the fertilized female flower develops into a slightly pear-shaped nut 1 to 2 inches long. The skin sheathing the hull is usually quite thin, a bit less than ⅛ inch, and as it dries, it becomes unpeeled part-way down the hull. Pignut hickories start to bear nuts when they are around 30 years old; the prime nut-producing age is between 75 and 200, with some trees as old as 300 years still producing fruit.

In pignut hickory, some nuts are sweet-tasting and others are insipid or bitter—from the same tree, no less, which doesn't inspire the prospective forager to gather bucketfuls and devote the time and energy needed to extract the small nutmeats, especially if he or she can drive down into the valley and pick from beneath shagbark hickories. The nuts may be 70 or even 80 percent fat. Squirrels, chipmunks, raccoons, and other wild animals avidly eat the kernels of pignut hickory, and at one time farmers turned their pigs loose to feed on them, a practice that gave rise to the tree's common name. Another moniker is broom hickory, bestowed by early settlers who fashioned brooms and scrubbers out of narrow splits of the wood. As with all of the hickories, the hard, heavy wood is excellent fuelwood.

Mockernut Hickory *(Carya tomentosa).*
Mockernut hickory ranges from southern New England west to Iowa, Missouri, and Arkansas, and south to Florida and Texas. In general the species makes its best growth in the Ohio River Basin and in Missouri and Arkansas. Mockernut hickory is abundant from Virginia southward, where it becomes the most common member of the hickory tribe.

In New England mockernut hickory occurs in Massachusetts, Rhode Island, and Connecticut; old range maps show it in Vermont and New Hampshire, but it probably does not grow there or in Maine. In the northern part of its range, mockernut hickory is found mainly on drier soils of ridges and hillsides and less commonly in moist woodlands; it rarely comes up in alluvial bottomlands. The tree becomes 50 to 75 feet tall, with a diameter of about 2 feet, but it can get considerably larger. The current national champion for the species, as recognized by the American Forestry Association, grows in Upper Marlboro, Maryland; it stands 108 feet tall and has a trunk circumference of 178 inches. The largest mockernut hickory recognized in Connecticut is 85 feet tall and has a 115-inch circumference.

In the mature tree the dark gray or light gray bark remains tight and deeply furrowed. The large, rounded buds on the twig ends look as if they

The white-breasted nuthatch will sometimes wedge a hickory nut into a tree's ridged bark, then use its beak to hammer the shell apart.

are covered with grayish brown felt; those terminal buds are a good diagnostic for picking out this species in winter. The leaves, 8 to 12 inches long, are compounded of seven to nine leaflets. Foliage and twigs are resinous and fragrant. The Latin species name *tomentosa* describes the hairy, matted-wool quality of the leaf stalks and the undersurfaces of the leaflets, characteristics that make this tree easy to identify when in foliage.

Flowers appear in May, when the leaves are about halfway emerged. Female and male flowers appear on the same tree. Male hickory flowers release copious amounts of pollen, which is carried about by the wind. Fertilized female flowers develop into nuts, which hang on the twigs singly or in pairs. Mockernut hickory may gets its name because, although its fruit appears to be nice and plump, the nutmeats are disappointingly small, covered as they are by a thick green husk and a large hard shell. The nutmeats taste sweet.

A mockernut hickory can live for 500 years. Trees between the ages of 40 and 125 bear nuts and yield good seed crops every two to three years. Fourteen southern Ohio trees monitored for six years produced an average annual crop of 6,285 nuts. Many wild animals eat the nuts, including squirrels, black bears, foxes, rabbits, beavers, mice, ducks, turkeys, and quail. Squirrels transport nuts away from the parent tree and store them underground; unrecovered nuts sprout and become new trees.

A mockernut hickory seedling sends down a 1- to 3-foot taproot during its first growing season. Most mature trees have long taproots and few lateral roots, and are quite wind-firm. Because the flinty, hard bark is fairly thin, it provides little insulation against fire, and the high temperatures generated by forest fires can kill mockernut hickories.

The wood has a large proportion of white sapwood; for that reason, the tree is sometimes called white hickory and whiteheart hickory. As useful as that of any other member of genus *Carya*, the wood is made into tool handles (including scythes), ladder rungs, furniture, flooring, baseball bats, and skis. It also goes into lumber, pulpwood, and charcoal. Mockernut hickory is considered an excellent wood for smoking hams.

Bitternut Hickory *(Carya cordiformis).*
Many autumns ago, as an enthusiastic but
neophyte forager, I paused beneath a small
hickory tree and filled a bucket with smooth,
pale nuts that had already shed their husks.
Back home, I started shelling the nuts.
Before I had gotten too far along on my task,
I decided to taste one of the nutmeats. I
popped the kernel into my mouth—and
spat it out immediately. The nut was incred-
ibly bitter, and a few cautious taste tests per-

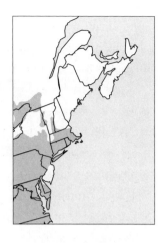

suaded me that the rest of the batch was just as bad. Thus was I introduced
to bitternut hickory.

When mature, bitternut hickory stands 50 to 75 feet tall, with a trunk
diameter of 1 to 2 feet; some specimens grow as large as 100 feet and have
a trunk 2½ to 3 feet broad. Stout side branches grow upward; these sprout
slightly drooping branchlets, resulting in a broad, rounded crown. The
bark is light gray, tight, and a bit scaly or roughened by shallow fissures and
narrow ridges. The leaves are 6 to 10 inches long and have seven to nine
(rarely eleven) leaflets. Each leaflet is 2 to 6 inches in length, the smallest
leaflets of all the hickories. In winter the twigs end in sulfur yellow buds.

C. cordiformis ranges farther north than any other hickory (marginally
farther than shagbark hickory) and is the most abundant hickory in
Canada. It occurs from Quebec to Minnesota and south to Florida and
Texas. In New England it is found in western Vermont, the Connecticut
River Valley, Massachusetts, Rhode Island, and Connecticut (an extremely
large specimen, growing in Wethersfield, Connecticut, stands 106 feet tall
and has a trunk circumference of 117 inches). Across its range, bitternut
hickory is probably the most common and uniformly distributed of all the
Carya species. It thrives in moist, fertile soils along streams and rivers, in
woodlots, and on mountain slopes. More than any other hickory, it prospers in alkaline soils, such as those derived from underlying limestone formations. It makes its best growth in rich soils of the lower Ohio River

Basin. It can be found growing with white oak, black oak, northern red oak, bur oak, and shagbark hickory. In central New England it grows alongside white ash, butternut, basswood, American elm, and sugar maple.

Trees thirty years old and older produce nuts in abundance. Heavy nut crops arrive every three to five years, with smaller crops in between. When mature, the fruits are 1 to 1½ inches long; they hang by themselves or in clusters of two or three. It's believed that most wild animals find the tannin-infused nuts unpalatable, although rabbits have been seen eating the kernels. Apparently the tree depends on gravity and on water transport for the dispersal of its seeds.

Bitternut hickory develops a dense root system and a pronounced taproot. It sprouts prolifically from the stump and the roots following logging. In forest stands *C. cordiformis* grows at about the same rate as chestnut oak, white oak, sweet birch, and beech, and more slowly than northern red oak, tuliptree, black cherry, and sugar maple. When they decompose, the leaves of bitternut hickory release much calcium into the soil.

The wood is judged slightly less strong than that of the other hickories. It is reputed to be the best of its clan for smoking meat. Settlers pressed an oil from the nutmeats, which they used as a remedy for rheumatism and as lamp fuel. Today the wood goes into furniture, flooring, paneling, dowels, tool handles, ladders, crates, and pallets.

Holly

American Holly *(Ilex opaca)*. American holly is the only broad-leaved evergreen tree native to New England. Our other evergreens—pine, hemlock, spruce, and fir—have needlelike leaves. The holly's leaves are oblong and broad, thick and leathery, 2 to 4 inches in length, their scalloped edges armed with sharp prickles: the familiar green used for Christmas decorations. The upper surfaces are dark and glossy; the undersides of the leaves are a paler shade of green and show a prominent central rib. Individual leaves remain on the tree for two or three years before falling, so that the holly ever wears a green cloak.

The bark is a pale greenish gray with a surface neither furrowed nor scaly, but much roughened by small bumps and warts. The tree's overall shape is generally that of a pyramid. American holly ranges from West Virginia and southern Missouri to Texas and Florida. It is common in New Jersey, Delaware, and Maryland, growing as an understory tree in coastal floodplain forests. The range of *I. opaca* extends just into southern New England, in coastal areas of Connecticut, and eastern Massachusetts.

Foresters believe that the species is slowly extending its range northward and farther into the region's interior.

American holly reaches its greatest size on well-drained, moist soils in Alabama, Arkansas, Louisiana, and eastern Texas. In the South holly regularly grows as tall as 50 feet and occasionally reaches 100 feet. In the Northeast most American hollies are shrublike. The largest specimen known in Connecticut is 46 feet tall and has a 49-inch trunk circumference and a 19-foot crown spread. In its southern range *I. opaca* usually occurs in small, pure stands or mixed in with pines, hickories, magnolias, sweet-gum, and sassafras. Holly was a favorite of George Washington, who sowed its brilliant red berries and transplanted small sprouts from the woods to beautify Mount Vernon, his Virginia estate.

American holly flowers from April to June. The small blossoms are pale greenish or white. A tree is either male or female; only the females produce the flowers that develop into berries. Some botanists believe there are three or four male hollies for every female. The pea-size berries remain on the branches into winter, and many birds feed on them, including ruffed grouse, bobwhite quail, wild turkey, thrushes, gray catbird, northern mockingbird, brown thrasher, eastern towhee, cedar waxwing, yellow-bellied sapsucker, and pileated woodpecker. The birds scatter the trees' seeds in their droppings. The dense foliage of American hollies provides resting and nesting cover for many birds. Bears, raccoons, skunks, foxes, and small rodents occasionally eat the fruit, and deer sometimes browse the trees' leaves.

American holly has never been an important commercial lumber tree in the Northeast, but holly is cut for its wood in parts of the South. The heartwood and sapwood are both chalky white, and the heartwood is said to resemble ivory. The wood is heavy and hard, its growth rings practically indistinguishable. It cuts smoothly and readily takes dyes and stains. Holly has been used for furniture parts and cabinet inlays, knife handles, scroll work, measuring scales and rules, ship models, and musical instruments: piano keys, violin pegs, and fingerboards are often made of holly, dyed black in some instances to resemble ebony.

More than a dozen kinds of holly are recognized in the United States. About half of the species are evergreen and half are deciduous, dropping their leaves and standing bare over winter. All produce red berries. Three small, shrubby species occur in New England: largeleaf holly *(I. montana);* common winterberry holly *(I. verticillata),* also known as black alder; and smooth winterberry holly *(I. laevigata).* English holly, *I. aquifolium,* is the only other evergreen holly in the Northeast. It grows to 30 feet tall and has a smaller leaf than the American species. A popular ornamental, it has been planted in hedges, yards, and formal gardens.

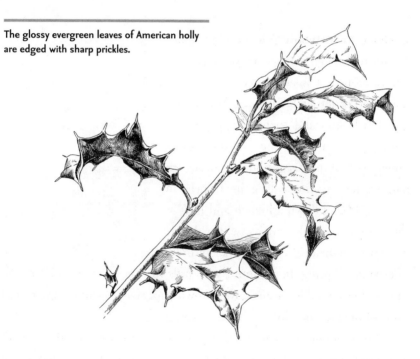

The glossy evergreen leaves of American holly are edged with sharp prickles.

Hornbeam

Eastern Hornbeam *(Ostrya virginiana).*
Scattered through our woods in northeastern Vermont is a smallish tree that hides in
the shade of loftier hardwoods. While hiking, I will stop and spend a few pleasant
moments examining the shreddy, gray-
brown bark of the eastern hornbeam, which
reminds me of some wild animal's pelt. In
winter I'll bend down a branch and look at
the hornbeam's male catkins, which dangle
in triplets, tight in their dormancy, waiting

to expand in spring. In autumn I will ruffle the tree's papery, rattling seed
cases—they resemble clustered tiny brown-paper bags—whose nutlets feed
some of my favorite birds.

Hornbeam means "hard tree." The word came across the Atlantic with
early immigrants who knew—and who used the wood of—a related tree in
England. Other names for *O. virginiana* are hop hornbeam ("hop" comes
from the resemblance of the pendent fruit clusters to the fruit of the cultivated hop plant, used in brewing beer), leverwood, and ironwood (ironwood is also attached to *Carpinus caroliniana,* another small tree of the
eastern forest; probably the two species are best described using their Latin

names alone). *O. virginiana* and *C. caroliniana* both belong to the large birch family, Betulaceae, which includes the birches and alders.

Hornbeam ranges from Nova Scotia west to southern Manitoba and the Black Hills of South Dakota, and south to Florida and Texas. Although its range is extensive, nowhere is it a particularly abundant tree. It is found in most of New England, but not in eastern Massachusetts or southern Rhode Island and Connecticut. Hornbeam grows in the understory of hardwood forests and along woods edges, on dry, gravelly slopes and ridges, and on moist sites in stream valleys. It makes its best growth in cool, shady places and thrives on limestone soil. The species is more common in oak-hickory forests than in beech-birch-maple woods.

Mature hornbeams rarely become taller than 30 feet or broader across the trunk than 18 inches. Two large specimens standing 63 and 67 feet tall,

The fruit of eastern hornbeam (top) looks like a loose, papery pine cone. Ironwood (bottom) sets out a series of three-pointed bracts, each bearing a single nutlet.

respectively, are listed in the current *Maine Register of Big Trees*. In hornbeam, the crown tends to be high, open, and rounded, formed by wide-spreading branches that support ascending branchlets. Tough and resilient, the branches resist damage from wind, snow, and ice. The thin bark is made up of many small, flat scales that are usually loose at both ends while remaining attached to the trunk in the middle.

The birchlike leaves are 3 to 5 inches long, dull yellowish green above and paler green below. Long oval in shape, they have sharp tips and double serrations: large marginal teeth further divided into smaller teeth. The leaves stand at the ends of short, hairy leafstalks, and they feel like flannel between the fingers. They turn a dull yellow in autumn.

Hornbeams begin to flower and fruit at around age twenty-five. As the leaves unfold in spring, the 2-inch-long male catkins extend their pollen-laden stamens. Female catkins flower on the same branch, blooming fully approximately one month after leaf emergence began. The female catkins are usually paired on a single stem and are shorter and smaller than the male structures. Wind takes care of pollination.

In summer the growing fruits are green; as they ripen in September and October, they turn brown. The loose, papery cones are about 2 inches long and 1 inch wide. They are composed of a dozen or more bladderlike bracts, each holding a single flat nutlet. Each bract expands to become a buoyant, inflated sac about ¾ inch long. During fall and early winter, the sacs detach from the stem, and the wind disperses them. Ruffed grouse eat the nutlets, as do wild turkeys, pheasants, quail, finches, grosbeaks, woodpeckers, and squirrels. Grouse also eat the buds and male catkins in winter. White-tailed deer browse on foliage and twig tips, but not very avidly. Beavers readily cut and eat hornbeam; a study in Ohio found that *O. virginiana* was the third most utilized food after alder and aspen.

Hornbeam seeds usually germinate during the spring after they are shed. Seedlings grow rapidly, even in the shade, and may be 7 feet tall after five years. As a mature tree, hornbeam has a slow to medium growth rate. In some areas, foresters try to poison or grub out hornbeams in favor of more commercially valuable species. That approach ignores the tree's value to wildlife and its contribution to the diversity of our forests. Donald Culross Peattie, who often assigned human characteristics to trees, called hornbeam "serviceable and self-effacing." He pointed out, in *A Natural History of Trees,* that as an understory species the tree "gives shade or, rather, redoubled shade to the wild flowers and the mosses."

Hornbeam will die if flooded: *O. virginiana* was the third most flood sensitive of thirty-nine tree species compared in a Tennessee study. Cut, burned, or injured trees send up sprouts from dormant buds on the trunk; they do not sprout from the roots. Studies have shown that hornbeam is very sensitive to air pollutants such as sulfur and nitrogen oxides, chlorine, and fluorine. Reports John Eastman in *The Book of Forest and Thicket,* "Because it cannot tolerate salt, winter salting of roads and subsequent soil leaching make this a tree that is seldom seen from a car window."

The wood of the hornbeam is extremely hard—harder even than hickory and black locust, although not quite as unyielding as flowering dogwood. It is considered 30 percent stronger than white oak and weighs fifty pounds per cubic foot. Native Americans made bows from hornbeam. Settlers used it for ox yokes, fenceposts, tool handles, mallets, rake teeth, sled runners, and levers for moving heavy loads.

Ironwood

Ironwood *(Carpinus caroliniana)*. Ironwood is a small, often crooked tree whose
smooth, thin bark looks like it was shrink-
wrapped onto the trunk. Visible beneath the
bark, the wood is fluted and ridged like a
tensed muscle—hence the colloquial name I
first learned for the species, musclewood.
The currently accepted title, ironwood,
describes the wood's hardness. And for many
years this tree was called hornbeam, which
connected two old words: *horn,* meaning

"hard" or "tough," and *beam,* cognate with the German *baum* (as in *tan-
nenbaum*), or "tree." Adding to the confusion, *C. caroliniana* has a couple
of other aliases: blue-beech, for the way its slick bark resembles that of
American beech (the beech's bark is pale gray, whereas that of ironwood is
a darker bluish gray tinged with brown), and water beech, since it often
grows in swamps and along lakes and streams.

Ironwood ranges from southern Maine and Quebec west to Minnesota
and Iowa, and south to Florida and Texas. It also grows in Mexico and
Central America. Found in every New England state, it is absent from
northern and eastern New Hampshire and northern Maine.

Ironwood is a fairly common member of the understory in oak-hickory and beech-birch-maple forests. It grows best on rich, moist sites but can tolerate a range of habitats, including dry hills, slopes, and ridges. In parts of its range, ironwood forms pure stands in abandoned fields. Smaller than the closely related eastern hornbeam, ironwood generally grows 10 to 30 feet tall, with a trunk 8 to 12 inches in diameter. Botanists consider ironwood to be a slow-growing and a rather short-lived tree. The current national champion for the species, cited by the American Forestry Association, stands 75 feet tall in Westchester, New York.

When ironwood grows as a single-trunk tree, its crown becomes wide and round-topped, with ascending upper branches. Near their ends, the side limbs may dip downward. Often, though, ironwood forks near the ground and takes on a multitrunked, shrubby form. The leaves are egg-shaped, with rounded or wedge-shaped bases, 2 to 5 inches long, and have pointed tips and doubly saw-toothed margins. Dull, dark blue-green above, the leaves are a paler green below. On their undersurfaces, small hairs cloak the veins and vein angles.

Male and female flowers appear on the same branch, in April or May, just as the leaves are unfurling. The male catkins are ½ inch long, the female catkins ⅔ inch. Wind spreads the male pollen to the female flowers. During summer, the female flowers develop into small nutlets enclosed by leaflike bracts, which are loosely stacked in pairs along slender stalks. The fruits ripen from August to October. The nutlet is about ⅓ inch long, and its attached bract, or wing, looks like a miniature, thin-lobed maple leaf. The graceful, three-pointed bract functions like the blade on a maple samara, giving the seed the buoyancy it needs to travel on the wind. The clustered bracts may remain hanging on the tree into winter.

Large seed crops arrive at three- to five-year intervals. The nutlets can germinate on top of leaf litter and establish themselves in the shade beneath mature trees. Seedlings growing in wet muck will survive if the soil dries out for at least part of the growing season. Although shade-tolerant when young, ironwood needs an opening in the canopy—a taller tree felled by disease or wind—to achieve its full size. Because of its small stature and

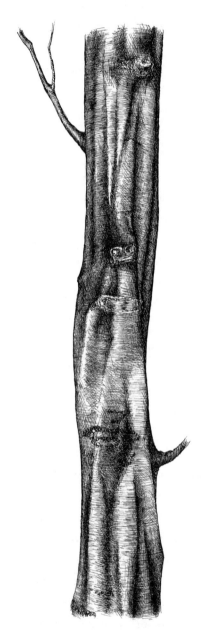

protected position in the understory, ironwood rarely gets uprooted by wind. Particularly in the South, when overstory trees are removed by logging, ironwood may grow in densely, preventing the larger trees from reestablishing themselves.

Songbirds, ruffed grouse, ring-necked pheasants, bobwhite quail, wild turkeys, and squirrels eat the seeds, buds, or catkins of *C. caroliniana*. Hares, rabbits, beavers, and deer nip off leaves, twigs, and stems. Chickadees and other small birds take shelter and build nests in cavities in dead ironwoods.

Early settlers made leak-proof bowls and dishes out of the tough wood, which, wrote William Wood in 1634 in his book *New England's Prospect,* "requires so much paines in riving as is almost incredible." The wood is close-grained, hard, and heavy at forty-five pounds per cubic foot. Since the trunk is small, the tree is rarely sawed into boards; instead, people fashion ironwood into tool handles, levers, wedges, mallets, and plowshares. It can be burned as fuel, and charcoal made from ironwood was once used in making gunpowder. Despite its strength, the wood rots quickly when in contact with the ground.

In three seasons ironwood is easy to overlook. But for a brief span in autumn, when its foliage turns scarlet and jack-o'-lantern orange, this small tree stands out brilliantly in the eastern woods.

Juneberry

Juneberry *(Amelanchier* species). Three times a year, the small, unobtrusive trees known as juneberries strongly state their presence. In early spring their gauzy blossoms are some of the first arboreal flowers to brighten the winter-drab woods. In June and July the early-ripening fruits attract many wild foragers—and some human ones as well. And in October their bright yellow-to-red foliage becomes part of the grand and colorful mosaic that is the eastern deciduous forest.

Juneberries are also known as shadbushes. They belong to family Rosaceae, which includes hawthorns, plums, apples, cherries, and mountain-ashes. Botanists have long puzzled over whether there are many juneberry species or a range of variable and hybridized forms best regarded as a single species. The various types differ in stature and in characteristics such as leaf shape and color, and the fineness or coarseness of the teeth edging the leaves.

Several juneberry variants are clearly shrubs. The most treelike of the tribe is downy juneberry *(A. arborea),* which grows 20 to 40 feet tall and occasionally surpasses 50 feet, with a trunk 8 to 16 inches in diameter, rarely as large as 24 inches. Downy juneberry ranges from Nova Scotia west to Minnesota and south to Florida and Oklahoma. It is found throughout New England. Don't look for groves of juneberries; they usually stand as solitary trees in the forest understory or as a clump of several individuals. Juneberries grow in both dry and moist habitats along the borders of woodlands and the edges of woods roads, in thickets, on stream banks, and on cliffs.

The juneberries possess alternate leaves; they are arranged along the twig not opposite each other but staggered back and forth, one on the left, the next a bit farther along on the right, and so on. The leaves of downy juneberry are about 3 inches long, have saw-toothed edges and sharp-pointed tips, and sometimes exhibit a heart-shaped base. They are dull green above and paler beneath. The "downy" part of this tree's name refers to a silvery white sheen found on all new growth—leaves, sepals, pedicels, flower stems—for a brief period in early spring, and to a matting of hairs on the undersides of the leaves.

The trunk is usually straight and slender, with little taper, or it may twist and turn in its ascent, as if the plant were straining toward the sun. The crown is shallow and narrow, with numerous fine sprays of branches. The bark is gray and fairly smooth; with age, it develops shallow furrows and low, narrow ridges running vertically on the trunk, producing a marbled appearance of gray and black areas interlaced. In winter the bark is a good identification mark, as are the dormant leaf buds: long and pointed, shaped much like those of American beech, often two-toned in red and green and covered with numerous overlapping scales.

Early settlers bestowed the names shadbush and shadblow on the juneberry: When the tree's flowers burst forth in April, people knew it was time to go to rivers and streams and set nets for shad swimming up from the Atlantic to spawn. The frost-resistant flowers of juneberry are white, about 1¼ inches across, and airy looking with their five thin blades. Some trees bear great masses of the showy blooms, which appear just before or as the leaves come out. In certain wooded areas, flowering juneberries stand like puffs of smoke beneath the still-bare crowns of taller trees. The blossoms hang in drooping clusters and release a nectar whose scent can be enjoyed by standing downwind of a tree on a breezy day. And they are perfect, which means they have both male and female parts. Insects, mainly small wild bees, pollinate them. *Amelanchier* species can also produce viable seeds in the absence of true fertilization through a process of asexual reproduction called apomixis.

The fruits of *A. arborea* ripen in June and July. They look like tiny apples about ¼ inch or ⅓ inch across. They are a rich maroon or purple, sometimes with a whitish bloom on the surface. Their insides are stocked with many small, rather soft seeds. Fruits from some trees are dry and bland, while others are juicy and sweet.

I once happened onto a juneberry that a bear had worked over. The bruin's claw marks crosshatched the 20-foot tree, and the bear had broken many branches and hugged them inward toward its perch to gobble up every last fruit. In addition to bears, mammals ranging from chipmunks to foxes relish the fruit. Birds flock to ripe juneberries: gray catbird, brown thrasher, mockingbird, robin, thrushes, cedar waxwing, towhee, titmouse, blue jay, crow, woodpeckers, flicker, wild turkey, ring-necked pheasant, ruffed grouse—the list goes on and on. Both mammals and birds disperse the trees' seeds in their droppings. Deer, moose, rabbits, and snowshoe hares browse on twigs and foliage.

Native Americans of many tribes ate juneberries and blended the dried fruits into venison and bear meat when making pemmican. The fruits are excellent as preserves and as pie filling: Juneberry pie is said to taste like sweet cherry. The foraging guru Euell Gibbons wrote in *Stalking the Wild Asparagus*, "I'm sure that God put Juneberries on earth for the use of man, as well as for the bears, raccoons, and birds. Let's get our share!" I applaud Gibbons's sentiment but usually find that the local wildlife has beaten me to the punch.

An old rural name for the plant is serviceberry, sometimes rendered "sarviss." Sarviss is thought to be the original form, derived from *sorbus,* a Latin taxonomic name for the related mountain-ash. A more colorful story holds that "service" refers to the memorial services that circuit preachers performed in spring, around the time of the juneberries' blossoming, to commemorate settlers who had not survived the preceding winter.

Juneberry grows slowly and lays down hard, strong, close-grained wood. At forty-nine pounds per cubic foot, it is one of the densest of the eastern hardwoods. The wood, dark brown and often tinged with red, tends to develop checks, or cracks, and to warp as it cures. Indians fashioned it into lance shafts, and settlers used it for tool handles. According to *Native Trees of Canada,* published by the Forestry Branch of the Canadian government, the wood is "sold in small quantities as 'lancewood' for fishing rods." Juneberries are planted as ornamentals and are used as grafting stock for pears and quince shrubs.

Maple

Red Maple *(Acer rubrum)*. Whatever the season, red maple shows its namesake color, vividly or subtly. In winter the buds and twig tips are crimson. In spring the trees' flowers open, contributing a reddish-pink tint to the faintly greening landscape. The leaves unfurl ruddily in April and May. When they assume a summertime green, their leafstalks remain touched with red. And in autumn the leaves of many red maples become scarlet—some of the brightest foliage in the woods.

Red maple is a medium-size tree. When mature at seventy or eighty years, it is normally 50 to 60 feet tall, with a trunk 1 to 2 feet in diameter. On an excellent site, red maple can become 100 feet tall and 3 to 4 feet in diameter. *A. rubrum* grows from Nova Scotia west to Manitoba and Minnesota, and south to Florida and Texas—essentially all of eastern North America. Red maple occurs regionwide in New England; it is more abundant now than in the past, since there is not a strong market for red maple and timber cutters do not seek it out. *A. rubrum* is also a common tree in the Mid-Atlantic states and the Upper Midwest, and some authorities judge it the most abundant tree in eastern North America. In various parts of its range, the species is known as scarlet maple, swamp maple, water maple, soft maple, and white maple.

As with all the maples, red maple has opposite leaves, directly across from each other on the twigs. The leaves are 2 to 6 inches long and nearly as broad. They generally have three (sometimes five) lobes, with the notches between the lobes relatively shallow. Coarse teeth rim the leaf margins. The bark on a young red maple is thin and smooth, often a pale gray color similar to that of American beech. As the tree ages, its bark darkens and breaks up into rough, shaggy ridges, some of which peel away in long plates.

Red maple is one of the first trees to flower in the spring—earlier during warm springs, and later when winter is reluctant to loosen its grip—with flowering completed by the time the leaf buds open in May in New England. (I have seen red maples blooming in south Florida swamps as early as December, their trunks and limbs bedecked with air plants and lichens, and sharing the muck with such exotic trees as poisonwood, strangler fig, and gumbo-limbo.) Most flowers grow on branches in the sunlit crowns of the trees, but one can usually find blossoms at eye level, often on smaller specimens growing along the edges of clearings. The male flowers are airy, pollen-bearing clusters of yellow and pink; the female flowers, destined to become the fruits, are larger and more substantial, hanging at the ends of slender, deep red stems. Some trees have only male flowers, some have only female flowers, and a few present flowers of both sexes on separate branches.

The wind, and perhaps a few wild solitary bees, pollinate red maple flowers. Pollination is timed to take place before the emergence of leaves, which might shield the flowers from the wind and prevent the successful transfer of pollen. Fertilized female flowers ripen into winged fruits, called samaras or keys, ½ to 1 inch long and attached in opposing pairs at the ends of the drooping stems. At first the fruits are bright red; later they fade to brown. A samara consists of a small seed and a thin, papery wing. Red maple produces the lightest seeds of all the maples. In May and June the samaras flash through the air and flutter to the ground. Most of the seeds

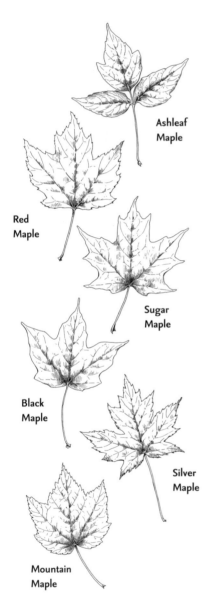

Shown here are the leaves of six species of maples found in New England. (See the section on striped maple for an illustration of its distinctive leaf.)

Ashleaf
Maple

Red
Maple

Sugar
Maple

Black
Maple

Silver
Maple

Mountain
Maple

geminate within a week, although some, particularly those landing in shady places, may lie dormant for a year and sprout the following spring.

Red maples are true generalists, growing "on a wider range of soil types, textures, moisture, pH, and elevation than any other forest [tree] species in North America," write Russell Walters and Harry Yawney in the USDA Forest Service's *Silvics of North America.* Of all the maples, red maple shows the greatest tolerance of different climatic conditions. Red maples thrive in chilly peat bogs, on river islands, on dry, rocky ridges, and in old farm fields. In Pennsylvania, West Virginia, and Ohio, red maples have seeded themselves onto strip mine spoil banks. An ideal habitat is a moderately well-drained, moist site at a low or intermediate elevation. Red maple is often planted as a street tree in cities and towns and as a shade or specimen tree on lawns.

In wetlands red maples produce short taproots and long, well-developed lateral roots. Where the soil is dry, the taproot becomes longer while the laterals remain short. Generally, the root system is horizontal and in the top 10 inches of soil. Temporary flooding does little harm to red maples. In one study, sixty days of flooding slowed tree growth but only slightly; in another investigation, red maple root systems recovered rapidly after saturated bottomland soils dried out again. Red maples can weather drought by halting their growth, then resuming it when moist conditions return.

With their thin bark, red maples are severely damaged by fire, and even a moderate blaze can kill a mature tree—although not its roots, which are likely to send up many vigorous shoots. Red maples also sprout from the stump after they are cut down. Connected to a complete root system, the sprouts grow faster than seedlings.

Red maple is moderately tolerant of shade—more so than the true pioneering species like the aspens and pin cherry, less so than slower-growing trees such as sugar maple and American beech. Red maple can be a dominant tree in the canopy on some sites. In a typical northern hardwood forest—a common silvic type in New England—sugar maples usually start to replace red maples after about eighty years.

Red maples seldom live longer than 150 years, and most die long before that age. Red maples wound easily, from their own branches dying and self-pruning, or breaking under a load of ice or wet snow; from other trees battering against their crowns during storms or falling against them; and from woodpeckers drilling for insects, and sapsuckers and squirrels chiseling and gnawing through the bark to start the flow of sweet sap. In *A. rubrum,* such wounds do not heal readily, and a large area of cambium (the layer of living tissue between a tree's outer bark and its inner wood) usually dies back before new growth can seal off the breach. Many different species of fungi invade red maple through wounds. The result is often heart rot, leading to a wind-snapped trunk or a fallen tree.

Black-capped chickadees will pick out the rotten wood from a maple stub and build a nest in the open-topped cavity or in an area just below the break. A number of hole-nesting birds take advantage of red maple's propensity to become hollow, and many other birds nest in the trees' branches. Porcupines perch in red maples, eating the bright flowers in spring; they also relish the bark. Deer and moose browse on twigs, leaves, and sprouts. Red maples produce huge quantities of seeds: a crop nearly every year, and a bumper crop every two years or so. Trees with trunks only 8 inches in diameter can bear up to 90,000 seeds. Songbirds, squirrels, and mice gorge on the seeds, and the rodents store them for winter food.

Humans put red maple to many and varied uses. We cut it for lumber and fuel, and fashion it into furniture, plywood, flooring, kitchenware, and clothespins. The wood is fairly soft and not particularly strong, and it weighs about thirty-eight pounds per cubic foot when dry—about 88 percent of the weight of its close relative, sugar maple. A craftsman friend of mine builds award-winning rocking chairs. He makes the frame, rockers, armrests, headboard, and seat out of red maple, which he buys from mills under the designation soft maple (as opposed to hard maple, which is sugar maple). He shaves the back-cushioning ribs from black walnut. The contrast between the two woods is stunning: the walnut a deep, lustrous brown, the maple pale gold to nearly bone white. My friend picks through boards to find ones with a tiger-striped grain pattern. I see such figuring from time to time in red maple I split for the woodstove; usually I set those billets aside to enjoy for a while, picking them up and turning the wood back and forth to catch the light, so that the grain winks light and dark, like flames dancing.

In autumn red maples light up the hills and mountainsides and flare up along the edges of swamps in hues grading from yellow-orange to deep burgundy. Weather and soil moisture affect the color's brilliance each year, and soil chemistry also may have an impact: Researchers suggest that the more acidic the soil, the deeper the red coloration. The scientists believe that most of the trees turning orange are females, while the males display that signature flaming red.

Sugar Maple (*Acer saccharum*). The sugar maples on the southern edge of our land are tall and stately. A road winds among them, where sleds were drawn fifty years ago to gather the trees' sweet sap in early spring. Nowadays, our farmer friend collects the sap using plastic tubing and bulk tanks. Throughout the winter, we snowshoe and ski along the road. In summer the trees' verdant crowns offer a shady retreat during hot spells. And in autumn the trees turn a vivid orange, contrasting with the evergreen firs and hemlocks that dot the grove. My wife calls the old maples "the queens of the forest."

Sugar maple ranges from Nova Scotia to Manitoba, Minnesota, and Missouri, and south in the Appalachian Mountains to North Carolina and Tennessee. Throughout New England the species grows in moist woods, ravines, bottomlands, and on wooded slopes. It does best on rich, well-drained soil but can manage on thin, nutrient-poor ground. *A. saccharum* is not found in swampy or extremely dry settings. People have planted sugar maples in cemeteries, parks, farmyards, and lawns, and along town streets.

In nature, sugar maple grows in pure stands and also mixed in with black cherry, basswood, yellow birch, American beech, northern red oak, eastern hemlock, and many other species. It is more common among the northern hardwoods than in oak–hickory forests. Also known as rock maple or hard maple, *A. saccharum* achieves its largest size in central New England, New York, northern Pennsylvania, and the Great Lakes region. An old-growth tree can reach 120 feet in height and have a trunk 5 feet in diameter. A large sugar maple in the Mohawk Trail State Forest in western Massachusetts is thought to be the tallest of its species in New England: 136 feet tall with a girth of 11.4 feet. Most mature maples are much smaller than that, at 40 to 70 feet high, with a trunk 2 to 3 feet across at breast height.

Growing in the open, a sugar maple sends up a short trunk support-ing stout, erect branches that form a round-topped crown. In a woods set-ting, a tree produces a long, straight trunk and a shallow crown; often such a tree will self-prune or shed its lower branches for more than half its over-all height. On the trunk, black chevrons like upside-down Vs mark the points of attachment for branches, and for scars where boughs formerly grew. Sugar maple has gray-brown bark. As the tree's trunk thickens, the bark splits into deep channels separated by long, irregular, vertical plates or flakes, which may break loose and flare out on one side. Sometimes this rugged, whiskery aspect causes people to mistake sugar maple for shagbark hickory.

The leaf shows a clean geometric shape; Canadians have chosen it as the emblem for their national flag. Think of a hand with the fingers splayed: The leaves are generally five-lobed, with each intervening notch U-shaped at the base. (The notches in the red maple's leaf, which has a similar shape, end in Vs.) Like the red maple leaf, the sugar maple leaf has toothed margins, but the teeth are fewer and not as sharp. The leaves are generally 3 to 5 inches in length and as wide as they are long, or slightly wider. They are dark green above and pale green below. The undersides may be glaucous, covered with a whitish waxy bloom. On some leaves the veins are hairy.

Sugar maples generally do not flower until they are more than twenty years old. The flowers bloom just before and as the leaves are unfurling—in April or May, depending on the latitude. The greenish yellow male and female flowers occur in separate clusters within the tree, scattered along the twigs and at the twig ends. In some trees certain limbs send forth only male flowers, and other limbs produce only female flowers. Male flowers often greatly outnumber the female ones. Scientists long believed that sugar maple flowers were pollinated solely by insects. Wild solitary bees do feed on the nectar and incidentally pollinate the blossoms; however, recent studies have shown that wind can also bring about pollination when insects are excluded from the flowers.

Over summer the female flowers develop into paired samaras. A samara consists of a small seed-carrying vessel attached to a papery wing about ½ to 1 inch long by ⅓ inch wide; the overall length is 1 inch to 1¼ inches. The fruits ripen around September and begin falling just before the leaves let go. As the twinned samaras come twirling down, winds can carry them 100 yards or farther. Usually only one of a pair carries a viable seed. Large, mature trees can produce huge numbers of samaras. Bumper crops arrive every two to five years—a pulsing of seed production that often leads to even-aged stands of sugar maple. In a Michigan study conducted during a good seed year, an estimated 70,000 samaras per acre landed in a ten-acre clear-cut near sugar maple trees.

The seeds overwinter in the leaf litter. If the weather becomes warm and dry too early in spring, the seeds may fail to germinate. Seeds contain considerable energy resources, enough to let their roots penetrate through heavy leaf litter and reach the soil beneath. In spring the seeds often sprout and their paired leaves start to photosynthesize before all of the snow has melted in the woods.

In the dense shade of a mature woodland, sugar maple seedlings grow a scant amount each year, starved for sunlight—waiting. In *The Trees in My Forest,* University of Vermont ecologist Bernd Heinrich describes how he homed in on a hole in the leaf canopy created by a mature tree falling. On the sunbathed ground beneath the gap grew a mat of sugar maple seedlings, averaging 4 to 5 inches tall. Heinrich pulled up seventy-one seedlings in a 4-square-foot plot. "[This] density of nearly eighteen seedlings per square foot covered an area of some five hundred feet," he writes, "and, in total, the 'hole' where the tree had fallen must have contained more than ten thousand seedlings." Probably only one of the seedlings would survive to replace the fallen tree; some were dead

The sap of the sugar maple, collected in buckets or through plastic tubing, is boiled down to make syrup and sugar.

already. Heinrich cut the seedlings' thin stems with a razor blade and counted their annual growth rings under a microscope. "In the sample of thirty-five that I examined, the growth rings indicated ages of six to ten years."

Sugar maples can live in dim light; they actually conduct their maximum photosynthesis when under about 25 percent of full sunlight. Among the larger broad-leaved trees, only American beech is as shade tolerant as sugar maple. Young sugar maples are easily killed by fire, but windfires are uncommon in sugar maple stands because of the high moisture content of the leaf litter in those shady settings.

The roots of *A. saccharum* go somewhat deeper than those of other maples. Strong, wide-spreading lateral roots branch extensively and can reach out to twice the diameter of the tree's crown. The roots release a chemical that may slow the growth of yellow birch, a frequent competitor. After about 150 years, the upward growth of sugar maples ceases or becomes negligible. Mature trees often live for 200 years, and some reach 400 years.

Sugar maple samaras sometimes remain hanging on their stalks into winter. Evening grosbeaks, which migrate south into New England during many winters, feed avidly on the seeds, as do nuthatches and finches. Red, gray, and flying squirrels, chipmunks, and mice hoard and eat the seeds. Deer and rabbits browse on sugar maple buds and vegetation; porcupines feed on bark and new spring leaves. Red squirrels use their sharp incisor teeth to gnaw wounds in trees, causing a flow of sap that dries on the bark; the squirrels return to lick up the sugar left after the sap has evaporated. Yellow-bellied sapsuckers peck feeding wells in the bark. On warm spring days gnats and flies are attracted to the sugary sap pooling in the wells, and migrating birds—warblers, flycatchers, hummingbirds—nab the insects.

Syrup and sugar made from the sap of *A. saccharum* (and a few other trees) were the only sweeteners available to the original human inhabitants of North America. Members of the Iroquois and Chippewa tribes collected the sap in vessels, then concentrated it by letting it freeze and removing the ice to get rid of excess water. They also boiled the sap in small batches by filling elm-bark containers and troughs hollowed into logs, and adding fire-heated rocks to steam off the water. European settlers adopted and advanced the sugar-making technology. No other type of sugar was widely available during the colonial era, and maple successfully competed in price with cane sugar until the second half of the nineteenth century.

Sugar maple sap is collected by drilling holes through the bark into a tree's sapwood, then inserting a hollow tap, or spile, which guides the sap into a lidded bucket or a plastic tube that carries the liquid to a tank. The sucrose that makes sap sweet was manufactured by the previous year's leaves and is stored in horizontal cells in the trunk. Sugar content varies among individual trees, ranging from 2 to 7 percent; a device called a refractometer can be used in the field to test sap sugar levels. Early sap flows usually have the highest sugar content of the year. Across southern Canada, New England, New York, northern Pennsylvania, northern Ohio, and the Great Lakes states, maple sugarers go to work in February and March. Some are backyard hobbyists who make enough syrup for their own needs. At a modern commercial operation near Johnson, Vermont, some 80 miles of plastic tubing conduct sap from 12,000 taps, and 120,000 gallons of sap yield 3,000 gallons of maple syrup. From Virginia south—because there is little of the freeze–thaw weather that stimulates heavy sap production, and because trees shift rapidly from dormancy to leafing out in spring—maple sap generally is not collected for syrup.

Warm, sunny days followed by subfreezing nights spur a tree to convert to sugar the carbohydrates stored in the stem wood. Sugar maple sap contains small bubbles of carbon dioxide; as the day warms, the bubbles expand, forcing the sap out of the tapholes. Tapping removes ten to twelve gallons per taphole during the sugaring season. Around forty gallons of sap, on average, yield a gallon of syrup. A season's tapping can drain off 15 percent of a tree's carbohydrate reserves; nevertheless, some sugarbushes—the traditional name for a stand of maples used for sugar production—have trees that have been tapped for 175 years with no loss in vigor or in the quantity or quality of sap produced.

Maple syrup is nothing short of ambrosial. Our friend who taps our grove gives us a couple of gallons each year. I enjoy the syrup best on wild blueberry pancakes and admit to taking a teaspoonful, neat, every now and then, both for the taste and for the energy boost it provides.

The value of the sugar maple extends beyond nourishing wildlife and people. The wood is hard, tough, and close-grained, the heartwood a warm tawny color, the sapwood—which is frequently 3 to 4 inches thick—white with a reddish tinge. The wood polishes to a bright gleam. It weighs forty-three pounds per cubic foot, dry weight. Products made from sugar maple are legion and include boxes, crates, clothespins, shoe lasts, toys, veneers, rulers, bowling lanes, gymnasium floors, rolling pins, cutting blocks, knife racks, tool handles, and bowls. Hard-maple flooring in a Philadelphia store withstood foot traffic longer than did a marble floor installed at the same time. Recently, a Canadian company has been making baseball bats out of sugar maple. Major-league sluggers claim the resilient wood propels the ball farther than white ash, the orthodox choice for bats, and doesn't crack as readily.

Sugar maple wood is in demand for fine furniture and cabinetry—particularly the decorative types known as curly maple, quilted maple, and bird's-eye maple. In those variants, it is believed, fungal growth causes changes in the structure of the wood fibers, yielding wavy figuring, dramatic ripples, and dots resembling the eyes of birds. Sugar maple makes an excellent firewood: It is the wood of choice for heating your home in the realm of the northern hardwoods. It burns hot, lasts a long time, doesn't throw off sparks, emits a pretty flame, and leaves little ash residue.

A. saccharum cannot tolerate polluted air; for city plantings, the imported Norway maple *(A. platanoides)* does better. Salt, used to melt the ice on paved roads, can kill sugar maples. Far more dangerous to the species as a whole is the ongoing problem of acid rain and snow, which ecologists term "acid deposition." Across the northeastern United States and southern Canada, the health of sugar maples has declined markedly in the last half century; the culprit is probably acid deposition, caused by power plant and industrial emissions farther west that are carried to the Northeast on the wind. The acid leaches out key elements from the soil, including calcium and magnesium, which trees need to grow. Acid deposition may kill or disable mycorrhizal fungi, microorganisms that mingle with the roots of trees and improve their ability to take in water and nutrients.

Scientists, foresters, and maple sugar producers report thinner foliage, dying branches, and decreasing growth rates in sugar maples. Trees that are under stress change colors and drop their leaves earlier. They are also more likely to die from drought, insect defoliation, and wood rot fungi. According to Charles Little in *The Dying of the Trees,* sap from pollution-hit sugar maples "contains aluminum, manganese, iron, sodium, and barium, while healthy elements such as calcium and potassium are absent."

Sugar maples are fairly resistant to insects, but recent irruptions of the pear thrip—a flea-size pest, accidentally imported from Europe, that feeds on the leaf buds—have killed many trees. Scientists warn that global warming has the potential to banish the cool-adapted sugar maple from parts of the Northeast, including much of New England, during the twenty-first century.

Black Maple *(Acer nigrum).* Black maple is either an ecotype, or physiological race, of *A. saccharum;* or, according to some taxonomists, it represents a separate species. The leaves of this variation on the sugar maple theme are 5 to 6 inches long and dark green; their undersurfaces are velvety. They have three lobes rather than the five typical of sugar maple. Rutherford Platt, in *Discover American Trees,* notes that black maple leaves suggest "sketches of sugar maple leaves simplified, with clean, straight edges, no fancy teeth."

Black maple ranges from southern Canada and scattered sites in New England (five of the region's six states have black maple, with no stands recognized in Rhode Island) west to South Dakota, Iowa, and Kansas, and south to North Carolina, Tennessee, and Arkansas. Black maple thrives in warmer, drier habitats than sugar maple; west of the Mississippi River, *A. nigrum* becomes more common than *A. saccharum.* Scientists suggest that black maple developed during an earlier warm and droughty, or exothermic, climatic era. In the Northeast black maple hybridizes readily with sugar maple. The growth habits, wood, and sap of black maple differ little or not at all from those of sugar maple. Some ecologists speculate that black maple will become more common in the Northeast and sugar maple will decline as a result of global warming.

Silver Maple *(Acer saccharinum).* Arborists describe the foliage of silver maple as having a cutleaf shape, with prominent sinuses—notches, to the layperson—angling in deeply from the margins of the leaf blade toward the center. The leaf's main central lobe is narrower at its base than farther toward its tip, a key identification feature. This central lobe is divided into three lobes. Adding to their intricacy, the leaves are doubly saw-toothed: The margins of the leaf have teeth, each of which sports its own smaller serrations.

Silver maple leaves are 2 to 10 inches in length and are nearly as wide as they are long. I measured one recently: The vegetative or photosynthetic portion, known as the blade, was 4 inches long; the free stalk, or petiole, was a generous 3½ inches. In addition to being long, the leafstalks of silver maple are supple and slightly flattened, like those of aspens and cottonwoods. These attenuated stems let the trees' leaves spin and sway even in a light breeze. The leaves' upper surfaces are dark green, and their bellies are pale; the trees' crowns riffle as zephyrs pass through them, with the foliage turning silver, then green, then back to shimmering silver again. It is the silvery color of the leaves' undersides that earn the tree its name.

Most silver maples grow 40 to 60 feet in height and achieve a 3-foot trunk diameter. Truly big specimens can be 120 feet tall, with a trunk diameter of 5 or more feet. I once measured a great silver maple whose bole divided into four upward-slanting limbs; below where those treelike limbs diverged, the trunk had a circumference of 22 feet—three people could not have touched fingertips around the trunk.

On a typical silver maple, the trunk is short, dividing into lateral branches that fork freely, forming a broad crown. On many trees, the lower side branches droop, then curve upward at their tips. Silver maples growing on swampy, frequently flooded land—such as that along Lake Champlain in western Vermont—often develop a trunk having a large, swollen-looking, buttressed base, with prominent water stains evidencing extended periods of flooding. The buttressing effect may help hold the tree up in the sodden ground. When lakeside forests are flooded, the silver maples standing in the still water look much like cypress trees in a southern swamp.

Some call the silver maple's crown ragged and do not consider it aesthetically pleasing, and perhaps it cannot compare with the symmetrical fountain shape of an American elm or the horizontal robustness of an open-grown white oak. But when he considered large, mature silver maples, Donald Culross Peattie, in his *A Natural History of Trees,* saw "dignity and lively grace."

The bark of *A. saccharinum* is smooth and gray on young trees. Older specimens have brownish gray bark furrowed into thin flakes that remain fastened to the trunk at the center while curling away from it at both ends. The twigs when broken or crushed emit a pungent, rather unpleasant odor.

Silver maple occurs from New Brunswick west to Minnesota and south to Florida and Oklahoma. The Ohio Valley is considered to be the center of the species' range; there, deep, fertile, damp soils provide an ideal growing substrate. The species is found throughout most of New England, with the exception of Rhode Island, eastern Massachusetts, and the eastern coast of Maine. Silver maples grow on flat and gently sloping land, but not on steep slopes or in high elevations in the mountains. Swamp borders, river islands, and lake edges support silver maples, and many of the trees have been planted to create shade in cities and towns. Other names for the species are river maple, swamp maple, white maple (because of the wide, pale sapwood), and soft maple.

Sycamore is a frequent companion of silver maple in streamside and lakeside habitats, as are American elm, red maple, black ash, basswood, northern hackberry, black willow, and other lowland species. Silver maple is the fastest growing of all the maples, achieving full stature in less than a century; some authorities also consider it the tallest of the maples.

A. saccharinum is one of the earliest of our trees to flower. In March or April, well before the leaves emerge, separate sprays of male and female flowers appear, both sexes on the same tree or one sex only on a single tree. The greenish or reddish flowers are about ¼ inch long; they are inconspicuous and are situated high in the tree. The wind pollinates the female flowers. The resulting samaras hang in pairs; they ripen quickly, becoming light brown. They are the largest samaras of any maple: 1½ to 3 inches. They consist of an oblong seed that may exceed ½ inch in length, attached to a thin, papery vane. The samaras twirl down during a two- to three-week period in May, just as the tree's leaves are expanding.

When hard frosts damage the flowers, seeds may be few; usually, though, silver maples bear prolific seed crops. Wood ducks, grosbeaks, wild turkeys, and squirrels eat the seeds, which come along at a time when other foods may be scarce. Those that land on suitable soil germinate quickly. Growth is most rapid during a tree's first fifty years, when it may add ½ inch of trunk diameter per year. The root system spreads and usually remains quite shallow. Silver maples can withstand temporary flooding, but fire easily kills them. The branches are brittle and apt to break during wind and ice storms, opening portals for fungal spores to enter and cause decay. Individual trees rarely live beyond 125 years.

The wood weighs thirty-three pounds per cubic foot. Pale, almost white sapwood surrounds the light brown hardwood. A bit softer than red maple, and somewhat brittle, the wood has been used for cheap furniture, packing crates, and paper pulp. Silver maple sap, although sweet, contains less sugar than that of sugar maple; nevertheless, syrup can be made from it.

In autumn the leaves of most silver maples turn a wan yellow, often with a hint of green—sober dress, compared with the fiery foliage of sugar maple and red maple. Peattie wrote that the "orange and scarlet tints are quite absent," but a photograph in *The Audubon Society Field Guide to North American Trees,* by Elbert L. Little, shows a silver maple leaf that's a bright orange-yellow. On a September day on a rocky promontory jutting out into Lake Champlain in western Vermont, I met with a small silver maple whose leaves were turning brilliant orange and red—colors almost as bright as those of red and sugar maples.

Striped Maple (*Acer pensylvanicum*). Of all the trees in forest and field, which has the handsomest bark? Perhaps paper birch, with its pale, shreddy wrapper, a white beacon in the woods. Or sycamore, patched and dappled like the hide of some great, mute animal. Or shagbark hickory, whose whiskery plates suggest strength and ruggedness. I like the bark of all those species—and another, belonging to a much smaller and less impressive tree: striped maple, named for its streaked, multicolored bark.

Both trunk and branches of striped maple are an overall brownish or olive green, interrupted with vertical stripes of paler green, each stripe brightening to white at the center. The stripes occur where the tree's expanding girth has split the outer bark. As a striped maple ages, the background color of its bark becomes a pale brownish gray, and the greenish white stripes may show mahogany-colored edges. Small warts and horizontal ridges are scattered across the smooth-textured surface. On old trees, the bark is darker and rougher, with less prominent striping.

Striped maple ranges from Nova Scotia west to Michigan's Upper Peninsula, and south in the Appalachians to Georgia. In New England it grows throughout Maine, New Hampshire, and Vermont; in central and western Massachusetts; and in western Connecticut. This small, slender tree has a trunk that generally divides within a few feet of the ground into several limbs, whose side branches zigzag out to spread their leaves over a broad area. Striped maple grows in cool, rocky woods, particularly on north-facing or shaded mountain slopes and in damp ravines.

Other names for the tree are moose maple and moosewood, because moose browse on it freely, and goosefoot maple, because of the way the leaf is shaped: three pointed lobes and a rounded base, like the foot of a big goose seen in outline. Most leaves are 5 to 7 inches long. Fine teeth serrate the margin, and three prominent veins extend upward from the base, one through the center of each lobe. Some leaves are lightly haired on the undersurfaces, which are paler than the upper sides and may show a tint of rust-brown. In autumn the leaves turn a rich golden yellow. The rose-colored winter leaf buds are large—the terminal ones are about ½ inch long—and perched on short stalks.

In the Northeast a mature striped maple may grow 20 to 30 feet tall and have a trunk diameter of 6 to 12 inches. Most individuals are stunted, subsisting in the limited light of the forest understory, where they reach only 10 to 15 feet tall. In New England really big specimens approach 60 feet in height. The largest striped maple currently known in North America is 77 feet tall and has a trunk 44 inches in circumference; it grows in Tennessee, in Great Smoky Mountains National Park. In the wild, striped maple achieves its greatest stature and girth in the mountains of Tennessee and North Carolina.

A. pensylvanicum flowers in late April and May, after the tree's leaves have fully expanded. The flowers are borne at the twig ends in narrow clusters dangling on slender, drooping stalks. Some authorities deem striped maple's flowers inconspicuous, but the keenly observant Donald Culross Peattie termed them a "brilliant canary yellow" in *A Natural History of Trees*.

The sex expression of striped maple is both variable and changing. Some trees put out male and female flowers. Other trees produce only female flowers, and still others bear only male flowers. The same tree may be male one year, female the next. In a Massachusetts study, scientists found that 4 percent of trees put forth both male and female flowers, and 96 percent bore either male or female flowers; of the latter, there were eight female trees for every male. Trees producing female flowers often were less healthy than those making male flowers. Perhaps the less vigorous trees' "strategy" was to produce a smaller number of female seeds, each of which presumably had a higher likelihood of becoming a tree, compared with the huge numbers of male pollen grains, statistically much less likely to fertilize a female blossom.

Striped maples fruit each year. Large, productive trees can yield several thousand fruits, which are typical for maples: paired samaras, or keys,

Buck deer often rub their antlers on the trunks of striped maple. The shape of the leaf earns the tree its nickname "goosefoot maple."

joined at the seed, with a thin, wind-catching wing attached to each seed. The fruits ripen in September and October and fall off and disperse in October and November. If a samara lands on crusted snow, the wind may blow it several miles from the parent tree.

In forest shade, striped maple spreads out its branches and arranges its leaves to capture stray shafts of sunlight—sunflecks, in the parlance of tree scientists—that come flickering down through the canopy as the sun moves across the sky and as breezes shift the leaves of taller trees. *A. pensylvanicum* has no need for deep roots to anchor itself because the hardwoods towering above it blunt the wind and provide protection against storm damage. Its shallow, spreading root system lets a striped maple take in soil moisture and nutrients efficiently. A striped maple may gain as little as 12 inches of height in ten years. It can survive for a hundred years, completing its entire life cycle in the forest understory.

Striped maple also prospers in small openings, and if logging or some other disturbance fells its taller neighbors, striped maple responds quickly to the increased light by putting out additional leaves and growing vigorously upward. When large trees are wiped out in forest stands that include abundant striped maples, *A. pensylvanicum* can become a dominant species, shading out the seedlings of other hardwoods for years.

Moose and white-tailed deer browse on twigs, buds, and leaves. Cottontail rabbits, snowshoe hares, and beavers eat the bark, especially in winter. A study in Maine found that ruffed grouse eat the seeds; rodents probably also consume them. Buck deer seem to seek out striped maples for polishing the velvet off their antlers prior to the late-autumn breeding season; many specimens I encounter are marked with healed-over buck rubs, as these scarrings are known.

The pale wood of striped maple weighs thirty-three pounds per cubic foot. It is soft and weak. Because the trunk is spindly, loggers find no use for it, although cabinetmakers sometimes inlay it into darker woods. In colonial times farmers fed both the green and dried leaves to cattle, and in the spring they turned their stock loose in the woods to eat the young shoots. In *New England Natives,* Sheila Connor notes that striped maple can be a handsome tree to plant: "With its attractive bark, arching branches, and large drooping leaves," she writes, "this small native maple can add year-round interest to the cultivated landscape."

A maple even spindlier than striped maple is mountain maple *(A. spicatum)*. Although it grows large enough to be considered a tree in the South, in New England it exists primarily as a shrub, rarely achieving a height of 25 feet. As its name implies, mountain maple grows in uplands, often near streams and freshets in rocky woods. Its thin, smooth bark is usually dark or greenish in color. Its leaves include three or five lobes and have coarsely saw-toothed edges. In autumn the winged samaras often turn a brilliant red before fading to a pinkish or yellowish brown. Like striped maple, *A. spicatum* is also known as moose maple because those large browsers readily eat its leaves and branchlets.

Ashleaf Maple *(Acer negundo)*. Ashleaf maple is a small- to medium-size tree that usually grows in floodplains and on the edges of streams, lakes, and swamps. Found from coast to coast and from Canada to Guatemala, it is the most widespread of the maples. The species' range centers on the bottomland hardwood forests of the lower Ohio and Mississippi river valleys, where it grows along with silver maple, eastern cottonwood, sycamore, hackberry, and several willow species.

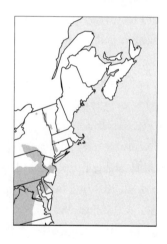

Ashleaf maple is widely known as box-elder. The USDA Forest Service range maps show the species occurring naturally in western Vermont, southern New Hampshire, western Massachusetts, and western Connecticut, but ashleaf maple is found in other parts of New England as well, both because people have planted it in urban and rural settings and because the tree, a prolific seeder, has spread on its own. *A. negundo* is tough enough to survive in the woods I own in northeastern Vermont, where winter temperatures sometimes plummet to -30 degrees Fahrenheit and lower.

The formerly accepted name, box-elder, is cobbled together and, as George Petrides notes in his *Field Guide to Eastern Trees,* "fails to indicate proper taxonomic relationships." It seems that *box* refers to the fact that *A. negundo* is sometimes planted to create a hedge, as is a popular unrelated species, Eurasian boxwood. It's also possible that the link comes from the tree's whitish wood, which resembles that of Eurasian boxwood. *Elder* stresses the similarity between box-elder's foliage and the leaves of elderberry, a common North American shrub. Ashleaf maple is a better, more accurate name. *A. negundo* is indeed a maple, which can be inferred from its opposite leaves and paired winged fruits, also called samaras or keys. And its toothed compound leaves do suggest the leaves of ash trees.

Ashleaf maple thrives in moist, fertile soils, yet it is hardy enough to grow in drier, poorer habitats, including disturbed sites such as spoil banks, old factory yards, and vacant lots. Across its extensive range, it withstands extremes of temperature, drought, and wind. Floods can choke its roots for a month without killing it.

Tough though it may be, ashleaf maple is short-lived, at least for a tree, with an average life span of sixty years; individuals rarely achieve a full century. Ashleaf maple grows rapidly, especially during its first fifteen to twenty years, making it a popular choice for landscape planners needing quick shade for parks and city streets, or a farmer wanting a windbreak or a shade planting in a pasture or near a livestock or poultry barn. Some people in the East consider *A. negundo* little more than an invasive weed tree and try to eradicate it.

Ashleaf maple can become as tall as 70 feet, with a 3-foot-diameter trunk, although 50 feet in height and 2 feet in breadth are probably more usual. The short, tapering trunk supports a bushy crown that is deep, broad, and rounded. The thick bark has many narrow ridges, broken up by fissures that become furrows as the tree ages. The roots spread wide but remain shallow. Storms and snow often knock off the brittle branches and twigs, which litter the ground beneath the tree.

This is the only maple that has compound leaves. Each leaf is 4 to 10 inches long and consists of three to five leaflets, 2 to 4 inches in length, ovate or elliptical and long-pointed at the tip, with coarsely toothed edges. The dense foliage is light green in summer and turns a dull yellow in autumn.

Flowers, male or female, grow on separate trees. The small yellow-green blossoms cluster on slender, drooping stalks; they appear before or along with the leaves in spring. By summer's end, the female flowers have ripened into clusters of paired samaras, each 1 to 1½ inches long, with a curved wing and a plump, nutlike seed. Winter winds gradually strip the samaras from their twigs. At least some of the fruits usually hang on through the winter; squirrels and birds, especially pine and evening grosbeaks, feed on them.

The seeds need full sunlight to sprout and grow. Ashleaf maple is less shade tolerant than other maples. If a young, vigorous tree is cut down or otherwise damaged, it will send up shoots from the stump or root system.

The wood weighs only twenty-seven pounds per cubic foot. Pale sapwood and heartwood blend together and are nearly indistinguishable. Ashleaf maple is not, and never has been, an important lumber tree, even in the heart of its range around the Ohio and Mississippi Rivers. People have used the soft, weak wood for paper pulp and fashioned it into barrels, woodenware, and, as one source reports dismissively, "cheap furniture" and "easily broken toys." Woodworkers like its figuring, often invested with green and pink highlights, and turn bowls from it. The Crow Indians of the Great Plains tapped the trees and boiled the sap to make sugar, even though the sap of ashleaf maple has a much lower sugar content than that of sugar maple and an acidic taste to boot. *A. negundo* is also called Manitoba maple, sugar ash, or—again the object of insult, judged wanting in comparison with the grander *Acer* species—bastard maple.

Mountain-Ash

American Mountain-Ash *(Sorbus ameri-cana)*. On rocky mountainsides near my home in northeastern Vermont—and in old overgrown fields and fencerows, too—mountain-ash trees raise their multiple stems toward the sun. American mountain-ash, also called American rowan, is hardly an impressive tree, but it offers color and interest in all seasons.

Its leaves appear in May and are soon followed by flat-topped sprays of creamy white flowers that almost match the old bone color of the exposed granite rock shelving the mountains hereabouts. In summer the leaves are a shade of yellow-green all their own. By autumn, when the leaves turn golden yellow, the fertilized flowers have developed into bright red fruits. If birds do not eat them, the fruits hang on the branches into winter, contrasting vividly with the somber hues of bare trees, snowcapped rocks, and stormy skies.

American mountain-ash is unrelated to the ash trees of genus *Fraxinus,* which are common in New England. Mountain-ash can be a shrub with several stems arising from the same root system, or it can take the form of a small tree, rarely topping 20 feet, with an 8- to 12-inch trunk diameter.

The biggest mountain-ashes are 50 or 60 feet tall and have a 2-foot trunk diameter; the reigning national champion (the biggest tree that anyone has reported nationwide to the American Forestry Association) is in West Virginia. *S. americana* ranges from Newfoundland west to Manitoba and Minnesota; throughout most of New England (with the exception of eastern Connecticut, Rhode Island, and eastern Massachusetts); and south in the Appalachians to North Carolina.

The compound leaves are 6 to 10 inches in length, composed of thirteen to seventeen leaflets; the leaflets are 2 to 4 inches long and up to an inch in width, lance-shaped and with toothed margins. They attach to a central stem, or rachis. The twigs are stout, grayish to reddish brown, hairy when young, and marked by large leaf scars. The thin, light gray bark varies from smooth to slightly scaly.

Mountain-ash grows in cool, moist woods openings and on the banks of lakes and streams. It favors acidic soil. Mountain-ash occurs singly or in small groups, along with other shrubs and trees that want the additional light that bathes old fields and the forest's edge. *S. americana* is slow grow-

Cedar waxwings feed on the fruits of mountain-ash.

ing and fairly short-lived. Moderately shade-tolerant, it can hang on for a time after taller trees rob it of direct sunlight.

In spring up to a hundred pale blossoms open on each upward-facing flower panicle; often a healthy mountain-ash will put out many such inflorescences. The panicles are 3 to 5 inches across; the individual flower is ⅛ to ¼ inch in diameter and has five petals. The flowers contain both male and female reproductive organs. They attract insects that inadvertently transfer pollen from the male to the female structures. In *The Trees of My Forest,* which sets down observations made on his wooded land in Maine, the ecologist Bernd Heinrich writes concerning the long-horned beetles of family Lepturinae: "There are 250 different species of this relatively small group. . . . In the spring dozens of different ones crawl and feed in the flowers of the mountain ash nearby, undoubtedly pollinating them. By taking part in the life cycle of these trees they ensure plenty of red berries that feed migrant flocks of cedar and Bohemian waxwings in the fall."

Each berry is technically a pome: a miniature apple about the size of a pea. The fruit's pulp is bitter, and it has a low fat content, perhaps explaining why the pomes are not a favored treat for birds. However, since the fruits persist into winter, foraging birds often get around to feeding on them after they have cleaned up other, more desirable foods. In addition to waxwings the following birds eat mountain-ash fruits: ruffed grouse, yellow-bellied flycatchers, thrushes, and grosbeaks. Sometimes the fruits ferment, and the birds get an alcoholic jolt from consuming them. Martens and fishers are also reported to eat the fruit, and moose browse on mountain-ash foliage, twigs, and bark.

The wood weighs thirty-four pounds per cubic foot, and I have not found a reference to any commercial, practical, or even whimsical use. In my mind, the tree is singularly valuable because it enlivens the rocky ledges near my home and because it puts forth lovely white flowers and red fruits.

Mulberry

Red Mulberry *(Morus rubra).* To observe
frenetic avian activity, station yourself in a
mulberry grove when the fruit is ripening in
early summer. Birds will be everywhere, gob-
bling down the sweet crop: grackles, starlings,
cardinals, robins, catbirds, mockingbirds,
thrashers, thrushes, orioles, waxwings, woodpeckers—even crows, clambering about
clumsily on the springy boughs. The birds
call stridently, scold one another, and go flapping through the dense foliage, trying to get
at the luscious red to purple-black drupes.

Red mulberry ranges from southern New England (where it grows in
parts of Vermont, Massachusetts, Rhode Island, and Connecticut) west to
Minnesota and south to Florida and Texas. It makes its straightest, tallest
growth in damp coves and river valleys of the southern Appalachians,
where it can become 70 feet tall and have a trunk 3 feet in diameter. In the
northern part of its range, red mulberry is often shrublike, although some
individuals reach a height of 40 to 60 feet.

Red mulberry grows mainly in rich, moist soils of lowlands and
wooded slopes, in the company of American elm, red maple, box-elder,

white ash, and other species. It is moderately tolerant of shade. The mature tree has a short trunk that branches into a broad, dense, round-topped crown. Mulberry leaves are 3 to 5 inches long and almost as broad. They alternate on the twigs. The leaves have coarse, saw-toothed edges and prominent veins. They are dark green above, with a sandpapery texture and soft hairs growing on their undersides. The leaves come in several different shapes, the most common of which is oval with a pointed tip. Particularly on sprouts and young twigs, leaves may develop one or several side lobes. (The only other tree with irregularly shaped foliage is sassafras, whose leaves have smooth edges.) The bark is brownish, sometimes tinged with red, and fissured into scaly plates. The twigs, when damaged, exude a milky sap.

In May or June red mulberry puts out clusters of tiny flowers, male and female flowers generally on separate trees although occasionally on different branches of the same tree. The wind carries male pollen to the female flowers. The fruits, green at first, ripen around July. A mulberry is about an inch long; it looks like an elongated blackberry, composed of multiple thin-skinned fruitlets (each developed from a separate flower) whose sweet, juicy flesh surrounds a small seed.

The fruits don't have to be fully ripe for birds to eat them, but in an unripe state they are dangerous to humans because they contain hallucinogenic compounds and can cause severe indigestion. Squirrels, woodchucks, foxes, skunks, opossums, and raccoons feast on mulberries, competing with the birds and with humans who pick the nutritious ripened fruits to make juices and preserves. Through their droppings, birds and mammals disperse the seeds.

Because it is generally a small tree with a short trunk, people have not found many uses for mulberry wood. The wood resists rotting in contact with the soil, and so it is sometimes used as a fencepost. It resembles black walnut when polished and has been fashioned into furniture and coffins. In olden days, Choctaw Indians in Louisiana wove cloaks out of the fibrous inner bark of stump sprouts that sprang up where mulberries had been cut down.

Oak

Northern Red Oak *(Quercus rubra)*. Northern red oak is one of the largest trees in the Northeast. A mature specimen will tower up 70 to 90 feet, with a 2- to 4-foot trunk diameter. There are red oaks on record 150 feet tall, with trunks 5 feet across. The classic woods-grown red oak has a long, straight trunk topped with ascending branches supporting a small, narrow crown. When a red oak grows in the open—in a field, on a lawn, shading a city street—it  forks nearer to the ground, its short, thick trunk dividing into stout branches holding up a deep, spreading crown. Many species of hardwoods display these contrasting growth patterns. But in red oaks, the difference between a tree that must compete for light and one that gets plenty of sun is particularly striking.

Northern red oak is one of the northernmost of the oaks. (Bur oak grows marginally farther to the north in Canada's Manitoba province.) Red oak ranges from Nova Scotia west across southern Canada to Minnesota, south through the Carolinas to Georgia and Mississippi in the east, and to Kansas and Oklahoma in the west. It is regionwide in New England. Red oak has been widely planted in England and western Europe, where it has become naturalized and is now expanding its range. Red oaks thrive under a variety of moisture conditions and soil types. The common name describes the color of the tree's wood. Southern red oak *(Q. falcata),* a separate species, grows from New Jersey and Pennsylvania southward.

Genus *Quercus,* the oaks, numbers around eighty-five species in North America. Botanists separate the oaks into two broad categories: red oaks and white oaks. In New England, prominent among the red oaks are northern red oak, black oak, scarlet oak, and pin oak. Members of the white oak group include white oak, swamp oak, chestnut oak, post oak, bur oak, and chinkapin oak. The leaves of species in the red oak group have angular lobes that end in bristle tips, in which the veins jut out beyond the leaf margin in the form of needlelike projections. These points, some scientists suggest, may help drain away moisture, thwarting fungal growth that might cloud the leaf's surface and disrupt photosynthesis. Leaves of trees in the white oak group have rounded, flowing margins on their lobes, which are not equipped with bristle tips. It takes two years for the acorns of trees in the red oak group to mature; white oak acorns ripen in a single growing season.

The leaves of northern red oak are 5 to 9 inches long by 4 to 6 inches wide. They are divided into seven to nine lobes, each of which may end in several points equipped with bristle tips. The gaps, or sinuses, between the lobes extend about halfway in from the leaf's margin to its midrib. When unfurling from their buds, the young leaves are pink. By summer, they are dull green on their top surfaces; often the midrib has a yellowish or reddish tint. The foliage of red oaks turns different colors in fall, including dark red, orange, and bronze; the leaves on some trees simply become dull brown before dropping off. Leaves may remain hanging on their twigs into winter.

Members of the red oak group hybridize readily, with trees from one species exchanging pollen with trees from another, closely related species. This situation results in individuals whose leaves and other vegetative and reproductive structures are intermediate in form between those of their parents—halfway between the leaves of red oak and black oak, for example. This situation can cause confusion for amateur botanists, and it prompted Donald Culross Peattie to make the following pronouncement in his book, *A Natural History of Trees:* "The leaves and acorn cups of Red Oak are so variable that it is hard to identify the tree, hard to describe it, and hard to illustrate it with certainty." Leaves may vary in shape on the same tree. In addition, the leaves of a seedling or a sucker shoot may be different—usually larger, and with shallower sinuses, giving a greater overall surface area—than the leaves of a mature tree.

On young trees and stems, the bark is greenish brown and smooth. Mature northern red oaks have thick, dark brown bark, whose surface is broken up by shallow fissures into long, vertical ridges that run into and

The acorns of northern red oak drop during autumn; they lie dormant on the forest floor until spring, when they germinate.

connect with each other. Often the ridges are broadly flat-topped. They look like they've been pressed down by a clothes iron, and their smooth surfaces shine with reflected light. The inner bark, just below the hard outer layer, is a light reddish color.

Red oaks prefer moist soil, which can be sandy, loamy, rocky, or with a strong clay component. They do not grow in swamps. Because their leathery leaves retard water loss through dessication, they grow well on dry, windy ridges. Wide-spreading lateral roots—and, in some cases, deep-plunging taproots—anchor the tree and procure water. *Q. rubra* is the fastest growing of the oaks. In one year a seedling can rise 19 inches. The same seedling at age ten can be 18 feet tall. And by age fifty, the resulting tree may tower up 50 to 60 feet. Red oaks are intolerant of shade when young. Both youthful trees and adults sprout prolifically from the stump or root system if logging or fire kills the aboveground portion of the plant. Although red oaks withstand cold better than most other oaks, they are more susceptible to drought than their *Quercus* relatives, and extended dry periods can kill them. On a good site a red oak may live 300 years or longer. Red oaks grow in pure stands or mixed in with maples, beech, basswood, white ash, sweet birch, tuliptree, black cherry, hickories, pines, and other species.

Flowers emerge in May, when the leaves are about half developed. The yellow-green male flowers are borne on a slender, hairy string 4 to 5 inches long; the structure is technically known as an ament and is also called a catkin. The female flowers are an unobtrusive pale green, rounded and smaller than the dangling male catkins. The male flowers usually are concentrated in a tree's upper branches, while the female blossoms emerge lower in the tree. The male flowers put out tremendous quantities of yellow pollen, which drifts and blows freely through the air. In a predominantly oak forest, the pollen will cover all flat surfaces and lie in a skin on the backwaters of streams and lakes.

Red oak acorns are a lustrous medium brown color and are furred with minuscule pale hairs. The nut has a flat base and a narrow tip. The broad, shallow cup looks like a saucer; it covers less than one-third of the base of the nut and is made up of many tightly overlapping reddish brown scales. Red oak acorns range from about ¾ to 1¼ inches in length—about as big as the last joint of your thumb. Great variation occurs in red oak acorns: in their color, shape, size, and weight. The ecologist Bernd Heinrich checked a series of acorns in his 300-acre Maine woodland and found weights ranging from 0.85 to 7.47 grams; notes Heinrich in *The Trees of My Forest*, "If, for example, gray squirrels disperse and bury the smaller acorns more than the larger nuts, then trees growing where the squirrels are abundant will reproduce more if they have small nuts."

Red oak acorns mature at the end of their second growing season. The nuts fall just before the leaves let go of their stems. The falling leaves bury the acorns, hiding some of them from foraging wildlife while leaving others exposed for seed-dispersing animals to find. The acorns don't germinate until the following spring, in contrast with the white oaks' strategy of immediate autumn germination.

Oaks often seem to be in some sort of mysterious synchrony, with many trees—even of different species—producing bumper crops in the same year. A superabundance of acorns overwhelms seed-eaters such as deer, bears, mice, chipmunks, and squirrels, so that some nuts remain to sprout. Large acorn crops spur population increases in deer mice and other rodents, whose populations then plummet in years when acorns are scarce. Ruffed grouse, ring-necked pheasants, bobwhite quail, wild turkeys, woodpeckers, crows, blue jays, tufted titmice, white-breasted nuthatches, brown thrashers, towhees, and grackles all eat acorns. The nuthatch uses its beak to hammer the shell open. The wild turkey swallows acorns whole and lets its muscular gizzard break up the nuts. The grackle has a hard ridge or keel in the roof of its mouth; using its bill, the bird rotates an acorn against this projection to slice through the nutshell.

Blue jays flock to forests where red oak acorns are plentiful. A jay will load its expandable throat and esophagus with several nuts, then fly back to its home territory and there bury the acorns beneath leaf duff, soft soil, or grass, to be eaten in winter and spring. Acorns that jays fail to recover, and that squirrels do not dig up and pilfer, germinate and may become new trees. Scientists believe that blue jays' transporting and burying of acorns helped oak trees march northward after the last ice age ended, around 10,000 years ago, when the *Quercus* species remained only in the South. Squirrels are major seed dispersers for all the oaks, including northern red oak. Acorns from trees in the red oak group, of which *Q. rubra* is a member, contain high levels of bitter-tasting tannins. Where red oak and white oak acorns lie side by side, squirrels tend to eat the white oak acorns immediately and cache the red oak acorns for future use.

Native Americans of many tribes had different ways of dissolving the water-soluble tannins from the nutmeats of red oak acorns. They buried the acorns in the mud of a swamp for a year, stored them beneath sand in fresh water, and pounded them into a meal and let a stream run through the fragments.

More than a thousand species of insects are known to eat red oak foliage, including moth caterpillars, leaf miners, June beetles, and walking sticks. Other insects lay eggs in the developing flower; the larva then lives in the nuts and chews its way out through the shell, leaving a telltale hole.

By far the most destructive insect pest is the gypsy moth, whose caterpillar larvae can defoliate millions of acres of oak forests each year. A Eurasian insect, the gypsy moth was brought to Massachusetts in the mid-1800s by a French entomologist who wanted to breed hybrid silk moths and establish a silk industry. Some of the moths escaped, and the insects have been expanding their range ever since, first throughout New England and then farther south and west. The leading edge of the infestation passed through central Pennsylvania in the late 1980s; I was living there at the time in a home surrounded by thirty acres of woods. I could hear the sound of the caterpillars' droppings, like a light rain pattering on the forest floor, as the insects ate all the leaves off all the oaks. Gypsy moth caterpillars may denude whole forests by early summer; often the trees leaf out again, squandering valuable energy. If moth populations remain high and larvae strip trees several years in a row, the stress may ultimately kill the trees, which perish within one to three years of defoliation. In my woods more red oaks died than any other species, perhaps because they could not withstand the dual burdens of repeated defoliations and several years of drought that unfortunately followed.

Red oak wood is strong, heavy, and hard. The heartwood is a light reddish brown, the sapwood paler. The wood weighs around forty pounds per cubic foot, dry weight. In the past, people considered red oak wood inferior to that of white oak. The red was lighter, more difficult to season without twisting and cracking, more porous, and not as rot resistant. It went for rough construction, clapboards, and slack cooperage (barrels not meant to hold liquids). Today red oak is used for railroad ties (its porosity helps it soak up preservatives) and paper pulp. The better grades now bring a much higher price than white oak. Its attractive golden color and handsome grain pattern make red oak a top choice for furniture, cabinets, flooring, and house trim. Because red oak is fairly tolerant of sulfur dioxide and resistant to damage from ozone, it has been widely planted as a street tree in urban areas.

Black Oak (*Quercus velutina*). Black oak can be difficult to distinguish from northern red oak, with which it freely hybridizes. Black oak is found from Maine to Florida and from Wisconsin to Texas, a distribution that is slightly more southerly than that of northern red oak. In New England black oak occurs in southern Maine and New Hampshire; in southern and northwestern Vermont (the Champlain Valley is at the northern limit for the species); and through-out much of Massachusetts, Connecticut, and Rhode Island, where, along with red oak, black oak can become a dominant tree in the hardwood forest. Other names for black oak are yellow oak and yellowbark oak.

Black oaks grow best on rich, well-drained soils, but they also live on sandy and rocky ridges and slopes. On the better sites, they can become 150 feet tall and produce a trunk 4 feet in diameter. A more typical size at maturity is 60 to 80 feet and a trunk 2 to 3 feet in diameter. Trees in rocky habitats, or growing in soils with a heavy clay component, rarely live beyond 200 years.

Black oak leaves strongly resemble those of northern red oak but are somewhat thicker, wider at the top sinuses, and more of a yellow-green color on their undersides. They are also quite variable; it's said that no other oak species produces so many differently shaped leaves on the same tree. The bark is darker (the tree's name comes from its nearly black bark) and lacks the broad, glossy-topped ridges of northern red oaks. Large black oaks that I have examined—and had identified for me by trained foresters—possessed thick bark broken by deep fissures, most of which ran vertically but some of which crossed the trunk, making for an extremely rough, almost checkered surface. Also, many had twisted, thick limbs and multitudes of twigs, which made them look like the kinds of trees often depicted standing next to haunted houses.

Black oaks start to produce acorns at around age twenty and reach full productivity when forty to seventy-five years old. The acorns take two years to mature, ripening from late August into October of their second year of development. Most trees bear bountiful acorn crops every two or three years. Squirrels, smaller rodents, white-tailed deer, bears, and wild turkeys devour most of the acorns in years of good production, and they get essentially all of the acorns in years when crops are slim. Squirrels and blue jays, which store acorns by burying them, help to spread *Q. velutina* over large areas.

Acorns that are missed by foraging animals germinate in the spring after they have fallen. The ones lying in direct contact with bare soil, and those that have been buried by rodents, are most likely to produce seedlings. Black oaks seedlings can tolerate drought more readily than northern red oak seedlings, and they are about as drought tolerant as white oak. It is usual for the seedlings to die back from drought, too much shade, fire, deer browsing, damage from falling trees or branches, or some other cause; should a seedling be killed, one or more dormant buds near the root collar will send up sprouts. Young black oaks may die back and resprout several times before becoming established, so that the root systems of black oak saplings may be ten to twenty years older than the trees themselves.

The inner bark of black oak is yellow to orange. It is charged with tannins; in the past, people used it to dye cloth yellow and to tan leather. Two old names for *Q. velutina* are dyers oak and tanbark oak. During the colonial era, black oak bark was exported to England for use in the dying industry. The wood is not distinguished from that of red oak and is used for furniture and trim.

Scarlet Oak *(Quercus coccinea).* Scarlet oak seems to both celebrate and prolong autumn each year. Even as the red maples are dropping their vermilion foliage, fires begin to smolder among the scarlet oak's greenery. Soon the tree becomes a rich maroon—a red with depth and staying power. As autumn wanes, and the leaves are stripped from the other species of oaks, color remains in the tight-clinging leaves of the scarlet oak, a diminished red like the dregs of last night's
wine. Finally the leaves go brown; but even then, as the first snows fall, they remain attached to their twigs, ragged, sere, talkative, refusing to let go.

Scarlet oak belongs to the red oak group. It occurs in the southern parts of Maine, New Hampshire, and Vermont and in Massachusetts, Connecticut, and Rhode Island. From New England, it ranges south to South Carolina, Georgia, Alabama, and Mississippi. It is found in all or part of every state east of the Mississippi River, with the exception of Wisconsin and Florida; west of the Mississippi, it is limited to southern Missouri. A hardy, fast-growing tree, it takes root on dry slopes and ridges, often on sandy or stony soil. The best specimens thrive on deeper soils that have accumulated at the bases of slopes. On poor sites, *Q. coccinea* seems to grow more rapidly than its other oak associates, which include northern red, black, white, and chestnut oaks.

A medium-size to large tree, scarlet oak usually tops out at 70 to 80 feet. At maturity, its trunk is about 2 feet in diameter. The trunk is often straight and has a noticeable taper to it. The crown tends to be rounded, open, and shallow. Branches high in the tree stretch upward, while those in the middle and lower parts stand out horizontally or droop toward the ground. As a scarlet oak grows taller, its lower branches may become shaded out and die; often they remain attached to the trunk, barkless stubs jutting out and giving the tree an unkempt, even unhealthy, appearance. The bark of scarlet oak is dark, thin, and broken into grooved fissures, which stand between ridges neither as rough as those of black oak bark nor as flat-topped as those of red oak.

The leaves are 3 to 6 inches long by 2 to 5 inches wide and strongly resemble pin oak leaves. They are deeply divided almost to the midrib into seven (rarely nine) lobes. The lobes broaden toward their tips and end in several bristle-tipped teeth. The notches, or sinuses, between the lobes have

Scarlet oak (left) is a member of the red oak group, whose leaves have lobes ending in sharp bristle tips. White oak (right) belongs to the white oak group, whose leaves lack the bristle tips.

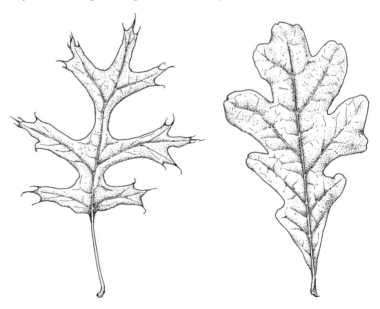

broad, rounded bottoms deeper than those of any other oak, except perhaps pin oak; they give the scarlet oak's foliage an angular, ragged appearance. The leaves are a bright shining green above and a paler yellow-green below, and usually have tufts of hair in the angles where the veins diverge from the midrib.

The leaves, when they come out in May, are bright red. When the leaves are about one-third developed, the flowers open, both sexes on the same tree: male flowers attached to dangling catkins 3 to 4 inches long, and reddish female flowers on short stalks. The wind blows pollen, released by the male flowers, to fertilize the female flowers. Scarlet oak hybridizes with northern red oak, *Q. rubra,* and with scrub oak, *Q. ilicifolia.*

A scarlet oak acorn takes two growing seasons to develop and mature: a flower fertilized in May of one year becomes a ripe acorn by autumn of the year following. The acorn of *Q. coccinea* is short-stalked or seated directly against the twig; it stands solitary or as one of a pair. The acorn is egg-shaped, ½ to 1 inch long, ⅜ to ⅞ inch in diameter, and reddish brown. A deep, bowl-shaped cup encloses a third to half of the nut; the cup is formed of smooth, close-fitting scales that often end in a fringe around the cup margin.

Seed production in scarlet oaks varies greatly from year to year; occasionally the trees produce bumper crops. Scarlet oak is a member of the red oak group, all of whose acorns contain bitter-tasting tannin compounds, likely evolved to deter mammals from eating them. However, the digestive systems of some acorn eaters, including squirrels, have become adapted to resist the ill effects of tannins, which can interfere with protein absorption. Squirrels, deer, bears, chipmunks, mice, wild turkeys, blue jays, and other birds all relish scarlet oak acorns. Squirrels and jays scatter-hoard the nuts, burying them beneath leaves and in loose soil. Unrecovered acorns sprout, perpetuating the parent trees.

Of four common New England oaks—scarlet, red, chestnut, and white—scarlet is the least tolerant of shady environments. Scarlet oak seedlings grow in open woods or in areas recently cleared of forest vegetation by windthrow, ice storms, fire, or logging. Once the canopy closes, with trees linking their crowns overhead, scarlet oak seedlings can arise only beneath gaps, where sunlight reaches the forest floor. For this reason, scarlet oak tends to fade from the scene and become uncommon in mature woods. Because its bark is thin, scarlet oak is easily damaged by fires, even blazes of low intensity. If the tree is not killed outright, its bark may be breached, allowing pathogens to enter. After it has reached adult size, scarlet oak is often attacked by fungi, leading to heart rot, which weakens the trunk so that a windstorm later snaps it.

A friend of mine cruises timber for a small sawmill, and he often gripes when, at a timber sale, foresters mark scarlet oak simply as red oak, the way it has traditionally been sold and marketed. The wood of scarlet oak is strong, heavy (forty-six pounds per cubic foot), and coarse. It is considered inferior to that of northern red oak and brings a lower price at the mill because it often has large knots that make it difficult to saw out for furniture stock, flooring, and interior house trim. Scarlet oak has gone into farming implements, boats, wagons, and barrel staves, with a few trees sound enough to provide stock for finer products. These days, my friend tells me, a market exists for railroad ties up to 24 feet in length, used in switching yards where a single track divides into two. Scarlet oak, which often has a long, straight bole, finds an application there.

Pin Oak *(Quercus palustris)*. Look for pin oak in wet woods and river bottomlands and on the edges of swamps. Pin oak's species name, *palustris,* is a Latin word meaning "of the marsh" or "marsh loving" and points to the tree's preferred habitat: palustrine, or swampy, ground. This medium-size oak grows best in soil that is saturated for part of the year, such as lowlands that flood in late winter and early spring. Pin oak also grows on clay soils underlying poorly drained upland sites.

Pin oak belongs to the red oak group, along with northern red oak, black oak, scarlet oak, and several other species. It ranges from central New England west to Iowa, Missouri, and eastern Kansas, and south to North Carolina in the east and Oklahoma in the west. A mature pin oak stands 50 to 90 feet tall and has a trunk 1 to 3 feet in diameter; the largest specimens on record exceed 100 feet in height and possess trunks more than 5 feet in diameter. A very large specimen in West Haven, Connecticut, stood 108 feet tall when measured in 2002.

I have a special fondness for deciduous trees in winter, when one can see and truly apprehend the form of an individual specimen. Winter-bare pin oak is one of my favorites. Unlike other oaks, Q. palustris sends up a central stem that does not fork. This mastlike shaft rises straight to the top of the tree, narrowing as it ascends. The trunk appears thick, relative to the size of the branches projecting from it. Branches near the crown fan upward, those near the middle of the tree extend horizontally, and ones lowest on the trunk dip downward, reaching back toward the ground. The overall shape is roughly conical. Filling in this complex, distinctive symmetry is a host of short, strong, flexible twigs that resemble pins closely enough to have earned this oak its most widely accepted common name. Two other folk names are water oak and swamp oak.

The angular leaves of pin oak strongly resemble those of its close relative, the scarlet oak. They are 4 to 6 inches long and 2 to 4 inches broad. Five to seven tapering lobes, each with a few sharply pointed teeth, stand separated by deep clefts; these gaps between the lobes extend almost the whole way to the midrib and are rounded at the base. As a member of the red oak tribe, pin oak sports tiny bristle tips at the ends of the lobe teeth. The leaves are a shiny dark green above and light green below; on their undersurfaces, at the angles where the conspicuous side veins join the midrib, are tufts of pale hairs. The leaves turn a rich deep red in autumn; some usually hang on the tree, dead and brown, into winter.

The bark is gray to gray-brown, hard, thin, and fairly smooth, broken by shallow cracks. Between the cracks, low ridges stand covered with small scales. The bark on young trees is smooth and shiny, light brown to reddish in color.

Pin oaks flower just as they are putting out leaves in spring. Individual trees have both male and female flowers. The male flowers are grouped in dangling, hairy catkins; the bright red female flowers stand at the ends of short stalks. Wind carries the male pollen to the female flowers. The resulting acorns take two years to ripen. A pin oak acorn is about ½ inch long and equally broad, notably rounded in shape. A scaly, saucer-shaped cup covers between one-quarter and one-third of the nut. Inside the acorn lies a pale yellow kernel full of bitter-tasting tannin compounds. Despite their bitterness, the acorns are eaten by deer, squirrels and other rodents, wild turkeys, woodpeckers, and ducks, especially mallards and wood ducks, which walk about on land picking up the nuts. In *The Book of Swamp and Bog,* the Michigan naturalist John Eastman reports finding pin oak acorns

The lower branches of pin oak droop toward the ground, giving the tree a distinctive silhouette.

cached by blue jays in the ragged seed heads of cattails.

Pin oak has a shallow, fibrous root system; although it does not send down a taproot, the tree is fairly resistant to summer drought. A shade-intolerant species, it pushes up quickly in wet areas where logging has removed other trees. Pin oaks as young as twenty years can produce acorns; the trees rarely live longer than a century. In poorly drained soil, pin oaks may grow in nearly pure stands. They also mix with hardwoods such as American elm, silver maple, red maple, hackberry, basswood, and shagbark hickory.

The wood is fairly heavy, at forty-three pounds per cubic foot, dry weight. It has a reputation for badly warping and checking, or cracking, while it cures; thanks to the tree's prolific branching habit, many small knots interrupt the grain. Pin oak is used for rough construction, railroad ties, barrels, crates, and pallets. The stubby, pinlike twigs were once used as pegs to hold together the squared-timber frames of barns and houses. The old farmhouse we remodeled in northeastern Vermont has a red spruce frame, and the pegs holding it together are oak—if they are pin oak, they may have been brought in from elsewhere, because *Q. palustris* does not grow locally.

Pin oak, with its intricate and graceful form, makes an eye-catching street or lawn tree. Since its root system is shallow, pin oak is easier to transplant than other oaks, and its capability to grow fast allows the tree to fill a site quickly. *Q. palustris* is disease-resistant and wind-firm, and it tolerates polluted air fairly well. I particularly admire specimens in their middle years: old enough to have developed those elegant, drooping lower branches, yet not so large that they have broadened and lost that conical, upward-striving silhouette.

Scrub Oak *(Quercus ilicifolia).* Scrub oak, also known as bear oak, is a shrub or a small tree that forms extensive, and in some cases almost impenetrable, thickets on rocky hillsides, sandy barrens, and mountain plateaus. Scrub oak ranges from Maine to North Carolina and west to western Pennsylvania and Virginia. It is found in part or all of the six New England states and is particularly abundant on Cape Cod. Botanists place it in the red oak group.

Scrub oak can be fully mature and yet stand only 2 feet high; most specimens never get taller than 4 to 8 feet and have stem diameters of 1 to 3 inches. A few individuals become treelike, reaching 20 feet tall. Scrub oak may cover areas that have been swept by fire or logged repeatedly. Over time, taller species—scarlet oak, chestnut oak, red maple, aspen—may ascend above the scrub oak and form a new forest.

The leaves are 2 to 5 inches long, with a wedge-shaped base. Needle-like extensions of the veins tip the sharp, angular outer lobes. The leaves are dark green and glossy above, pale and densely furred below, and leathery to the touch. They turn yellow and brown in autumn and often cling to the twigs into winter. The small, ½-inch-long, rounded acorns taste so bitter that they are said to be shunned by all wildlife except bears. Dense stands of scrub oak offer escape and resting habitat to deer, black bears, and other animals.

White Oak *(Quercus alba)*. Several years ago, while living in Pennsylvania, I cut down a small white oak. Dead at least five years, it would, I knew, make excellent firewood: hot-burning, long-lasting fuel to keep the stove pumping out heat through a cold winter's night. After bucking the tree into stove lengths, I noticed how dense the annual growth rings were on the log closest to the stump. I left that billet unsplit, and when I got back home, I fetched a ruler and a hand lens.

The billet measured 8½ inches in diameter. Starting from the center, I began counting my way outward. The rings were so narrow in places that I needed the magnifying lens to distinguish them. At every tenth ring, I made a pencil mark. By the time I reached the outermost rings on the log, my count was one hundred. I lost a few rings at the perimeter, laid down during the last years of the tree's life, now flaking away and obscured by wood rot. So the tree was at least 105 and maybe 110 years old.

The white oak had been a seedling around 1890. It grew slowly during its first several decades; one ten-year span measured only ¼ inch, the rings so narrow they almost blended into each other. According to an elderly neighbor, much of the land in the vicinity had been logged between 1928 and 1930. Obviously the white oak was too small to be worth cutting then. I could see how the growth rings widened markedly after the logging: Some measured a full ⅛ inch, which meant that the tree, flourishing in the suddenly abundant sunlight, expanded its girth by ¼ inch a year, ten times as fast as it had grown before the logging. Things slowed down again for the white oak in the 1940s, when other trees apparently outstripped it in the race upward to become part of the forest canopy. Indeed, another white oak, now 13 inches across, and a tall black oak, its trunk a strapping 22 inches in diameter, both towered over the dead white oak's stump.

The small white oak had survived a gypsy moth infestation in the 1980s, when every oak in the woods was stripped of its leaves two years in a row. However, I could not tell which growth rings might have reflected the gypsy moth scourge: Everything was so crowded together, there at the end, as the tree's life dwindled and finally wound down. Perhaps the stress caused by the defoliations represented the final straw.

White oak ranges from southern Quebec to Minnesota and south to Florida and Texas. In New England this long-lived tree grows in the southern districts of Maine, New Hampshire, and Vermont, and in the Lake Champlain valley of northern Vermont; it is found throughout Massachusetts, Connecticut, and Rhode Island. Although it grows in sandy and gravelly soil, and in relatively dry settings, white oak does best in rich, deep, moist soil. The species thrives in lowlands, hill country, and mountains, sometimes occurring in pure or nearly pure stands. White oaks do not colonize bone-dry ridges (chestnut oaks replace them there) or poorly drained flats and wet bottomlands, to which swamp oak and pin oak are better adapted.

Q. *alba* is the exemplar of the white oak group, a complex of oak species whose leaves have rounded instead of angular lobes and lack the pointed, needlelike extensions at the lobe ends, called bristle tips, that distinguish the red oaks, the other major oak group. Because they contain fewer tannin compounds, white oak acorns are not as bitter-tasting as the acorns of the red oaks. White oak acorns mature in a single growing season, whereas those of red oaks take two growing seasons to ripen.

Under normal conditions, a white oak will become 70 to 80 feet tall, with a trunk 3 to 5 feet across. The potential exists for greater growth: There are records of specimens 150 feet tall, with trunks 8 feet in diameter. In a closed forest stand, the trunk of a white oak typically becomes tall and straight, with little taper; the limbs cluster at the top of the tree, forming a compact crown. White oaks that grow in open terrain look like another species altogether. Ten to 20 feet above ground level, the trunk divides into many stout branches, which twist and crook as they extend outward to 50 or more feet, and upward to form a deep, broad crown, often with an irregular shape but sometimes quite symmetrical and covering an impressive area. Look for such behemoths in farm fields, where they were left to provide a patch of cooling shade for the plowmen and the horse and ox teams of yesteryear.

White oak leaves are 4 to 9 inches long by 2 to 4 inches wide. They have three to nine (usually seven) ascending lobes that are blunt-tipped and separated by deep, round-based gaps. The shape suggests the part of a topographic map you would get if you snipped along a single contour line surrounding a hilly upland drained by numerous streams. Leaves in the tree's crown often are slender, with deep lobes; those on lower branches tend to be broader and less deeply lobed. The leaves are bright green above and gray-green or whitish green on their undersurfaces. They turn a deep dark red in autumn, a hue similar to that of scarlet oak, although not usually so brilliant. Often some of a white oak's leaves remain attached to their twigs into winter.

The tree gets its common name from its pale bark, not nearly as white as a paper birch's bark but nonetheless a very pale brownish gray in some individuals. The bark is composed of many small irregular scales or patches that often are only loosely attached. On small branches, the bark may be light green, reddish green, or almost silvery and not patchy. Extremely pale, almost white, roughly circular areas on the trunk are harmless surface fungi, saprophytes that get nourishment from dead and decaying organic matter. Black, stringlike strands beneath the sloughed-off bark of a dead white oak are the mycelia of *Armillaria mellea,* a root-rot fungus whose gilled fruiting bodies are the choice edibles known as honey mushrooms.

In May the crowns of winter-bare white oaks gradually turn red and then fade to a silvery pink as the new leaves emerge and expand. When the

Farmers of yesteryear left white oaks standing in fields to provide shade for plowmen and their horses and oxen.

leaves are about a third developed, the trees set out flowers. Male flowers are creamy-green, clustered on hairy, stringy, drooping catkins 2 to 3 inches long; the short-stalked female catkins are shaped like spikes. Flowers of both sexes blossom on the same tree. The wind blows the male pollen to the female flowers. The resulting acorns are a shiny pale brown, oval, and rounded at the tip. They range in size from ½ to 1 inch long, averaging about ¾ inch; a bowl-shaped cup encloses the nut's base for a quarter of its overall length. The nuts take about four months to ripen, falling off in September and October.

Lacking a strong tannin defense, white oak acorns germinate soon after they fall; before freezing weather arrives, their first small roots have penetrated the soil, with the shoot remaining dormant until the following spring. Animals avidly search out the sweet-tasting nuts, which, at about 6 percent protein and 65 percent carbohydrates, constitute a high-energy foodstuff. More than 180 species of birds and mammals consume white oak acorns, including squirrels, chipmunks, mice, deer, bears, raccoons, blue jays, wild turkeys, quail, grouse, woodpeckers, nuthatches, and ducks.

Native Americans of many tribes gathered white oak acorns, whose low tannin content made the nuts more palatable than red oak acorns. The Indians boiled the nuts to remove the water-soluble tannins, then ground them into a meal used to bake bread. Acorns from some white oaks are sweet enough to eat out of hand.

Growing in open light, a white oak as young as twenty years may produce nuts. Trees between the ages of 50 and 200 are the most prolific acorn producers. In Virginia, botanists monitored a single 69-year-old white oak and found that it bore more than 60,000 acorns in one year; the tree was 69 feet tall and had a 25-inch trunk diameter. Typical good production for a mature forest-grown tree is probably closer to 10,000 acorns. A stand of white oaks can yield more than 200,000 acorns per acre. Several years may pass when trees bear few or no acorns; they produce bumper crops once every four to ten years. Investing resources in vast quantities of acorns on an irregular schedule is a strategy that overwhelms seed predators: By dropping more acorns than the local wildlife can consume, trees improve the odds that at least some of their acorns will germinate and sprout. How trees synchronize their acorn production is a mystery science has yet to unravel.

Of all the oaks, *Q. alba* is the most shade tolerant, sprouting fairly readily even beneath the canopy of a mature forest, which allows the species to maintain its numbers or increase in a wooded stand. Seedlings and saplings grow slowly, waiting for a taller tree to die and come crashing down; then they press toward the light. White oak seedlings, saplings, and even pole-size trees are able to persist under a shaded forest canopy for more than ninety years—which is about the age of that smallish, stunted white oak I cut up for firewood a few years back.

After one growing season, seedlings may be 3 to 4 inches high, with a taproot ¼ to ½ inch in diameter, reaching down more than 12 inches. As the tree enlarges, the central taproot is replaced by several deep, spreading lateral roots, usually within 2 feet of the ground surface, plus a system of fibrous rootlets. White oak grows faster than hickory and beech, and slower than tuliptree, black walnut, white ash, and sugar maple. Among the oaks, white oak grows faster than chestnut but not as rapidly as scarlet, northern red, and black. Young white oaks sprout prolifically when cut down or damaged by fire. But once the trees' trunks get to be more than a foot in diameter, the likelihood of such stump sprouting falls to only 15 percent. White oaks are extremely long-lived: trees 600 years old have been recorded.

White oak wood is pale brown, with lighter sapwood. Extremely strong, hard, and heavy, it weighs forty-six pounds per cubic foot when dry. Old books about trees often characterize white oak as "the most valuable of all oak wood"; today, red oak and black oak exceed it in value because their ruddier color makes them more popular for furniture and flooring. In the past, sturdy, water-resistant white oak went into boats and ships; the nascent American navy built its famed heavy frigates, including the USS *Constitution,* with white oak keels and planks. Yankee sailors dubbed the *Constitution* "Old Ironsides" and boasted that her stout white oak hull turned aside British cannonballs during the War of 1812.

Because it resists decay, white oak has been used for log houses, barn and house frames, covered bridges, railroad ties (for which it was preferred over all other kinds of wood), and fences. Another name for white oak is stave oak, *Q. alba* being the traditional choice for barrel staves, especially for tight cooperage, vessels that hold whiskey and other liquids. Because the pores of white oak are plugged with woody cells, called tyloses, liquids cannot seep through them. Red oak, on the other hand, makes loose cooperage because its pores are not plugged with tyloses and are not watertight. In colonial days New Englanders exported white oak staves to winemakers in Spain, Portugal, and the Canary Islands.

Botanists have documented hybridization between *Q. alba* and seven other species in the white oak group, including these New England natives: swamp oak, post oak, bur oak, and chinkapin oak.

Swamp Oak *(Quercus bicolor).* Recently I found several swamp oaks growing at Little Otter Creek Wildlife Management Area, near Ferrisburg in Vermont's Lake Champlain Valley. (I was guided to the site by an excellent manual, *Wetland, Woodland, Wildland: A Guide to the Natural Communities of Vermont,* by Elizabeth Thompson and Eric Sorenson.) The trees grew scattered through a woods near a winding inlet of the large lake. They were rooted in ground that  squelched underfoot. They were typical for the species: 60 to 70 feet tall, their trunks approaching 2 feet in diameter, with grayish brown bark fissured into long, flat ridges that were broken up into small scales. Their leaves swayed in the breeze, showing dark green upper surfaces, then flashing back the sunlight from their bright, pale undersides—demonstrating why the species name *bicolor* was given to this lowland dweller.

The currently accepted name for this tree is simply "swamp oak," but I prefer an older moniker, swamp white oak, since it emphasizes the great similarity of *Q. bicolor* to the white oak, *Q. alba*. Swamp oak is neither as common nor as widespread as white oak. It ranges from Maine west to Minnesota, Iowa, and Missouri, and south to North Carolina and Tennessee. In New England it is found in southwestern Maine and adjacent New Hampshire, in the Champlain Valley in Vermont, in eastern Massachusetts, and throughout Connecticut and Rhode Island. It grows in wet woods along streams and on the borders of swamps, although not in the standing water of open swampland. Think of it as the counterpart to pin oak, the major wetland-dwelling species in the red oak group, swamp oak belonging to the white oak group.

Q. bicolor sometimes grows alongside pin oak. It also mixes in forest stands with American elm, hackberry, shagbark hickory, sycamore, black willow, silver maple, red maple, basswood, black ash, and several other species. A long-lived tree, swamp oak can survive for more than 300 years. Its wood is very similar to that of white oak and traditionally has been used in the same ways: barrel staves, ship parts, railroad ties, flooring.

Swamp oak leaves are 4 to 9 inches long. They look like the leaves of chestnut oak but with slightly deeper lobes. The lobes separate four to ten prominent, rounded marginal projections on each side of the leaf. The leaves have soft whitish hairs on their undersurfaces. Swamp oak's branches often show a distinctive pattern: upper ones abundant and erect, middle ones sticking out horizontally from the trunk, and lower ones curved down, intermingled with dead branches that may remain attached to the trunk for years. The smaller branches often shed their outer bark, in the manner of sycamore trees.

Swamp oak acorns stand in pairs at the ends of prominent woody stems an inch or so long. The nuts are ¾ to 1¼ inches long, egg-shaped, and have a bowl-like cup. Swamp oaks produce bumper acorn crops every three to five years. The sweet-tasting nuts are eaten by wild turkeys, squirrels, deer, ducks, and other animals that live in wetlands or dabble along the edges of those productive, valuable habitats.

Chestnut Oak *(Quercus montana).* Chestnut oak ranges from southern Maine, New Hampshire, and Vermont south through the rest of New England. It grows as far west as Michigan and in the Appalachians south to Georgia and Mississippi. The species reaches its maximum size on rich, moist soils of mountain slopes in the Carolinas and Tennessee. Chestnut oaks grow in lowlands but are more notable for colonizing dry uplands, including sandy, gravelly, and rocky sites. On 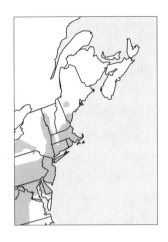 ridges they sometimes form pure stands. Two folk names describe the tree's classic habitat: mountain oak and rock oak. The Latin species name, *montana,* reflects this oak's affinity for mountains. An alternate binomial is *Q. prinus.*

When mature, a chestnut oak stands 60 to 80 feet tall, with a trunk 2 to 3 feet in diameter. Under excellent growing conditions, a tree can become 100 feet tall and 6 feet in diameter. In forest stands, where many individual trees shoot up in competition for light, a chestnut oak will become tall and straight; in a more open setting, the tree will fork low to the ground and form a broad, open crown. In the thin soil of a wind-scoured ridge, *Q. montana* can look like an oversize bonsai specimen, with a bent and twisted trunk and gnarled, crooked limbs. Add in the rough, blocky bark that is normal for the species, and you have a truly rugged-looking plant. The bark is thick, gray-brown to dark gray and sometimes almost black, broken into long, broad vertical ridges, sharp-angled uplifts that are themselves interrupted and offset by horizontal-running faults. At the bottoms of the fissures between the ridges, a layer of inner bark may show pale tan or cinnamon red in color.

The crenate leaves of chestnut oak resemble the toothed foliage of the American chestnut, a similarity that earned the oak its common name. The leaves are thick and leathery, 5 to 9 inches long by 2 to 4 inches wide, generally oval in shape, and bordered on each side with seven to sixteen coarse, rounded teeth, which lack the needlelike points adorning the teeth on the American chestnut leaf. In chestnut oak the leaves are a glossy green above, paler and slightly hairy on their undersurfaces. They turn yellow or bronze in autumn.

In May, when the new leaves are expanding, chestnut oaks put forth flowers, both male and female on the same tree. The greenish yellow male flowers look like bulky, ill-tied knots studding the hairy, stringlike, 2- to 3-inch-long catkins. The female flowers cluster in small groups on short stalks. As with all oaks, wind takes care of pollination. Chestnut oak is a member of the white oak group, whose acorns mature over a single growing season. The pollinated female flowers develop into acorns, which fall to the ground in September and October. In the spring, late frosts sometimes kill the flowers, reducing or eliminating acorn production for that year. Heavy seed crops occur every few years, with most trees in a given area simultaneously producing a bumper crop.

The dangling flowers of the chestnut oak appear in May, when the tree's leaves are about one-third developed.

The acorns hang singly or in pairs on the twigs. The oblong nuts are among the largest of all oak acorns, 1 to 1½ inches long and nearly 1 inch across. They are smooth, shiny, chestnut brown or light brown, with a thin cup made of knobby, hairy scales; the cup covers about one-third of the nut. Chestnut oak acorns are relatively low in tannin content (tannins are bitter-tasting compounds that deter some foliage- and nut-consuming animals), another trait of acorns from the white oak group. Some sources maintain that *Q. montana* has the sweetest-tasting acorns of all the northern oaks.

Years ago, while living on a mountainside in central Pennsylvania, in mid-November I picked twenty chestnut oak acorns at random from beneath a tree near my house. The nuts had fallen in September and October. It had hardly rained at all since September; nevertheless, nineteen of the acorns had germinated and sent a reddish, white-tipped rootlet plunging into the ground. The rootlets, or radicles, as botanists call them, were about ⅛ inch thick; one had extended almost 3 inches into the hard, dry soil and needed to be dug out with a pocketknife.

I opened one of the acorns by slicing its thin shell. The nutmeat, or embryo, was creamy yellow. It had a somewhat bitter taste, but was not so bitter that I had to spit it out. Boiling the acorns in water leaches out the soluble tannins, much improving the nuts' flavor. Indians of many eastern tribes relied on acorns from the white oak group as key foodstuffs. After treating the acorns to nullify the bitter taste, they ground the nuts into a mealy flour and baked it into a hard, nutritious bread.

Deer, bears, squirrels, chipmunks, mice, and woodrats eat chestnut oak acorns. If they have a choice, deer select the less tannic, sweeter-tasting nuts of chestnut and white oaks over those of red, scarlet, and black oaks (all of which belong to the red oak group), even though the acorns from the red oak species have a higher fat content. Bears gorge on acorns to build up fat for their winter hibernation. Turkeys use their large, clawed feet to rake away fallen leaves and expose the acorns of chestnut oak and other oak species. A turkey will swallow the acorns, even the larger ones, and let its gizzard—a muscular pouch that is part of the digestive tract—crush and grind the nuts into digestible pieces.

Although its acorns are low in tannin, the chestnut oak's bark has an extremely high tannin content, and in the past it was used to tan leather. The wood of *Q. montana* weighs forty-seven pounds per cubic foot, dry weight. It has dark brown heartwood and lighter-colored sapwood. People have used it for flooring, furniture, boat building, barrels, pallets, and rough construction. Fairly durable in contact with the soil, it finds application as railroad ties, mine props, and fencing. Its density makes it an excellent fuelwood.

Chestnut oak grows in mixture with many hardwoods and softwoods, including northern red oak, scarlet oak, black oak, and white oak; pitch pine, white pine, and red pine; black-gum; sweet birch; and red maple. Chestnut oak grows more slowly than red, black, scarlet, and white oaks on the same sites. Fairly shade-tolerant, chestnut oak seedlings can survive overtopping by other trees, and for that reason, chestnut oak can ultimately become a dominant canopy tree in its preferred habitat of dry slopes and ridgetops. In such places soils are thin and acidic. Beneath chestnut oaks, soil acidity is maintained by the continual breakdown of fallen oak twigs, bark, and leaves. Highbush and lowbush blueberries and mountain laurel, all acid-loving shrubs, commonly cloak the ground beneath chestnut oaks.

After it has been sawed down, a chestnut oak will sprout prolifically and persistently from the stump. At my Pennsylvania home I cut down several chestnut oaks when adding a woodshed to my garage, and after five years their stumps were still sending up sprouts—all of which were repeatedly browsed back by deer. Foresters estimate that 75 percent of chestnut oaks in the southern Appalachians came from stump sprouts rather than acorn reproduction; those numbers may also be accurate for parts of the Northeast. Because stump sprouts have a fully developed root system supplying them with nutrients, they grow much faster than seedlings that have arisen from acorns. In general, as trees grow older and larger, their ability to stump-sprout lessens.

Intense fires sometimes sweep across the dry ridges and exposed sites inhabited by chestnut oaks. The thick bark of *Q. montana* is an adaptation that lets the trees survive most fires. Many old trees have suffered wounds from fires, breaches in their bark that have let in wood decay fungi. A decayed bole may become hollow, leaving a shell of a tree that is still alive and growing. Hollow chestnut oaks provide dens for squirrels, porcupines, raccoons, gray foxes, black bears, and cavity-nesting birds such as screech owls, barred owls, woodpeckers, black-capped chickadees, and white-breasted nuthatches.

Parts of the Northeast, including southern New England, have an abundance of oaks. *Quercus* species resprout quickly from the stump following logging, and the region's forests were heavily logged in the eighteenth and nineteenth centuries, with oaks growing back over large areas. Also, a chief competitor, the American chestnut, was essentially wiped out by a fungus blight in the early twentieth century, and its place in the ecosystem was largely taken over by oaks.

In what is sometimes termed an oak monoculture, trees are at a heightened risk of attack from pathogens and insects. Many insects eat the leaves of *Q. montana*. June beetles sometimes strip entire trees. The gypsy moth, a Eurasian species accidentally introduced into Massachusetts in 1869, found few natural predators in the eastern forests, and it spread almost unchecked through the woodlands in the late nineteenth and early twentieth centuries. Repeated gypsy moth defoliations have killed many chestnut oaks and other oaks as well.

Post Oak *(Quercus stellata).* A species of dry habitats, including seashores and uplands, post oak is classified in the white oak group. It ranges from southern New England south to Florida and west to Oklahoma and Texas. This small tree usually grows no taller than 60 feet, with a trunk 1 to 2 feet in diameter. The largest post oak currently known in Connecticut grows in Greenwich; it is 48 feet tall and has a crown spread of 32 feet and a trunk circumference

of 61 inches. The species name, *stellata,* refers to starlike formations of tiny hairs on the undersurfaces of the leaves. (A magnifying lens is needed to verify this trait.) The leathery leaves have rounded lobes arranged in a shape often described as resembling a Maltese cross.

Post oak grows on poor, rocky sites more readily than white oak. On Cape Cod it joins black, red, scarlet, white, and scrub oaks, along with pitch pine, in the stunted forest arising from the sandy soil. Its heavy, hard wood earns the species an additional name: iron oak. Durable in contact with the soil, the wood finds use as fenceposts and railroad ties.

Bur Oak *(Quercus macrocarpa).* Bur oak is the northernmost American oak. A member of the white oak group, it grows from New Brunswick across Quebec and Ontario to Manitoba and eastern Saskatchewan. Its range also extends south through portions of New England (including central Maine, the Champlain Valley of Vermont, and extreme southwestern Massachusetts and northwestern Connecticut) to New York and West Virginia, and from eastern Montana south

to Texas. It is also called mossycup oak. Bur oak makes its best growth in the deep soils of the Midwest. It thrives in dry to moist soils that are neutral or limestone-sweet and often does well when transplanted to urban sites. An extensive root system helps bur oak survive drought.

The mature trees are 70 to 80 feet tall, with some individuals reaching a reported 170 feet. Bur oaks can live more than 400 years. Large bur oaks have stout, burly trunks and a broad canopy held up by thick, often crooked branches. Smaller branchlets bear corky, winged projections. The bark is gray and deeply ridged—intermediate in texture between the flaky bark of white oak and the roughly ridged bark of chestnut oak. Bur oak bark is thick enough to withstand hot-burning grass fires in prairie settings.

At its midpoint, the leaf of bur oak is divided—cut almost in half—by deep sinuses extending inward from each side; the upper half of the blade has shallower, more rounded lobes than the lower half. The acorns, up to 2 inches long, are the largest of our native oak species. They are clasped in deep cups whose shaggy outer ridges resemble the spiny burs or husks of American chestnut—perhaps another defense against fire. In western Vermont bur oak is found in a rare botanical community known as the Wet Clayplain Forest, where it grows on fertile soils in company with swamp oak, white oak, red maple, ashes, shagbark hickory, and American elm.

Chinkapin Oak *(Quercus muhlenbergii).* Chinkapin oak ranges from New England— including western Vermont, western Massachusetts, and Connecticut—south to Florida and Texas and west to Iowa and Kansas. Sometimes spelled *chinquapin* (the word comes from the Algonquian Indian tongue), this tree's name refers to the leaves' resemblance to the foliage of chinkapins, small trees in the chestnut family. Another name for chinkapin oak is yellow oak. At  maturity, chinkapin oak in the northern part of its range usually does not exceed 50 feet in height, although some specimens reach 80 feet, with a crown spread of 120 feet. (An oak of this magnitude stands near Oley, in southeastern Pennsylvania, near the birthplace of Daniel Boone. The tree, more than three centuries old, would have been standing when the pioneer Boone was born in 1734.)

The leaves are 4 to 9 inches long. They have wavy edges with sharp-pointed marginal teeth (but no bristle tips) and look like smaller versions of swamp oak leaves. The bark is gray and flaky. Like other oaks in the white oak group, chinkapin oak produces sweet-tasting acorns favored by many wildlife species. The wood is exceedingly heavy: fifty-four pounds per cubic foot, dry weight. Strong, hard, and durable, it has been used for fence rails, railroad ties, fuel, and general construction. It checks, or cracks, badly upon drying.

Pine

Eastern White Pine *(Pinus strobus)*. The tree was as tall as a sixteen-story building. It stood with a slight eastward lean to its trunk, the result of growing for more than a century in a prevailing west wind. It towered up just off a hiking path in the Mohawk Trail State Forest in western Massachusetts. Others of its kind populated the area, their thick, grayish brown trunks lifting feathery green crowns into a milky October sky. The wind sighed in the treetops high overhead.

The white pines in Mohawk Trail State Forest are not old-growth trees; they are old, and they are grown large, but they are not the original vegetation that stood on that particular site when Europeans first arrived in the New World. Among them stands the tallest measured white pine in New England at 158.6 feet high; the tree's girth is almost 10 feet.

The eastern white pine is named for its pale wood, light but strong in proportion to its weight. *P. strobus* ranges from Newfoundland west to Manitoba and south to Iowa, Indiana, Ohio, Pennsylvania, and, in the Appalachian Mountains, Georgia. *P. strobus* grows regionwide in New England, with the exception of the eastern reaches of Rhode Island and Massachusetts. In New England and New York, white pines occur mainly at elevations from sea level to 1,500 feet; in Pennsylvania, from 500 to 2,000 feet; and in the southern Appalachians, between 1,200 and 3,500 feet. *P. strobus* is the largest pine species east of the Rocky Mountains.

White pines usually grow in mixed stands with other trees, both conifers and hardwoods. People have also planted it widely for reforestation purposes and as an ornamental. White pine makes its best growth on fertile, moist, well-drained soil. It also arises from dry, sandy soil, rocky slopes, river and stream banks, and some wetlands; I can look out my office window and see a lovely straight white pine growing in a stream bottom not far from a stand of cattails. White pine favors slightly damper settings than red pine, a companion species over much of the white pine's range.

In full sunlight the crown of *P. strobus* forms a broad, irregular triangle. Usually the tree keeps its branches most of the way to the ground, rather than having them die and "self prune," or fall off. The trunk tapers upward; sometimes the crown forks into two or more uprights. The multiple tiers of branches descend slightly, then snub up at the tips. The twigs themselves finger skyward from the branches, the needles in bright green clusters underscored by the horizontal black lines of the limbs. A woods-grown white pine, in competition with surrounding trees, shoots up straight and tall, with little taper to its trunk, few lateral branches, and a small, conical crown.

Remember "five" to identify this species. It is our only pine to hold its needles in bundles of five. Usually it sends out five side buds clustered around a central top bud. The side buds become the branches that surround a pine's trunk in a whorled pattern, with one whorl for each year the tree has been alive (although the lowest whorls may be shed through self-pruning). The distance between the whorls shows how much vertical growth the tree added in a given year.

The needles are 2 to 5 inches long, slender and springy, light green to bluish green. Snip one in half and look at it in cross section with a magnifying lens. The form is triangular, the edges toothed. (You can also detect the triangular shape by rolling the needle between your thumb and forefinger.) The straight rows of tiny pale dots lining two sides of the needle are breathing pores. Needles remain on the tree for a year and a half—two growing seasons—before turning brown and falling off in autumn. A white pine sheds about half of its needles each fall. I have stood in the woods during a brisk breeze in October and watched the tan needles come snowing down.

On a young white pine, the bark is smooth. It becomes rough as the tree grows older, dividing into broad, scaly ridges separated by long, shallow fissures. The overall dark shade of the bark, which often has a purplish tinge, may be streaked by whitish gum or resin seeping down from wounds or where branches were snapped off by storms. A white pine usually sends forth three to five large roots, which spread outward and sink into the soil. There is no central taproot, but its lateral roots make the tree fairly wind-firm.

White pine (right) has horizontal boughs that often turn up at their ends; eastern hemlock (left) presents a looser, more irregular pattern of limbs.

In *P. strobus,* male and female flowers blossom on the same tree. The female flowers are bright pink, with purple-rimmed scales; they emerge high in the tree's crown. The male flowers are yellow, oval, and about ⅓ inch long, clustered at the base of the new growth of needles at the stem ends on the tree's lower branches. In spring the male flowers release their pollen, and the wind spreads it far and wide. The yellow pollen can be so abundant that it makes a haze in the air and forms a skin on the surfaces of ponds, lakes, and the backwaters of rivers and streams.

When the tiny male cones fall off in June, they litter the ground beneath the trees. The female cones are the ones that persist, grow larger, and bear the seeds. They take two years to mature, so for much of the year, a tree will have two sizes of cones. At first green in color and tightly sealed with resin, the cones ripen to a tan or light reddish brown hue. A mature cone is 5 to 10 inches long, cylindrical, curving, and borne on the end of a ½-inch woody stalk. The cone scales do not have prickles. Cones, usually shed in winter and spring, are most often found on the ground with the thin, rounded scales opened wide, showing that the seeds have been discharged.

White pine seeds are ¼ inch long, dark brown, and fitted with a thin, ½-inch, asymmetrical wing. The wind can carry them up to 700 feet in open areas. An old pine left in a pasture to give shade for livestock will spread its seeds—and its progeny—across the land; in this way does abandoned farmland become woods again. White pines as young as five to ten years can bear cones. Each cone contains an average of seventy viable seeds. Trees begin setting out good numbers of cones when they reach twenty to thirty years. A mature tree produces an average of 200 to 300 cones yearly, containing 14,000 to more than 20,000 seeds. Larger-than-average seed crops usually issue forth every three to five years, with fewer seeds produced during the intervening years.

Like those of many other pines, the seeds of *P. strobus* sprout prolifically on ground that has been cleared by fire. Seedlings also prosper on land disturbed by logging. Botanists classify *P. strobus* as a "gap-phase species," which means it will germinate in the shade cast by the forest canopy but will grow to maturity only if overstory trees die and fall, creating a gap in the canopy that lets sunlight reach the ground. White pine is considered more shade tolerant than the aspens, red oak, red maple, gray birch, and black spruce, and less shade tolerant than yellow birch, eastern hemlock, American beech, sugar maple, and balsam fir. Seeds of *P. strobus* germinate readily in abandoned fields and pastures, where existing low vegetation—grasses, ferns, blueberry shrubs, blackberry, and dewberry vines—provides a protective groundcover.

At first a white pine seedling grows slowly. Ten years may pass before it stands 5 feet tall, even in full sunlight. After that, growth takes off, and trees can be 60 feet high and have a 2-foot trunk diameter in only thirty years. A pine extends upward and outward from buds—called candles because of their cylindrical shape—on the uppermost shoot and the tips of lower branches. These growth structures are fragile: A bird landing on one can snap it off, changing the tree's future form. A white pine achieves all of its lengthening and produces its next year's growth buds in about a month during early summer.

On good sites white pines grow rapidly, increasing in height an average of 16 inches per year. When fully mature, a tree may tower up to 200 or more feet, but most are cut down before they achieve such a stature, and a 100-foot pine in today's forests can be considered a large specimen. Old-growth white pines can have trunks 6 feet in diameter, although 3 to 4 feet is more usual. Individual trees live 200 years and may reach and exceed 450 years. The Cathedral Pines of Cornwall, Connecticut, were once considered the largest stand of big pines in New England, with many 150-footers and one tree that measured 172 feet. A storm knocked down many of those pines in 1989.

Several diseases and pests plague the species. The white pine weevil, a beetle, lays its eggs in the growing buds. The larvae feed on the new tissue, killing the leading shoot. Side buds then compete to replace the leader, and the tree ends up with several stems or, if attacked repeatedly, with a deformed, bushy crown; such a specimen is known as a "cabbage pine." The weevil only attacks trees growing in direct sunlight and usually hits trees less than 40 feet tall. White pine blister rust is a fungus that apparently came from Europe on imported nursery stock. It invades the inner bark, causing cankers that can girdle branches or trunk and lead to the tree's death. To control blister rust, foresters grub out currant and gooseberry shrubs (hosts in which the fungus spends part of its life cycle) within a quarter mile of pines.

Early explorers reported vast veins of white pines growing in many parts of the Northeast. It is possible that those huge, pure, aboriginal stands had filled in areas devastated by hurricanes or forest fires. One area where *P. strobus* was particularly abundant stretched from eastern Maine south to northeastern Massachusetts and inland to the Connecticut River valley. White pine was the most highly sought-after tree when logging overspread the region in the 1700s and 1800s.

New Englanders found the wood useful in many applications, including house paneling and trim, doors, window sashes, furniture, cabinetry, shakes and shingles, matches, boxes, covered bridges, boat planking, ships' figureheads, and the masts and spars of sailing ships. In colonial times, three blows of an axe etched the King's Broad Arrow onto the trunks of the tallest, straightest white pines, reserving them for the Royal Navy; colonists' resentment of this practice fueled anti-British sentiment that led to the Revolutionary War. At the battle of Bunker Hill, American troops fought under a flag bearing the image of a white pine.

In the mid-1800s many acres of marginally fertile farmland were abandoned in New England as the American population shifted westward. White pines took over old fields in parts of southern New Hampshire, much of eastern Massachusetts, and portions of northeastern Connecticut and Rhode Island. When those timber stands matured in the late 1800s and early 1900s, a second wave of intensive logging brought new wealth to the region. Writes Sheila Connor in *New England Natives,* "During the first decade of the twentieth century, lumbermen cut more white pine in Massachusetts, in proportion to its area, than in any other state. Between 1890 and 1925, fifteen billion feet of pine lumber, 80 percent of which was harvested from abandoned Massachusetts farmland, was made into boxes and woodenware alone."

White pine wood weighs around twenty-five pounds per cubic foot when dried. It is widely used today for lumber and paper pulp. As a construction material, it saws easily, resists splitting, and holds onto paint. It's a handsome wood, aging to a rich golden yellow, often with ruddy highlights; this reddish orange wood is called "pumpkin pine," and some lumbermen believe it comes from pines that have grown in fertile, deep soil.

Hawks, owls, ravens, crows, blue jays, grackles, and a host of perching birds—mourning doves, flycatchers, grosbeaks, finches, warblers, and oth-

Four species of pine grow in New England. They bear their needles in bundles, the number of needles per bundle varying between the different species.

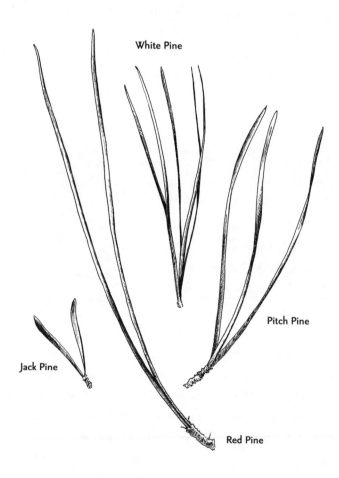

White Pine

Pitch Pine

Jack Pine

Red Pine

ers—hide their nests in the thick boughs of white pines. Black-capped chickadees, white- and red-breasted nuthatches, pine and evening grosbeaks, pine siskins, and red and white-winged crossbills eat the seeds, as do mice, voles, chipmunks, and squirrels. Red squirrels often cut down cones, then dismantle them starting from the bottom up. Sometimes they bury green cones in damp soil; if they stored the cones in open air, the seeds might scatter in the wind and be lost. Writes naturalist John Eastman in *The Book of Forest and Thicket*, "A red squirrel can strip an average-size cone (about forty-five seeds) in two minutes." I have watched the squirrels carry mushrooms—particularly the red-and-white fruiting bodies of *Russula emetica*—into white pines and store them by hanging them in branch crotches.

Porcupines, squirrels, and snowshoe hares eat the bark of white pine. White-tailed deer browse heavily on seedlings. Eastman reports frequently finding raccoon dung on the ground beneath large white pines; the raccoons "often use pines as daytime resting areas," he writes, "leaving scats on the ground before they climb."

Pitch Pine *(Pinus rigida)*. A pine knot is a curious object. A good-size one may be a foot long, curving, sleek, tapered at one end and blunt at the other end, heavy in the hand. If it has lain exposed on the forest floor, it will be covered with a skin of gray, weathered wood; black char marks may signal ground fires that swept through the forest in years past. A pocketknife scraped across the knot's surface exposes wood that gleams a rich golden brown. The dense  wood resists the knife's blade. It has a sweet, pungent aroma like the dust chewed out of a two-by-four when a saw cuts it. A pine knot is a stub that developed at the point where a branch diverged from a tree's trunk. Pitch pine forms knots that are particularly hard and enduring.

Pitch pine ranges from southern Maine to northern Georgia and from the Atlantic Coast west to southern Ohio and eastern Kentucky and Tennessee. It prospers in acidic soils, gravelly soils, and soils that are almost nonexistent, as on rocky ridges. Pitch pine is found throughout central and southern New England. It is the most abundant conifer on New York's Long Island, in the New Jersey Pine Barrens, and on Cape Cod, Massachusetts, where it colonizes salt marshes and sand dunes, often rising above an undergrowth of scrub oak. On sandy sites, pitch pines sink their roots deep: A tree whose trunk is only 4 inches in diameter can have roots that penetrate 9 feet down. Pitch pines also grow in freshwater wetlands, such as Maquam Bog east of Lake Champlain in northern Vermont, where groves of *P. rigida* are scattered across open peatland.

Pitch pine foliage varies from a deep forest green to a bright yellowish green, often with different tints on the same tree. The coarse-looking needles are borne on thick, twisted branches. The sparse branches form wide, roughly pyramidal crowns sprinkled with dead boughs and often with one or more living limbs jutting out at an odd angle. Pitch pines do not stand tall and straight; rather, they grow twisted and gnarled. On the trunks, interconnecting fissures break up the bark into irregular plates and flat-topped ridges. The plates and ridges are reddish brown, the fissures dark brown verging on black, a color that gives the pitch pine the alternate common name of black pine.

Pitch pine needles are 3 to 6 inches long. Next to red pine, pitch pine has the longest needles of New England's conifers. The twisted, stiff needles are held in bundles of three; the bundles emerge all along the warty yellowish brown twigs.

Pitch pine cones occur singly or in whorled clusters containing several cones. Half-opened cones present a roundish shape. A typical pitch pine cone is 1 to 3 inches in length and looks like "a squat, woody pineapple," observes Sheila Connor in her book *New England Natives*. On the cone a sturdy, curving prickle arms each woody scale. A pitch pine can produce cones as early as its third or fourth year. Even after shedding its seeds, a pitch pine cone may remain attached to its branch for several years.

A fire-adapted species, pitch pine benefits from blazes that kill competing hardwood trees such as oaks and maples. On a mature pitch pine, the bark is a full 2 inches thick a foot above the ground, providing excellent insulation and protecting the trunk against fire damage. If a conflagration blows up into a full-fledged crown fire, with flames leaping from tree to tree and turning each into a blazing pyre, a pitch pine may yet be able to survive. The tree's trunk and branches are studded with dormant buds, so that even if all its needles are burned, the tree can swiftly send out a new crop. (Most other needle-bearing trees die if they lose their foliage all at once.) If burned too badly, or if sawed down, a pitch pine—especially a young, vigorous tree 8 inches or less in diameter—will usually resprout, sending up new shoots from a zone known as the root collar, where the trunk and the root system merge. Even large pitch pines up to eighty years old can send out these basal sprouts. *P. rigida* is the only New England pine that will stump-sprout following fire or logging.

Pitch pines on dry sites, such as south-facing ridges or sandy coastal-plain forests that are repeatedly swept by fires, produce what scientists term serotinous cones. Resin tightly seals the scales of the cones, with the seeds inside remaining viable for many years. The cones do not release their seeds until extreme heat melts the resin. Serotinous cones are a pitch pine's ace in the hole: Should a fire become severe enough to kill the tree, its cones will open and scatter seeds. The seeds fall on ground newly scoured of hardwood saplings and grass, a perfect habitat for seedling pines. Pitch pine seeds can sprout and grow on soil that includes no humus whatsoever.

Pitch pine carries two seeds behind each cone scale. The seeds are oval, winged, and ¾ inch long. Sixty-five thousand of them weigh one pound. Many pitch pines produce both serotinous and nonserotinous cones. The nonserotinous cones open and distribute their seeds mainly in winter, when winds shake the seeds loose and blow them 100 feet or farther from the parent tree. Squirrels, grouse, quail, and smaller birds eat the seeds. White-tailed deer browse pitch pine seedlings, nipping off buds and twigs.

Pitch pine wood is hard compared with that of most other pines. It weighs thirty-five pounds per cubic foot, dry weight (a cubic foot of white pine weighs twenty-five pounds). Pitch pine lumber has been used for framing houses and barns. Because of its high resin content, the wood withstands decay, and carpenters have used it for house sills, boats, mill wheels, and buckets. Around 1800, the city of Philadelphia laid 45 miles of bored-out pitch pine logs as underground water pipes. Boxes, kegs, crates, railroad ties, mine props, and fence rails also have been made from pitch pine.

Another name that early settlers used for pitch pine was torch pine, and they called its wood candlewood. The settlers split the heartwood into long slivers, or splint lights, useful for lighting the way to the barn at night and for carrying fire from one part of the house to another. Torches were made by wedging pitch pine knots into the ends of hickory shafts. Some people used those lanterns to "shine" deer: transfix the curious animals at night, allowing them to be shot. (Another common name for pitch pine is jack pine, and it seems probable that the verb to "jacklight" a deer comes from this old poacher's practice.) Pitch pine wood makes excellent charcoal. Tar can be distilled from pine knots by heating them slowly in a pit and catching and refining the resin that flows out. In bygone years, pitch pine tar was considered to be an excellent axle grease; few wagons were seen without a tar bucket and paddle swinging from the rear axle.

New England's settlers often "boxed" or "milked" pitch pines by chopping out a section of the trunk and scoring a channel in the bark to convey the resin to a vessel. Many acres of coastal pine forest were cut to produce naval stores: pitch, tar, resin, and turpentine. Bereft of their trees, dunes began to shift, with windblown sand drifting onto farms, homes, and roadways. By the early 1700s, colonial governments had passed regulations to conserve pine trees and protect the land. In Massachusetts in 1715, no one could "cut, carry off, bark, or box any pine tree" without a permit; the fine for breaking the rule was 25 shillings for each tree damaged.

Pitch pines sprout readily on burned-over land; on clear-cut tracts where the soil has been broken up by machinery and the groundcover plants scraped off; and on abandoned fields. If fires keep sweeping such lands clear, pitch pines persist and may become dominant. *P. rigida* is the least shade tolerant of the eastern pines. If hardwoods overtop them, pitch pines may linger on; however, their seedlings will not sprout on a shaded forest floor, or where leaf duff accumulates too thickly for their tiny rootlets to penetrate. Because we have suppressed fire in our forests for many decades and allowed deer populations to burgeon in many areas, today the eastern woodlands offer much less suitable habitat for pitch pines than they did a century in the past. On Cape Cod, in places where fires and cutting have not taken place recently, pitch pines are gradually being shaded out by oaks, sassafras, and red maple.

Red Pine *(Pinus resinosa)*. Red pine is a tree of the north, with a range about 1,500 miles long by 500 miles wide. In Canada it grows from Newfoundland to Manitoba. Red pine occurs in the Great Lakes states, in New York, and in New England: Maine, New Hampshire, Vermont, Massachusetts, and northern Connecticut. In the East red pine extends as far south as northern Pennsylvania and the Appalachians of West Virginia, where it grows at elevations from 3,800 to  4,300 feet. Red pines are generally mixed in with trees of other species, but sometimes they occur in pure stands. In New England red pines grow on dry slopes and rocky ridges. In some areas, foresters have planted large stands of *P. resinosa*—so many that the planted stands probably outnumber the natural ones.

Red pine is a conspicuous tree, tall, straight, and colorful. The upper zones of the trunk and the thicker parts of the branches bear reddish orange bark; the color of its bark earns the red pine its name. The thick bark is covered with gray-brown, diamond-shaped plates separated by shallow interconnecting furrows. Where the outer surfaces of the plates flake off, the ruddy orangish layer is revealed beneath.

The shiny, dark green needles (darker than the needles of white pine) are straight, slender, limber, and bound in clusters of two. The needles are 4 to 6 inches long, the longest of any pine native to New England. In comparison, the needles of eastern white pine are 2 to 5 inches in length and packaged in bundles of five. A telltale feature of the red pine's needles is that when bent double, they snap crisply. Each needle remains attached to its twig for three to four years.

Red pines thrive in poorer soils than do white pines. They grow best in sandy or gravelly ground. They rarely occur in swamps, but sometimes they will edge wetland areas. As they grow, some individuals develop taproots: long central roots that probe deep for nutrients and moisture. Red pines have broad-spreading lateral roots that give good support and make the trees wind-firm.

Mature red pines stand 50 to 80 feet tall, with a trunk 1 to 3 feet in diameter. Huge specimens can become 150 feet tall and 5 feet in diameter. The tallest red pine found in New England in recent years grows in Mount Tom State Reservation in central Massachusetts. A bit more than 115 feet tall, it stands among large white pines. Big-tree authority Robert Leverett is a coauthor of *The Sierra Club Guide to the Ancient Forests of the Northeast* and a Massachusetts resident. He asserts that had the Mount Tom red pine been competing with others of its own species, it probably would not have grown taller than 100 feet. Other large New England specimens have been found in Vermont (95 feet) and Maine (96 feet). The tallest red pine known in America stands in Itasca State Park in Minnesota. It is 126 feet tall and has a 10-foot circumference.

A red pine can live for around 400 years. In a closed or densely grown stand, red pines become straight and free of lateral branches from ground level to about three-quarters of the way up the trunk. In the full sun of an open stand, side branches may bend down nearly to the tree's base, and the trunk may be forked or strongly tapering. Most red pine branches extend out horizontally and tilt up slightly near the tip.

Red pine's thick, many-layered bark helps protect the tree against fire damage; mature trees can be scorched as high as 40 feet without being killed, but if the fire or intense heat reaches the crown, the result is fatal.

Red pine is not as perfectly adapted to fire as pitch pine and jack pine, lacking the serotinous, or heat-activated, cones of those other two species, but whenever red pines occur in a pure or a near-pure natural stand, you can be fairly certain that a fire swept through the area in the past, suddenly baring the land.

Red pine flowers from April to June. The pollinated cones grow and develop, but actual fertilization of the seed embryos does not take place until the following summer, after about thirteen months have passed. The cones ripen by mid-August to October of their second year. They are chestnut brown, about 2 inches long, and have an ovoid-conic shape. Their scales lack spines or prickles. In dry weather the cone scales expand, and the wind blows the fully developed seeds out from behind the scales.

P. resinosa produces large quantities of lightweight, broad-winged seeds that can travel up to 900 feet on the wind. During a good seed year in a mature red pine stand, each tree will produce around two hundred cones. Good seed crops occur at three- to seven-year intervals, with light crops during intervening years and bumper crops every ten to twelve or more years. In a Michigan study, the soundness of seeds varied from 14 to 63 percent. After losing their seeds, the cones usually fall off the branches during spring and summer, although some may hang on for two or three years.

Red pines need direct sunlight to prosper. Hemlock and white pine seedlings may grow beneath red pines, but rarely the reverse. In a mixed stand, hardwoods such as northern red oak and sugar maple may grow taller than red pines, ultimately shading them out; other hardwood associates include red maple, beech, and paper birch. Natural stands of *P. resinosa* often have an understory that includes huckleberry, blueberry, shadbush, wintergreen, Canada mayflower, bracken fern, sarsaparilla, starflower, and trailing arbutus. In a planted, same-species stand, the ground beneath red pines is usually clear, except for fallen needles and small limbs that have died and dropped off the trees.

Cedar waxwings, red-breasted nuthatches, golden-crowned kinglets, Blackburnian warblers, and pine warblers are some of the forest birds that nest in *P. resinosa*. In the Great Lakes states, bald eagles often build their bulky stick nests in the tops of large, old-growth red pines. Because it produces seed crops fairly infrequently, red pine is less important as a food source for wildlife than some other conifers. Red squirrels, white-footed mice, red-backed voles, and chipmunks eat large quantities of seeds in the years when they are available. Deer, snowshoe hares, and porcupines feed on seedlings and bark.

Red pine wood is darker in color and harder than the wood of white pine; it is also heavier, at thirty-three pounds per cubic foot, dry weight, compared with white pine at twenty-five. The green or unseasoned wood of red pine, thoroughly impregnated with resin, is so dense that it sinks in water. Red pine gets used for general construction, structural framing members, flooring, outdoor furniture, and toys. Creosote readily penetrates the thick sapwood, and for this reason red pine is often chosen for treated poles and pilings. Shipbuilders use it for masts, spars, and other fittings.

P. resinosa is sometimes called Norway pine. Some sources claim that this title comes from the town of Norway, Maine, where red pine grew abundantly, but the nickname seems to have been in use before the town came into being. An alternate explanation is that early English explorers mistook the tree for Norway spruce, a valuable ship-building wood imported to Britain from Scandinavia. Red pine does not occur naturally in Norway or anywhere else outside of North America.

Jack Pine *(Pinus banksiana)*. Common and abundant in Canada, jack pine is a rare tree in New England, where it grows on scattered sites in northern New Hampshire and central and coastal Maine. Jack pine occurs from Nova Scotia west to the Northwest Territories. It has the most extensive range of any pine in Canada, and it grows farther north than any other pine: almost as far north as the limit of tree growth. In addition

to New England, its southern outposts include northern New York and the Great Lakes states. The largest stands of jack pine in the United States are in Minnesota, Wisconsin, and Michigan, but those parcels are small compared to the vast areas over which the tree grows in northern and western Canada.

Paleobotanists believe that during the most recent ice age, jack pine survived in the Appalachian Mountains south of 34 degrees latitude (approximately the latitude of Atlanta, Georgia) and in the western Ozarks. From those refugia, it spread north again as the ice retreated, reaching northern Canada after the relatively short span of 15,000 years.

Jack pine is no beauty. When mature, it generally has an open, irregular crown full of short, twisted branches. Its stocky, contorted form makes jack pine look like "an old crone of a tree," according to Donald Culross Peattie in *A Natural History of Trees*. Lower branches often die, and their snags remain attached to the trunk, adding to the scrubby appearance. Braided ridges and dark brown scales mark the thin bark. The needles are 1 to 1¼ inches long—among the smallest of the North American pines. They are dark green, blunt, slightly flattened, curved, and grow in pairs. An individual needle lasts for two or three years before dying and falling off the twig.

In jack pine the lower branches often die, and their barkless snags remain attached to the trunk for years.

Most jack pines are 40 to 60 feet tall and have a trunk 8 to 12 inches in diameter at breast height. On good sites, trees can become 80 and even 100 feet tall and more than 2 feet in diameter. The better habitats in New England are dominated by trees of other species, and jack pines here tend to be fairly small. The largest specimen reported from Maine is only 25 feet tall; however, its trunk is almost 3 feet in diameter. In the White Mountains National Forest in New Hampshire, jack pines grow on rocky summits, rock outcrops, and ledges.

Jack pines can survive on granitic rocks and sandy or gravelly soils—dry, infertile habitats where other trees cannot make a living. They grow best on well-drained, sandy loam. In deep soil the roots may extend down 9 feet, and most trees' root systems exceed the breadth of their needle-covered crowns. In the East, jack pine grows from near sea level to about 4,000 feet in elevation. Jack pine tolerates shade better than do the aspens and tamarack, but *P. banksiana* is still considered to be a shade-intolerant species. It often grows in pure, even-aged stands. Those stands begin to die off after about eighty years on the best sites and sixty years on poorer sites. The oldest jack pine reported to date stood near Lake Nipigon in Ontario; it was 230 years old.

The cones of jack pine are dull green or purple, ripening to a pale shiny yellow. They are 1½ to 2 inches long, with a pronounced curve along one side, giving them a pinched, lopsided appearance. A tree growing in full sunlight may produce cones when it is as young as five years; trees ranked together, in what foresters call "closed stands," require a few more years of growth before they start making cones. In the spring, small male flowering structures release yellow pollen; the wind carries the pollen to female structures that ultimately become the seed cones. Wind pollination is the norm. Up to a quarter of the female cones may become fertilized by male pollen from the same tree.

A seed cone takes two years to mature. Once it has ripened, a cone may open during hot, dry weather and shed its seeds, or it may stay closed for years, its scales cemented shut with resin. Cones can remain on the branches for twenty years or longer. (In some cases, branches have actually grown around the cones, encasing them in wood.) The long-lasting cones expand their scales and release their seeds only after a fire sweeps through the woods and melts the cones' resin. Cones that need a fire's heat to liberate their seeds are said to be serotinous. Some jack pines bear serotinous cones, and others do not. Trees in the southern portion of the species' range, including New England, are less apt to have serotinous cones than those farther north. Forest scientists have estimated that the total seeds stored in serotinous cones can exceed thirteen pounds or 1.6 million seeds per acre in well-stocked, mature jack pine stands. In forest stands where trees bear many serotinous cones, up to half of the cones in the sunny part of an individual tree's crown may open in the absence of fire. When a tree sheds its seeds, the wind may blow them several tree-heights away from the parent tree.

P. banksiana is considered a pioneer species. Two ideal surfaces on which jack pine seeds may land are bare mineral soil and burned forest duff free of competing weeds and seedlings. Jack pine seeds usually germinate fifteen to sixty days after falling. A seedling may grow 2 inches in its first year, stand 6 inches tall after two years, and be 1 to 3 feet tall after four years.

The wood of jack pine is weak, soft, and light, weighing twenty-nine pounds per cubic foot. Although scorned as a timber tree in the past—when loggers had plenty of larger, loftier white pines and red pines to cut—jack pine is now a valuable species. It goes into pulpwood, lumber, and round timbers. Because it takes on creosote readily, it is used for railroad ties and utility poles.

White-tailed deer and snowshoe hares eat jack pine foliage. Porcupines and meadow voles gnaw on the bark. And rodents, particularly red squirrels, eat the seeds, with the squirrels going to work on the ripening cones as early as midsummer. Jack pine plains provide habitat for ground-nesting birds, including common nighthawks and vesper sparrows. Another ground nester is Kirtland's warbler, an endangered species with a population estimated at 1,000 birds in recent years. Kirtland's warbler requires dense stands of young jack pines for nesting. In north-central Michigan—

the only place where the birds are known to breed—biologists create nesting habitat for the species through the controlled burning of jack pine stands.

P. banksiana was named in honor of Sir Joseph Banks, an English botanist who lived from 1743 to 1820 and who explored and collected plants in Canada and elsewhere around the globe. The scientific name was bestowed by a colleague of Banks, another English botanist named Aylmer Bourke Lambert, who published a *Description of the Genus Pinus* in 1803. Common names for jack pine include gray pine, scrub pine, and black jack pine.

Sassafras

Sassafras *(Sassafras albidum).* Curious leaves adorn this small- to medium-size tree. The leaves come in three patterns: a simple egg-shaped form; a leaf like a mitten, with a lobe thumbing off to either the left or the right; and a three-lobed variant, like a mitten fashioned by a knitter who absentmindedly added a thumb on each side. With the exception of red mulberry, no other New England tree has such variable foliage. Leaves of all three types can show up on the same sassafras tree, on the same branch—even on the same twig. Younger trees generally produce a greater number of lobed leaves than do older specimens.

The range of sassafras includes southwestern Maine, southern New Hampshire, southern Vermont, and essentially all of Massachusetts, Rhode Island, and Connecticut. The tree grows south to Florida in the east, and from southern Michigan to Texas in the west. It springs up in young woods, fencerows, abandoned fields, clearings, burned-over areas, sandy terrain, and forest edges. Sassafras is not a species of the deep woods, where trees with greater growth potential overtop it, shutting out the light and ultimately killing it.

In the Northeast, sassafras can be anything from a thicket-forming shrub to a tree more than 70 feet tall and 2 feet in diameter. On a poor site, such as a rocky mountainside where the soil depth is measured in fractions of an inch, a mature sassafras may have a trunk only 6 inches across. In the South, sassafras achieves its greatest stature: up to 80 feet tall and 4 or even 6 feet across the trunk. The species grows largest in the Great Smoky Mountains, on rich, moist, well-drained sandy loam.

The roots of sassafras run shallow, around 6 to 20 inches deep. They spread out and branch freely, forming a complex system. The short, stout trunk holds up a narrow, spreading crown. The gray-brown to reddish brown bark is scored with deep, vertical fissures separated by flat ridges. The branches of sassafras are brittle and contorted, wavy and twisting, ending in sprays of twigs. The leaves are 4 to 6 inches long, smooth and yellow-green on their upper surfaces and a paler chalky green below. In autumn they turn yellow, orange, rose, or red. The leaves on their long, slender stalks arise from graceful, upturned twigs; the twigs are covered with smooth, glossy green bark, which, scratched with a thumbnail, gives off a nose-tickling, spicy scent, as does the crushed foliage. When chewed, the inner bark becomes gummy or mucilaginous in the mouth, like the twigs of slippery elm. Chewing on the leaves stimulates salivation.

Sassafras puts out flowers in May. Male and female flowers resemble each other but grow on separate trees. The blossoms are greenish yellow and about ¼ inch across; they hang in drooping clusters at the ends of the twigs. Flies are the chief pollinators.

By autumn the female flowers have developed into ripe fruits known as drupes. A drupe consists of a fleshy pulp surrounding a seed. The fruit of the sassafras is elliptical in shape and about ½ inch long; dark blue and shiny, it sits at the end of a bright red, club-shaped stem, like a miniature, out-of-round golf ball perched on a tee. It seems that everything about sassafras is colorful in September and October: the foliage, which catches the eyes of hungry birds; the ruddy stems; and the dark blue fruits. Sassafras fruits have a high fat content, and they are relished by bobwhite quail, wild turkey, pileated woodpecker, several flycatcher species (phoebe, great-crested flycatcher, and kingbird), red-eyed vireo, catbird, and many others. I have found sassafras demolished by black bears, who pull down the branches and bite the fruits off, stems and all. Cottontail rabbits and white-tailed deer browse the twigs, and deer eat the leaves.

A number of insect species consume the foliage. Two common summertime feeders are the caterpillars of the spicebush swallowtail butterfly (bulky and green, with ferocious-looking eyespots behind the head) and the promethea moth (even fatter and more turgid-looking than the swallowtail larva, and studded with red bristles). The promethea larva often fashions its cocoon out of a sassafras leaf, curling the leaf lengthwise around its body and, using silk produced in its abdomen, firmly wrapping and anchoring both leaf and cocoon to the stem. Gypsy moth caterpillars and Japanese beetles are two unwelcome immigrant pests that have no difficulty digesting sassafras leaves.

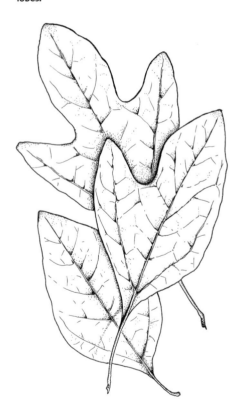

Sassafras leaves come in three patterns: single-lobed; double-lobed; and obovate, having no lobes.

The trees start producing fruits at around age ten. Individuals from twenty-five to fifty years of age yield the largest crops. Trees bear abundantly every year or two. Wildlife that eat the fruits disperse the seeds in their droppings; fruits that remain uneaten fall from their stems in late autumn. Most seeds germinate the following spring, although they have the potential to remain viable for up to six years. The best place for a seed to end up is a patch of moist, rich, loamy soil covered with rotting leaf mulch, in the open or along the edge of a wooded tract where sunlight bathes the ground. In full light sprouts may climb as high as 12 feet in three years. Seedlings in forest settings show some shade tolerance but need an opening in the leafy canopy to get the full sunlight they require for further growth. Sassafras reproduces itself more frequently and reliably by cloning, when an established tree sends up shoots, called suckers, from its root system. The cloning habit may lead to small thickets of sapling-size shoots, all of them genetically identical.

Sassafras roots produce chemicals that can suppress the growth of nearby competing plants, a botanical strategy known as allelopathy. Other trees that commonly grow near sassafras include black locust, scrub oak, flowering dogwood, elms, ashes, eastern redcedar, hickories, American beech, tuliptree, black-gum, red maple, and various oaks. Sassafras trees of all ages are highly susceptible to fire damage; fires and other injuries cause breaches in the bark, through which the spores of wood-decay fungi enter. Invasion by fungi leads to hollow trunks and limbs. Wild birds and mammals nest in the cavities of sassafras trees and shelter in those hidey-holes during bad weather.

The wood of *S. albidum* is soft and brittle; like the tree's leaves, twigs, and roots, it gives off a pleasant aromatic scent. A thin band of yellowish sapwood surrounds the orange-brown heartwood, which can show a pretty grain and figure. While curing, the wood shrinks less than any other North American hardwood. It is relatively light, at thirty-one pounds per cubic foot, dry weight. The wood does not rot readily in contact with the soil; in bygone days, people used it for fenceposts and split it into rails. They also made buckets, small boats, and dugout canoes from sassafras. Today, artisans occasionally craft the wood into cabinetry and furniture. Its fragrance is thought to repel clothing moths.

When burned, sassafras snaps and shoots off sparks, so some folks call it a poor fuel. When I lived in central Pennsylvania, my house was surrounded by a forest in which many sassafras trees grew, and I used the wood for kindling because it splits easily and burns with a quick, hot flame.

I have also made walking sticks from the light and durable wood, some of which I use these days when hiking over the hills of northern Vermont, where nary a sassafras stands.

The name "sassafras" is a sixteenth-century Spanish adaptation of a word used by Florida Indians. Explorers in North America eagerly sought sassafras, which they considered a panacea, a cure-all for a host of ailments, everything from malaria to lameness to kidney stones to venereal disease. Sassafras was the first cash crop shipped back to Europe by the earliest settlers. By 1622 the English Crown had obligated the colonists at Jamestown, Virginia, to annually ship thirty tons of sassafras to Britain, where preparations from the bark and roots were made into a popular drink. Superstitious people crafted boxes from the wood for holding Bibles—sassafras was supposed to ward off evil spirits—and some believed that a ship with enough sassafras in its hull would never wreck.

Over time, sassafras came to be regarded as less a wonder drug than a healthful tonic, traditional in springtime for thinning the blood, preparing the body to better withstand the coming heat of summer. Other names for sassafras include ague tree, chewing stick, cinnamonwood, and tea tree. Tea can be brewed from chopped-up pieces of the smaller roots or bark from the larger ones. The active chemical in aromatic sassafras oil, present in every part of the plant, is known as safrole. Safrole has been used to flavor root beer, chewing gum, candy, toothpaste, medicine, perfumes, and soap. Dried leaves of sassafras, powdered fine, make a tasty thickener known as filé, mixed into stews and gumbos in Creole and southern cooking.

Taxonomists place *S. albidum* in the laurel family, Lauraceae; sassafras is the only member of this group hardy enough to survive the cold New England winters. The fossil record shows that sassafras once grew in Europe but was wiped out there during the ice ages. Sassafras is closely related to common spicebush, *Lindera benzoin,* a berry-producing shrub. Two other relatives are cinnamon, a tree native to India and Sri Lanka, and camphor laurel, common in China and Japan.

Spruce

SPRUCES ARE QUINTESSENTIALLY NORTHERN TREES. These evergreens bear short, stiff, sharp-pointed needles that grow all the way around the twigs like the bristles on a stout cylindrical brush—or, as the nature writer Hal Borland put it in *A Countryman's Woods,* "like the hair on the tail of an angry cat." In contrast, pines present their needles in bundles (the number of needles per bundle varying among the different species), and hemlocks and firs have rows of needles fringing their twigs. Individual spruce needles are seated on small woody knobs called sterigmata; the knobs remain after the needles drop, giving the twigs a rough, bumpy appearance. Spruce needles are square when viewed in cross section.

Black Spruce *(Picea mariana).* Black spruce gets its name from the dark hue of its foliage. The needles are about ¼ to ⅓ inch long. Crushed, they give off a strong, resin-scented fragrance. Individual needles remain on the tree for seven to ten years. The twigs are covered with tiny hairs; strip off the needles and use a hand lens to verify this characteristic.

Black spruce has a large range, extend-

ing from Labrador west to Alaska, from the northern limit of tree growth (where black spruce is but a shrub) south to Wisconsin and Michigan, throughout most of New England and New York, and in isolated pockets in New Jersey and Pennsylvania. Black spruce is the dominant tree in the muskeg bogs of boreal Canada; another name for the species is bog spruce.

An intriguing habitat in which to view black spruce is a kettlehole bog, a feature of formerly glaciated landscapes such as New England. These wetlands came into being as the last ice age ended around 10,000 years ago, when glaciers that had invaded from the north began to retreat. Huge pieces of ice broke off from the great masses and became stranded; the weight of the ice chunks kept the land beneath them from rebounding as the glaciers withdrew. As temperatures warmed and the ice fragments melted, the kettle-shaped depressions they had caused became filled with water.

In a typical kettlehole bog, over time plants begin to encroach on the open water, starting from the pond's edges. A floating mat of sedges and mosses, especially sphagnum mosses, covers the pond like a jar lid. As the centuries pass and organic detritus builds up, the mat becomes thicker and

Black spruce (right) often grows in bogs, as does tamarack (left). Sphagnum moss carpets the bog surface, with heaths forming a shrub layer.

more compacted. Seeds of trees and shrubs blow onto the surface or are deposited there by animals. Venture out onto a quaking bog, as these sites are also known, and it will feel as if you are walking across a giant water bed. Trees jutting up from the sphagnum substrate—black spruce, balsam fir, tamarack, northern white-cedar, pitch pine, white pine, alders, red maple, and black-gum—may actually sway back and forth as you trek past. (Classic examples of kettlehole bogs include Black Spruce Bog, near Goshen, Connecticut; Widow Smith Road Bog, near Pascoag, Rhode Island; and Black Pond Bog, near Cohasset, Massachusetts. For a state-by-state listing of kettlehole bogs and other wetlands throughout New England, see *Bogs of the Northeast,* by Charles W. Johnson.)

On the open bog mat, *P. mariana* typically develops into a spindly tree with a triangular plume of dark bluish green foliage gathered at the top of the trunk; a forester friend of mine says they remind him of "the crooked finger of a witch." Such trees are not tall, usually around 30 feet. Some rise no higher than a human's head; when its roots do not contact mineral soil, a tree grows very slowly indeed.

In a bog setting, a spruce's roots usually do not probe deeper than a foot or two into the saturated substrate. They fan out near the surface, making a big footprint, something like a snowshoe, that helps protect the tree from being blown over. Some roots become shaped like I-beams, further strengthening them. As a spruce grows taller and becomes heavier, it may sink down into the bog; or water levels may rise when beavers dam a stream, or as decayed sphagnum builds up in the form of peat on the bottom of the pond. In such instances, a half-submerged spruce may send roots radiating out from its trunk, which in turn put down rootlets and send up shoots. Also, a tree may "layer," its lowest branches rooting and sending up shoots wherever they touch the bog surface. The shoots grow into trees. After several years, the taller parent—perhaps wind-toppled by this time, or with a snapped-off trunk—is surrounded by a ring of younger, shorter, genetically identical offspring.

On better, drier sites, black spruce may reach 100 feet in height, with a trunk 3 feet in diameter. In New York in the late 1800s, foresters used magnifying glasses to count the annual growth rings on stumps of logged-off black spruces. "In many cases it [was] impossible to count these rings, or 'grains' as the woodsmen term them, with the naked eye," wrote William F. Fox in *The Adirondack Black Spruce,* published in 1895. The foresters found that the average 12-inch-diameter black spruce was 128 years old; the average 24-incher was 195. One 29-inch stump had 321 annual rings.

Although it thrives best in full sunlight, black spruce is moderately shade tolerant: Its seeds will germinate and its seedlings will grow in the shade cast by larger trees. Two common competitors, balsam fir and northern white-cedar, are even more shade tolerant than black spruce and may prosper in the cool and gloom beneath a black spruce stand.

Black spruce can also eke out a living near the tops of high peaks. Recently, while hiking above the timberline in New Hampshire's White Mountains, I took a trail that angled downslope and found myself in a dwarf forest where shrubby black spruces mingled with balsam firs. The trees were knee- and waist-high, growing in a thin layer of soil, and they were severely pruned back by ice, snow, and winds. Scientists have bestowed a name on this ecosystem: krummholz, which is German for "crooked wood" or "crooked forest." In the krummholz, the trees' gnarled trunks bend and twist. They grow so densely and have such stiff branches that they form a nearly impenetrable thicket. Birds that nest in the subalpine krummholz include dark-eyed junco, blackpoll warbler, white-throated sparrow, and gray-cheeked thrush.

Black spruces flower in spring. Each tree produces both male and female blossoms. Wind-borne pollen from the male flowers fertilizes the females' reproductive structures. On a given tree, the female flowers chemically recognize and usually reject pollen from the tree's own male flowers, assuring cross-pollination that promotes genetic variation within the species.

The female flower is cylindrical and about ⅛ inch long. Fertilized, it develops into a woody cone, grayish brown and ½ to 1½ inches in length. A spruce sets cones mainly in its upper branches. The cones of black spruce, which dangle beneath the twigs, release their seeds during winter. The cones drop off the following spring, or they may remain on the branches for several years, gradually releasing seeds. The cones of some black spruces are partly cemented shut with pitch. If a fire burns through a stand of black spruce, the pitch melts and the cones shed copious seeds, which fall upon a charred and unvegetated seedbed, where they sprout readily. (For a more detailed discussion of this fire-survival strategy, known as cone serotiny, see the section on pitch pine.)

Red squirrels clip off black spruce cones, strip out the small, winged seeds, and eat them on the spot or store them for future consumption. Squirrels can remove up to 90 percent of the cones in a stand. Crossbills are birds that compete directly with red squirrels for spruce kernels. Research by wildlife biologists suggests that a crossbill needs to eat a spruce kernel about every seven seconds, all day long during daylight hours, to survive a typical northern winter. In northern New England and Canada, spruce grouse home in on black spruce and other conifers. The birds take shelter in the evergreens in winter and eat the trees' needles and buds. Deer and moose will browse on spruce if other, more nutritious plants are not available and will use stands of the trees as resting or escape cover.

Sharp-shinned hawks, Cooper's hawks, and northern goshawks hide their nests in spruces. Warblers and flycatchers nest and feed in stands of spruces; the different species of birds exploit separate niches in the stand, or even in a single tree, to avoid competing directly for limited resources. One warbler species may nest far out on a conifer's limbs, while another builds its nest close to the trunk. One type of flycatcher may hunt for insects high in the crown, while another related species patrols the lower branches. In parts of northern New England—including Victory Bog, just over the mountain from my home in northeastern Vermont—black-backed woodpeckers, boreal chickadees, and gray jays breed in spruce-fir woodlands.

A parasite of black spruce is the eastern dwarf mistletoe. Seeds of this plant are deposited on a tree branch in a bird dropping; after a seed germinates, it sends out a modified root that penetrates the host's bark, forming a connection through which the mistletoe draws water and nutrients. The injury and invasion weaken and stunt the parasitized tree and sometimes cause it to grow distorted bushy clumps known as witches' brooms. Crinkly-looking beard lichens often festoon the dead lower branches of black spruce. The lichens are not parasites but simply use the tree as a perch.

The wood of black spruce is pale and fairly heavy for a softwood at thirty-three pounds per cubic foot, dry weight. It is used for house framing and siding. When we remodeled an old farmhouse on our land, we sided it with quarter-sawn spruce produced by a small family-owned mill in Vermont's Mad River Valley. To make the siding, a saw is run along the top of a spruce log, cutting down to the log's center; the log is then rotated, and the saw makes additional passes, sawing out a series of clapboards that resemble thin slivers of pie. The quarter-sawn wood is extremely stable, unlikely to expand and contract, and so tends to hold on to paint—a bonus in a place with a harsh climate and great and rapid swings in temperature.

Spruce wood is also used for boat building, and the best knot-free grades are in demand for the sounding boards of pianos. According to *The Adirondack Black Spruce,* in bygone days the bark was peeled from standing trees "by woodsmen, guides or sportsmen, who use it for covering the roof or sides of their shanties." Today black spruce's chief use is for paper pulp. *P. mariana* is Canada's foremost pulp species, and each year millions of cubic feet of the wood are ground up and processed into paper.

Native Americans steeped black spruce needles in hot water to make a tea rich in vitamin C. They used the resin and poultices made from the tree's inner bark to treat sores and inflammations, and concocted a drink from the inner bark that relieved aches and pains. In the 1800s lumbermen brewed "spruce beer" from the sap. Until it was replaced by chicle (the coagulated juice of a tropical plant), black spruce resin was collected and enjoyed as chewing gum. When snowshoeing through our woods, I sometimes wake up my taste buds by peeling off some spruce resin and chewing it—carefully, since the stuff seems sticky enough to lift out tooth fillings.

Indians also used the long, pliant, tough roots of black spruce as thread for piecing together swatches of bark from the white birch, to form the skin of a birch-bark canoe. They heated spruce gum and painted it over the seams, making them watertight.

Red Spruce *(Picea rubens).* In the past some taxonomists considered red spruce to be a variety of black spruce, but today the two are classified as separate species. The needles of red spruce are marginally longer than those of black spruce; some twigs of red spruce are hairy and some are not, whereas those of black spruce are invariably hairy; and the cones of red spruce are larger, at 1¼ to 1⅝ inches long, more of a reddish brown color, and glossier. When crushed, the scent  of red spruce needles tickles the nose like that of an orange rind, while black spruce needles give off a menthol odor.

Red spruce has a more limited range than black spruce: from New Brunswick and southern Ontario south through New England to New York, New Jersey, and Pennsylvania, and in the high Appalachians as far as North Carolina and Tennessee. Red spruce makes its greatest growth in the southern Appalachians, where the air is more humid and rainfall more abundant than elsewhere in its range. Today the largest known red spruce stands in Great Smoky Mountains National Park; it is 123 feet tall, its trunk is 169 inches in circumference, and it has a 39-foot crown spread. By comparison, the tallest red spruce known in New England grows on Mount Greylock in western Massachusetts, an area of steep slopes and shallow soil; although the tree towers up 127 feet, the girth of its trunk is only 78 inches.

In New England red spruce grows at elevations from near sea level to about 4,500 feet. It is found in Maine, in most of New Hampshire and Vermont, in western Massachusetts and in isolated pockets elsewhere in that state, and in northwestern Connecticut. It is absent from Rhode Island. Red spruce can prosper in drier settings than can black spruce and white spruce. It often mixes with the northern hardwoods: beech, birches, maples, and associated trees, including white ash, balsam poplar, the aspens, balsam fir, hemlock, and white pine. Red spruce, white spruce, and balsam fir are the major softwood species in the northeastern spruce-fir forest, which covers some eleven million acres in New York and New England. In the mountains red spruce and balsam fir grow together at increasingly high elevations until, approaching timberline, they become low shrubs. Write Elizabeth Thompson and Eric Sorenson in *Wetland, Woodland, Wildland: A Guide to the Natural Communities of Vermont:* "At the very highest elevations of Montane Spruce-Fir Forest, just below Subalpine Krummholz [another forest type], black spruce begins to mix in with balsam fir, and red spruce is completely gone."

Red spruce flowers in springtime. The male flowers are bright red, and the female flowers are green tinged with purple. The fertilized female flowers develop into cones over summer. The cones ripen by September and October. Heavy seed crops are produced every three to eight years. The wind disseminates the winged seeds. Red spruce seeds will germinate on leaf duff, mineral soil, and rotten wood, but usually they fail to take hold on sod. On heavily logged land, dense bracken fern, raspberry canes, and hardwood sprouts may outcompete spruce seedlings, or the seedlings may remain beneath those competing plants until sufficient sunlight reaches them and allows them to begin a vigorous vertical growth.

A study in Maine found the average rooting depth for red spruce on a variety of sites to be 13 inches, with a maximum of 22 inches. Because its root system is shallow, red spruce is frequently uprooted by high winds. Red spruce has thin bark and flammable foliage, and fire can easily damage or kill a tree. Outbreaks of the spruce budworm destroy some red spruces, but since *P. rubens* puts forth its new growth and foliage somewhat later in the spring than balsam fir and white spruce, it tends to sustain less damage from the insect pest than do the other two species.

Air pollution continues to harm red spruces. Hub Vogelman, a scientist at the University of Vermont, first suggested acid rain as a cause of mortality among spruces on Camel's Hump, a peak in the Green Mountains.

Between 1965 and 1990, nearly three-quarters of the red spruces in Vogelman's study area died. Follow-up research suggests that an insect pest feeding on the tree rootlets may also have contributed to the trees' deaths. The air pollutants most damaging to trees are sulphur dioxide and nitrogen oxides. These chemicals are released by the burning of fossil fuels in factories and power plants in the Midwest and are carried east by prevailing winds. All along the Appalachian chain, red spruces at high elevations have suffered crown damage and a significant decline in growth rates, with air pollution the likely cause.

Spruce budworm, the caterpillar stage of a woodland moth, is a major pest of all the species in genus *Picea*. Budworms often build up their population in a nearby balsam fir stand, then shift to eating the needles of spruce after denuding the firs. In some areas, many spruce trees have been wiped out by spruce budworm.

The pale-colored wood of red spruce weighs twenty-eight pounds per cubic foot. Loggers market it along with black spruce and white spruce for use as paper pulp, lumber, and plywood. The wood is soft and can be worked easily with tools. Because of air pockets in its structure, red spruce is resonant; boards of the highest quality, with no knots and a uniform grain texture, are crafted into fiddles, guitars, mandolins, organ pipes, and piano sounding boards.

Mice and voles eat and store large quantities of red spruce seeds; they seem to prefer them to the seeds of balsam fir, which may explain the low ratio of spruce to fir seedlings in naturally regenerated forest stands. Red squirrels clip twigs and eat cone and foliage buds. Red spruce offers important winter cover to deer, moose, grouse, and snowshoe hares. Many songbirds nest and find shelter in spruce stands and in spruce trees scattered through hardwood forests.

In the southern Appalachians, red spruce often grows side by side with Fraser fir, a close relative of balsam fir. Plain-seeing mountain folk called the fir she-balsam because the resin-filled blisters interrupting the tree's bark reminded them of breasts; red spruce, which lacks the blisters, became he-balsam.

White Spruce *(Picea glauca)*. To my eye, white spruce is the handsomest of the spruce tribe. Steeple-shaped when young, full and symmetrical when mature, it puts forth thick foliage, often with a blue-green tint. Its lower branches bow gently toward the ground, then ascend at their tips; branches higher in the crown angle up, emphasizing the tree's skyward stance. In comparison, black spruce is narrower and more spindling, and red spruce has sparser boughs. I became familiar with white spruce only when we moved to northern Vermont, which is in the extreme south of the species' range.

P. glauca grows from Labrador west to Alaska. Although most of its transcontinental range lies within Canada, it extends south into northern Minnesota, Wisconsin, Michigan, and New York. In New England white spruce occurs in the northern third of both Vermont and New Hampshire and throughout Maine, except along the southwest coast. In company with black spruce and tamarack, white spruce stands at the northern limit of tree growth. It ranges above the Arctic Circle in the Northwest Territories, the Yukon, and Alaska.

The needles are ⅜ to ¾ inch long; they remain on the tree for five to ten years. As in all spruces, the needles are four-sided and sharp-pointed. Extending from short stalks, they spiral around the twig, but because they curve upward, they may appear to be crowded on the twig's upper surface. When crushed, they give off a smell like a skunk's musk—hence the tree's colloquial names, skunk spruce and cat spruce (cat urine having its own special pungency). To further verify white spruce, use a hand lens and examine a twig: If the twig is orange-brown and hairless, it comes from *P. glauca.*

When mature, white spruce stands 40 to 100 feet tall and has a trunk 1 to 2 feet in diameter. The species attains its greatest height on the eastern slopes of the Canadian Rockies, where individual trees can be 180 feet tall, with a 3- to 4-foot trunk. The trunk is often quite branchy; the crown is deep and symmetrical.

White spruce makes its best growth on deep, well-drained, moist soils along streams and near swamps. In fact, it can prosper in a wide range of sites, including those with acidic or alkaline soils. White spruce needs a dependable supply of well-aerated water and will not grow in soil saturated with stagnant water. It does well on dry sites if they are fertile, as are our old fields and forested land here on the Butternut Farm, where many white spruces grow. White spruce is also found on ocean cliffs, including those Down East along the Maine coast. White spruce grows faster than either black or red spruce, and generally it doesn't live as long. On a good site white spruce will live 100 to 250 years. Trees on marginal sites grow more slowly but live longer: A specimen sampled on the Mackenzie River Delta

White spruces are strongly conical and have dense foliage. The needles, four-sided and sharp-pointed, spiral around the twig.

in the Northwest Territories had 589 growth rings, and trees north of the Arctic Circle have been found to be almost 1,000 years old.

The roots of white spruce go 3 to 4 feet, and in floodplain soils and silt deposits they may extend as far as 10 feet. *P. glauca* rarely grows in pure stands. In New England it often mixes with black spruce, red spruce, balsam fir, paper birch, quaking aspen, balsam poplar, sugar maple, and other species. White spruce can become established in old fields; the seeds work their way down into the sod, and the resulting seedlings soon rise above the field grasses. In forests, seedlings take hold on rotted wood; on mineral soil deposited by floods; and on soil exposed where wind-thrown trees have kicked up out of the ground.

The seed cones of white spruce are cylindrical and 1 to 2½ inches long. Cone size can vary from year to year, depending on the weather during the previous growing season, the weather during cone growth and expansion, and the genetics of the individual tree. The shiny, pale brown cones hang at the ends of twigs, mainly in the upper part of the tree. About every four to six years, white spruces set out abundant cone crops; usually all of the trees in a local area simultaneously produce bumper yields. A cone contains 32 to 130 seeds, of which 12 to 60 or more will be viable. A single tree may produce 8,000 to 12,000 cones in a good year and shed around a quarter million seeds. Most of the seeds fall in September. They are dispersed by the wind. Cold, wet, snowy weather can cause the cones' scales to close before all the seeds have dropped; the cones then reopen when humidity lessens. Some cones detach from the branches soon after their seeds disperse, while others remain on the tree for a year or two.

Many northern birds eat white spruce seeds, including chickadees, nuthatches, juncos, crossbills, and sparrows. Red squirrels cut down the cones, chew them to pieces, and eat or store the seeds; biologists have estimated that squirrels can consume up to 90 percent of the annual seed crop in local areas. Deer mice, voles, chipmunks, and shrews also eat spruce seeds. Snowshoe hares and porcupines dine on needles and bark. Spruce grouse eat the needles. The foliage is not a key food for white-tailed deer and moose, but those browsers will turn to spruce if nothing else is available. (Biologists refer to spruce and other low-nutrition items as "stuffing" or starvation food.)

The dense evergreen foliage of white spruce gives winter shelter to wildlife. In spring many boreal birds nest among the boughs: black-backed woodpecker, boreal and black-capped chickadee, ruby-crowned kinglet, Swainson's thrush, purple finch, white-winged crossbill, and several warbler species, including Cape May, yellow-rumped, bay-breasted, and blackpoll.

The wood of white spruce is light and easy to saw. People have used it for framing lumber, log houses, timbers and beams in wooden boats, canoe paddles, musical instruments, boxes, and containers. Many tons of white spruce are pulped annually to produce paper. White spruce is probably the most important commercial tree species in Canada.

Sumac

Staghorn Sumac *(Rhus typhina).* Staghorn sumac ranges from Nova Scotia to Minnesota and south to North Carolina and Tennessee. It is widespread in New England. This shrubby tree often forms thickets in old fields, along roadsides and fencerows, and on stone piles. At maturity it may stand 30 feet tall, with a trunk 8 inches in diameter; the largest specimens approach 40 feet and 15 inches in diameter. Typically, though, most sumacs are much shorter—15 to 20 feet.

The plant comes by its name because its stout, widely forking twigs are cloaked with fuzzy hair, which makes them look like deer antlers in velvet; this trait is exhibited by one- to three-year-old twigs and is seen most easily when the leaves are off the plant in winter. The leaves are 16 to 24 inches long and compounded of eleven to thirty-one leaflets. Each leaflet is 2 to 5 inches in length, with toothed margins and a pointed tip. In summer the leaves are a smooth dark green with silvery undersides. They turn a fiery orange-red or a deep wine red in autumn.

The flowers appear in May or June: erect, greenish yellow cones 5 to 12 inches high, consisting of multiple, closely clustered blossoms. Male and female flowers are separate, and only plants with female flowers produce fruit. The fruiting head, called a bob, is a furry cone made up of hundreds of berries covered with sticky scarlet hairs; each berry, or drupe, contains a small, hard seed. Naturalists have recorded nearly a hundred species of birds eating sumac seeds. Some of the more prominent feeders are ruffed grouse, wild turkeys, bobwhite quail, crows, bluebirds, robins, catbirds, brown thrashers, and cardinals. Deer browse the stems and foliage, and cottontail rabbits eat sumac bark, especially in winter. If a rabbit girdles a stem, the stem may die, stimulating the plant's root system to send up new sprouts.

Sumacs are too small and their wood is too light to be of much utility. People have used the leaves, which are rich in tannin, to cure leather. Water

Staghorn sumac forms thickets in old fields, along roadsides and fencerows, and on stone piles. Female plants produce the cone-shaped, fuzzy fruiting heads.

pipes were sometimes made out of sumac stems by removing their interior pith. Short lengths of sumac were whittled into spouts, or spiles, and their cores bored out with a hot metal rod; they were then tapped into holes in sugar maples to convey sap into buckets. During the Civil War, when the Federal navy's blockade of secessionist ports prevented the importation of foodstuffs, including citrus fruits, Southerners dipped the acidic sumac bobs in water and created a new drink rich in vitamin C: pink lemonade.

Smooth Sumac *(Rhus glabra).* Smooth sumac is much like staghorn sumac except that its twigs and leafstalks lack hairs. It usually does not grow quite as large as staghorn sumac. Like staghorn sumac, it quickly establishes itself on roadsides and embankments, including sites with thin soil above bedrock, where its presence helps minimize erosion. The sumacs are members of the cashew family. A related shrub, poison sumac—*Toxicodendron vernix,* found from 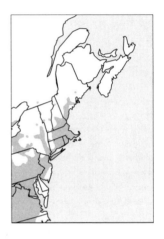 southwestern Maine south to Florida and Texas—produces a skin-irritating oil more virulent than that of poison ivy.

Sycamore

Sycamore *(Platanus occidentalis)*. To the sycamore goes the title of the most massive tree in eastern North America. In the 1700s George Washington and then, twenty years later, the botanist André Michaux, each measured the same old-growth sycamore on an island in the Ohio River. It was 40 feet, 4 inches, around the trunk, or about 13 feet in diameter. The age of that mammoth tree was not recorded, but sycamores can live for five centuries or longer.

Today large sycamores still stand rooted in the land, perhaps not as gargantuan as that Ohio specimen, but great trees nonetheless. Consider the one in Simsbury, Connecticut: At breast height, it is more than 27 feet in circumference; its uttermost twigs reach 95 feet into the air; and its canopy stretches across 146 feet. People have measured sycamores 168 feet tall. Most large ones are between 70 to 100 feet in height, and the average trunk diameter is 3 feet.

P. occidentalis ranges from Maine and Ontario west to Nebraska and south to Florida and Texas, with scattered specimens in the mountains of Mexico. Sycamores occur in every state east of the Great Plains except

Minnesota. In New England they can be found in the southern counties of Maine, New Hampshire, and Vermont and throughout much of Massachusetts, Connecticut, and Rhode Island. The species achieves its greatest size in the alluvial soils of the Ohio and Mississippi River drainages. It thrives in deep, moist, well-drained soils but also can grow on drier sites. Look for sycamores along streams, rivers, and lakes, and in old fields in areas with a reliable supply of groundwater. Sycamores grow singly or in small groups, rarely in extensive pure stands.

On stream banks and small islands, sycamores often shade out and replace pioneering shrubby trees such as alders and willows, especially after

The dappled, peeling bark of sycamore is a good identification mark for this tree, which usually grows along rivers and streams. Wood ducks nest in cavities in the trunks of older sycamores.

the soils that collect on those sites have been stabilized by the smaller trees' roots and have built up deeply enough to become well drained. Sycamores grow rapidly and sometimes reach 70 feet after only twenty years. In its favored bottomland habitat, *P. occidentalis* often grows near American elm, black ash, silver maple, hackberry, eastern cottonwood, and black willow.

The most striking characteristic of a mature sycamore is its bark: brown at the base of the trunk, and above that, mottled with patches of white, lemon, tan, and pale green. The crazy-quilt colors show through where irregularly shaped scraps of the outer bark have fallen off, or exfoliated. The upper bole and the branches are often a smooth, grayish white. The bark of very young trees is thin and smooth; the flaking commences when the tree is about four years old. As a sycamore ages, its crown becomes deeper and broader, composed of many wide-spreading, crooked branches.

Sycamore leaves look much like maple leaves. They are large and coarse, usually 4 to 10 inches long and 6 to 8 inches across, bright green above and pale green and covered with fine hairs on the underside. The hairs are light and sharp, and when they fall off as the leaves mature, they irritate the lungs of some people. Each leaf has three to nine lobes and prominent veins, and is toothed along the margin. In autumn the leaves turn dull yellow or tan before falling.

A sturdy, spreading root system makes the tree fairly wind-firm, able to resist strong blasts without toppling. If young sycamores are cut down, they sprout again from the stump. Slips or cuttings from vigorous stems send out roots and may grow into new trees. My favorite story about this sort of reproduction concerns a huge tree that grew near Philadelphia. When William Rodman was a young man, around 1745, he plucked a sycamore withe to use as a riding whip. Finishing his ride, he stuck the whip into the ground near a spring. The tree that grew from that slip became a leviathan with a girth of 29 feet, 4 inches; when a storm felled it in 1984, it was 239 years old.

In May sycamores send forth flowers and leaves simultaneously. Each tree produces both male and female blossoms, which are borne on separate stalks. The female flower is yellowish green, the male flower is dark red, and neither is conspicuous. The wind brings about the pollination of the female blossoms, which, by October, mature into ball-shaped composite fruits, each dangling from a slender stem. A fruit is about an inch in diameter and made up of many closely packed achenes: one-seeded, thin-walled nutlets about ¾ inch long. The fruits break apart during winter or the following spring. Wind scatters the nutlets, which have small tufts of hair that act as parachutes. The seeds are also carried by running water, to be washed up on stream banks, mudflats, and sandbars. Seeds and seedlings need direct sunlight to germinate and grow.

The seeds are not highly sought after by animals. Purple finches and goldfinches eat some, as do squirrels. Far more important to wildlife are the trunk cavities that develop in mature sycamores. Squirrels, opossums, and raccoons take shelter and nest in these nooks. Bats and swarms of honeybees house themselves in the holes. Owls and woodpeckers nest there. Occasionally I have been startled by a wood duck launching into flight out of a cavity in a sycamore, where this waterfowl species often nests; soon after hatching, the ducklings jump out and float down like tiny balls of cotton to a relatively soft landing on water or earth 20 or more feet below.

While traveling through the wilds of Kentucky in the early nineteenth century, the bird artist John James Audubon watched thousands of chimney swifts pouring into a hollow sycamore. "I remained," he wrote, "my head leaning on the tree, listening to the roaring noise made within by the birds as they settled and arranged themselves, until it was quite dark." He likened the rushing sound to "a large wheel revolving under a powerful stream."

Early settlers took advantage of the sycamore's propensity to become hollow with age. Some pioneers stabled livestock in the heart of a huge tree or took up housekeeping inside a great trunk until a cabin could be built. Saw off a section of hollow trunk, nail a bottom to it, and you've got yourself a cask. Tubs, troughs, cisterns, and containers of all sorts were fashioned out of hollow lengths of sycamores. Sound logs were sawn into cart wheels; the wood is extremely tough, its interlocking fibers preventing it from splitting. Native Americans made dugout canoes from sycamores; one such vessel is said to have been 65 feet long and capable of carrying 9,000 pounds.

Sycamore wood weighs about thirty-four pounds per cubic foot. The sapwood is white or yellow, and the heartwood is light brown to reddish brown. In recent times people have used sycamore for food containers, furniture, fenceposts, railroad ties, pallets, broom handles, butcher blocks, flooring, paper pulp, and plywood. Sycamore has been widely planted as a shade tree. But *P. occidentalis* can get too big to comfortably stand between sidewalk and street; thus the sycamore seen in an urban setting is probably a cultivated variety or a hybrid London planetree, an imported tree slightly smaller than our native species. The planetree has the added advantage of resisting anthracnose, a fungal disease that kills the leaves and twigs of sycamores. Sycamores can tolerate polluted air and compacted soil, adding to their popularity as city trees.

Sycamore goes by several names: buttonwood and buttonball, on account of its round fruit; American planetree; water beech; and whitewood. The name sycamore seems to have an Indian ring to it, but the word can be traced back through Latin and Greek; it describes a kind of fig tree. Our native species may have gotten its title from colonists who noted a resemblance between its leaves and those of sycamore maple, an unrelated tree in England.

Tamarack

Tamarack *(Larix laricina)*. Also called American larch, the tamarack is the only needle-leaved New England tree to drop its foliage in autumn. Other deciduous conifers include the baldcypress of the Southern United States and three genera of Asian trees.

My dictionary says that tamarack is a Canadian French word, probably of Algonquian origin. Another common name for *L. laricina* is hackmatack, perhaps derived from an Abenaki word meaning "wood for snowshoes." (Adding to the confusion, balsam poplar, a completely unrelated tree, is also called hackmatack by some people.)

At maturity tamaracks are generally 50 to 75 feet tall and 14 to 20 inches in diameter at breast height. A few trees achieve a height of 115 feet and a diameter of 40 inches. *L. laricina* has one of the largest ranges of all North American conifers. The species occurs from New Jersey, Pennsylvania, and Ohio to northern Canada, all the way to the northernmost limit of tree growth, where a tamarack may resemble a shrub and where individuals may cluster as densely as 13,000 stems per acre. Tamaracks range across the Great Lakes states and west to Alaska. In New England tamaracks are found throughout Maine, New Hampshire, and Vermont, and in western Massachusetts and Connecticut. They usually grow in acidic wetlands, and some trees ascend cool, north-facing slopes. Tamaracks require full sunlight and make their best growth in moist but well-drained loamy soil along the margins of streams, lakes, and swamps. People have planted tamaracks in parks and gardens. While tamarack seeds will not germinate in a well-tended lawn, the tree will usually survive if transferred there as a sapling.

For three seasons of the year, the tamarack is a subtly colorful tree. In late April and early May, just before and as it begins to renew its foliage, the tamarack puts forth female flowers that look like tiny purplish red rosebuds. The female flowers are fertilized by windblown pollen released by even smaller, golden-yellow male flowers.

It takes up to six weeks for a tamarack to don its full complement of needles. The needles are about an inch long, soft and flexible, sprouting from buds at the ends of short lateral spurs on the branches and twigs. Most of the needles stand in little tufts and fountain-shaped sprays. At first, they are a tender green-gold. As summer strengthens, they take on a frosty blue-green hue. And in autumn they change to a rich, luminous gold, which provides the last vestiges of fall color in many parts of our region. In October and November the needles let go and sift down to carpet the ground beneath the trees.

Tamarack needles stand in delicate sprays along the twigs and branches. The oval seed cones are less than an inch long.

When snowshoeing through boggy areas on our land, sometimes I tell myself to stop and examine the uncloaked tamaracks, which otherwise would scarcely claim my attention. The trees don't simply appear bare: They look dead, through and through. Their crowns—pyramids of warty twigs—hover insubstantially above the reddish brown trunks. With their foliage absent, I can study the trees' shapes: strongly conical, with upright trunks and straight, slender branches. The top branches angle slightly upward, while the lower branches stand parallel to the ground.

Some of the trees are covered with cones: shiny, pale brown ovals about ¾ inch long. They look like hemlock cones, except that tamaracks carry their cones upright on the surfaces of their twigs, rather than dangling them, as hemlocks do, beneath the branch ends. The cones developed from the female flowers that were fertilized in the spring. Their scales start to open from late August to mid-September, and they release their seeds during the next several months. The spent cones may hang on the tree for as long as five years.

In a good year a large, healthy tamarack can bear 20,000 cones containing 300,000 seeds. A typical stand may produce as many as five million germinable seeds. Tamaracks put out at least some cones each year, with prolific crops arriving every three to six years. In most habitats tamaracks reproduce through the spreading of their seeds, but in swamps in the northern part of the species' range, they also may layer: send down roots and put up vegetative sprouts where their lower branches touch the ground.

In a wetland a tamarack seedling often takes root on top of a tussock of sphagnum moss. *L. laricina* grows slowly in the bog environment, where its roots do not contact soil and where a tree may live 250 years before achieving a trunk diameter of 20 inches. On better sites, in direct sunlight, tamaracks shoot up quickly: 1½ to 2 feet per year for the first twenty or thirty years, with growth slowing sharply after individuals reach age forty to fifty and when the crowns of neighboring trees knit together. A tamarack must remain a part of the forest canopy to survive.

Even when fully leafed out, tamaracks with their feathery foliage allow light to filter through to the ground. A dense understory of shrubs and herbs often grows beneath the trees, including leatherleaf, creeping snowberry, common winterberry, spirea, sweetgale, poison sumac, and several species of blueberry and huckleberry. Tamaracks form mixed stands with black spruce, red spruce, balsam fir, white pine, and hemlock. Gray birch, yellow birch, red maple, black-gum, quaking aspen, and black ash are deciduous trees that often grow alongside tamaracks.

Of the thousands of seeds produced by a tamarack, half may be eaten by mice, voles, and shrews. Red squirrels cut down cone-bearing branchlets and stash the cones for future meals. Red crossbills perch in the trees and use their specially adapted mandibles to pry the cone scales apart; the birds then lift out the exposed seeds with their tongues. Porcupines gnaw on the bark, and snowshoe hares eat bark and the growing tips of seedlings. Ruffed and spruce grouse feed on buds and needles. A tamarack grove, especially one with other conifers and hardwoods mixed in, offers a range of feeding and nesting habitats for birds, particularly flycatchers and wood-warblers.

Native Americans used various parts of the tamarack as medicine and for rope, twine, caulking, and arrow shafts. John Josselyn, a naturalist and historian of the Massachusetts Bay Colony, wrote during the seventeenth century: "The Turpentine that issueth from the Larch Tree is singularly good to heal wounds and to draw out malice . . . of any Ach by rubbing the place therewith."

Tamarack wood is heavy for a conifer—around 35 pounds per square foot—and makes a decent fuelwood. Taking advantage of its inherent rot resistance, carpenters have used it for house sills. Eighteenth- and nineteenth-century boatwrights favored tamarack "knees"—a lateral root and a section of lower trunk, together forming a natural curve—for supporting the deck and tying the beam ends to a boat's hull. Newman Gee, a farmer in St. Albans, Maine, currently harvests tamarack knees and sells them to wooden-boat builders and restorers and for diagonal bracing in modern timber-frame homes. Tamarack wood does not split readily, making it a good choice for ladders, boxes, posts, poles, mine timbers, and railroad ties. In Alaska young tamarack stems are fashioned into dogsled runners, boat ribs, and fish traps. The beautiful reddish wood can be made into fine furniture.

People have wondered why the tamarack, practically alone among the conifers, goes to the expense of jettisoning in autumn all of the needles that it grew only six months earlier. Deciduous broad-leaved trees drop their leaves to prevent snow and ice buildup, and to conserve water during winter, when frozen ground may prevent water from reaching tree roots. Conifers, by the shape and placement of their boughs, avoid winter damage. And they need not shed their needles to conserve water because the needles are already adapted to retain the precious fluid.

As he explains in his book *The Trees in My Forest,* University of Vermont ecologist Bernd Heinrich analyzed the relative limb strength of various conifers. The limbs of eastern white pine are weak compared with those of spruce and fir, but the pine grows its limbs thicker in compensation—and, as an added safeguard, sheds about half of its needles each autumn, so that winter's snow and ice will not build up excessively on the remaining foliage. Writes Heinrich: "If tamarack limbs could accumulate as much ice and snow as spruce and fir limbs do, they would regularly be snapped off the tree. This rarely happens. Being deciduous, tamaracks can apparently afford to have weaker limbs." Heinrich stops his analysis there, leaving me to wonder how—or whether—tamaracks benefit from having weaker limbs.

Consider the three Asian coniferous genera that also drop their needles in winter. Millions of years ago, according to the fossil record, those or similar trees grew at high latitudes—north of the Arctic Circle, where no trees currently survive—during a time when the poles were not frozen and the earth was much warmer than it is today. In winter, balmy though it may have been, the polar night was long. It did the trees no good to hang on to their needles, spending energy keeping those tissues alive at a time when the leaves could return nothing to the plant because darkness prevented them from conducting photosynthesis.

Paleobotanists have suggested that those far-northern trees evolved to shed their useless foliage as the days shortened in autumn, and then grow new needles when the sun reappeared and strengthened in spring. Later, as the climate cooled, the trees retreated south—in the case of the tamarack, not very far south—and retained the leaf-shedding trait.

Tuliptree

Tuliptree *(Liriodendron tulipifera).* The tuliptree is an ancient plant. It has been part of the flora of North America since the Cretaceous Period, more than sixty-five million years ago, when the Gulf of Mexico stretched north to join the Arctic Ocean, when tyrannosaurs preyed on smaller dinosaurs, when the very first deciduous trees, including *L. tulipifera,* came to tower over the formerly dominant ferns and cycads.

Tuliptree is also widely known as tulip poplar or yellow poplar. However, it is unrelated to the poplars, which belong to the willow family. Taxonomists group tuliptree—sometimes simply called tulip—with that ancient sylvan clan the magnolias. Tuliptrees grew in Europe and Asia before the glaciers of the Pleistocene extinguished it on those continents. Today the species' natural range is confined to eastern North America, from southern New England—including parts of Vermont, Massachusetts, Connecticut, and Rhode Island—west to the Great Lakes states and south to Louisiana and Florida. The only other member of its genus survives in China.

A long, straight, slightly tapering trunk distinguishes this woodland stalwart. Mature tuliptrees are 50 to 100 feet tall and have a trunk 2 to 3 feet in diameter. A tuliptree currently reported from Bennington, Vermont, stands 116 feet tall; another from South Windsor, Connecticut, is 138 feet. A woods-grown tuliptree often does not have lateral branches for the first 40 or 50 feet of its bole. The crown tends to be rather narrow. The bark on young trees is smooth, while that of older specimens is scored with vertical furrows, similar to the bark of the white ash but lacking the latter's distinctive diamond pattern. The bottoms of the fissures in tuliptree bark show light gray to white, a paleness that is often visible from quite a distance.

The tuliptree leaf has an ancient or primitive appearance. It is 3 to 6 inches long and equally broad, with a widened, squared-off tip indented with a central notch, ahead of four (sometimes six) short-pointed, paired side lobes. The shape somewhat suggests a maple leaf; early English settlers likened it to an "old woman's smock." The leaves alternate along the stems. Thanks to their long, pliant stalks, they flutter whenever a breath of air is moving. A shiny dark green in summer, they turn bright yellow in autumn.

Tuliptrees thrive in deep, moist soils of valleys and low slopes, and also in drier mountain settings, where you can sometimes pick them out from afar, with their whitish bark, standing taller than their neighbors and often clustered around a spring seep or a stream course. On good sites where sunlight is ample, seedlings can become 10 to 18 feet tall in five years. Historically, the tree made its best growth in the cove forests of the southern Appalachians, where old-growth specimens approached 200 feet in height; such mature trees were 250 to 300 or more years old. In the 1870s the naturalist Robert Ridgway documented many giant tuliptrees along the Wabash River in Indiana. He measured the trunks of eighteen that had been cut down by loggers: The trees averaged 143 feet in length and 6.2 feet in diameter.

Tuliptrees flower in May and June. The blossoms—which call to mind both the cultivated tulip and the water lily—open at the ends of the leaf-bearing twigs. The flower, not quite 2 inches deep, is composed of six thick, broad, yellow-green petals, each with a blush of orange at the base.

Cupped within the petals, the male pollen-bearing structures fan out around a central overlapping cluster of female pistils, which later become the seeds. A copious nectar flow attracts beetles, flies, native bees, and honeybees, which pollinate the blossoms. (Tuliptree is an important honey-producing flower.) The Swedish scientist Peter Kalm, collector of many American plants in the 1700s, bemoaned the fact that the tuliptree's flowers "have no scent to delight the nose." Borne high up in the tree, the blossoms are rarely seen; human hikers are more apt to notice the yellowish petals of the spent flowers lying on the ground.

In September or October the fruit matures into a 3-inch cone-shaped packet of winged seeds, or samaras. The long, flattened samaras detach and

The tall, straight, swift-growing tuliptree yields valuable wood often used for house trim. The inset shows a cross section of the seed cluster, containing stacked samaras.

spin away on the wind, which may scatter them to a distance equaling five times the tree's height. When scientists monitored a North Carolina tuliptree having a trunk diameter of 20 inches, they found that the tree produced 3,250 cones and 29,000 seeds in one year. A study of nineteen southern Appalachian tuliptree stands revealed an average of one and a half million seeds shed per acre. Several years ago, while traveling in Maryland, I saw a pure and extremely dense stand of tuliptree saplings; it appeared that they had arisen from seed falling on an abandoned farm field. After releasing its seeds, the cone's core stands upright on the bare twig, often lasting into winter. Seeds can stay viable in the forest litter for up to seven years. Squirrels, mice, and some songbirds—particularly cardinals and finches—eat tuliptree seeds.

More than forty insect species attack *L. tulipifera,* but few cause significant damage. Even the ravenous gypsy moth caterpillar leaves tuliptrees alone: In years when oaks and other species are totally defoliated, the only greenery left in the woods may cling to tuliptrees, as well as flowering dogwood, mountain laurel, and wild grapevines. Sapsuckers often drill into tuliptree bark, ringing the trunk with dense bands of their sap-collecting excavations.

Another name for tuliptree is canoewood. Several Native American tribes made canoes from the tree, using fire, stone hatchets, or seashells to hollow out the trunk. The massive but lightweight dugouts could carry twenty paddlers and their provisions. Legend has it that Daniel Boone floated his family down the Ohio River, leaving Kentucky for the Spanish Territory in the late 1700s in a 60-foot tuliptree canoe.

In the original forests of America, the tuliptree was second in girth only to the sycamore. From the southern colonies in 1709 came the report of John Lawson, surveyor general to the British lords proprietors of the Carolinas, of a hollow tuliptree "wherein a lusty Man had his Bed and Household Furniture, and liv'd in it, till his Labour got him a more fashionable Mansion."

Tuliptree wood is easily cut with hand tools. Settlers used it for cabin logs, shingles, wainscoting, and, since it imparts no taste to water, well linings. Other past and present applications include interior house trim, furniture, boxes, chests, crates, toys, and paneling. The wood, weighing twenty-six pounds per cubic foot, is among the lightest of the hardwoods. Because it has a fine grain and contains no resins, it takes paint well. It is very stable when cured and is the top choice for drawer sides in cabinets and cases. The pulp is made into high-quality book paper.

Tuliptree has been a popular species with Europeans since they first met it. Thomas Jefferson particularly fancied the tree, planting it on the grounds of his summer home in Bedford County, Virginia, and sending quantities of the seeds to fellow horticulturists in France.

Tuliptree has much to recommend itself: its regimental straightness, its flowers glinting like candles on the vernal boughs, the distinct and beautiful shape of the leaf, the golden accent it brings to the autumn woods—and the sense that it is an ancient tree, a true forest elder.

Walnut

Black Walnut *(Juglans nigra)*. Black walnut raises its burly trunk and stalwart limbs
above rich bottomland soil and on fertile
hillsides. It ranges from southern New England—portions of western Connecticut,
western Massachusetts, and western Vermont—across extreme southern Ontario to
Minnesota, Nebraska, and Kansas, and
south to Florida and Texas. The closely
related butternut, *J. cinerea,* is more common in New England, extending farther to
the north and growing at higher elevations than black walnut.

On a good site a black walnut can become 70 to 100 feet tall and have
a trunk 2 to 3 feet in diameter; black walnuts in North America's rich
primeval forests are said to have stood 150 feet tall, with trunks 6 to 8 feet
in diameter. At present, the largest black walnut known in Vermont stands
in North Hartland in Windsor County; it is 115 feet tall and more than 5
feet in diameter. Woods-grown black walnuts develop straight trunks and
gradually jettison their shaded-out lower branches through a process
known as self-pruning. In the open—along a woods edge or in a fencerow

or an abandoned field—black walnut forks low, its branches sprawling outward, sometimes drooping almost to the ground.

Like the hickories to which it is related, *J. nigra* has compound leaves that alternate along the twigs. In its entirety, the leaf of a black walnut measures 1 to 2 feet long. Each leaf consists of thirteen to twenty-three leaflets attached to a central stalk called a rachis. The leaflets all line up opposite each other, except for the terminal one at the rachis tip. Each leaflet is 3 to 4 inches long by about 1 inch wide, stalkless, and shaped like a long spearhead with finely saw-toothed edges. Black walnut leaflets are hairless above and covered with many short, soft hairs on their undersurfaces. Crushed, they release a spicy scent. The leaflets are yellow-green to dark green above and paler beneath; they turn yellow in autumn, when black walnuts are among the first trees to have their foliage turn color and fall.

As the tree's common name implies, the bark of black walnut is dark: dark brown, charcoal gray, on some specimens approaching black. The bark is thick and rough, broken up by deep fissures running lengthwise with the trunk. You can get a real sense of the blackness of the bark by looking at the tree's leafless limbs silhouetted against the sky; note also the telltale zigzag twigs. Should you take a sharp knife and slice through a black walnut twig, you will see that its pith is chambered, interrupted by light brown partitions lined up like ladder rungs. (Butternut also has chambered pith, but the partitions are closer together, darker, and heavier; the hickories have solid, unchambered pith.)

In deep, rich soil black walnut sends down a large taproot and further buttresses itself with several substantial side roots. On most trees, the root system equals or even doubles the diameter of the leafy crown. When botanists excavated a nine-year-old black walnut in Indiana, it already had a taproot more than 7 feet long and lateral roots extending beyond 8 feet. Black walnut thrives on moist, sandy loam, and especially on soil having a limestone origin; it grows more slowly on acidic and shale soils. It does not survive for very long in poorly drained, swampy ground, although a mature tree can withstand up to three months of flooding during the growing season. Black walnut does not flourish in places where its roots stub up against shallow bedrock or on dry ridges and slopes. Seedlings need abundant sunlight and will not grow in the deep shade of the forest understory. On a good site a young tree can add 3 to 4 feet of height per year; in twenty years it may be 40 to 50 feet tall and have a trunk 6 to 10 inches in diameter at breast height. Black walnut grows faster than the oaks and slower than tuliptree and white ash.

Black walnut flowers in May, before the leaves have fully unfurled. A late frost can damage the flowers, ruining the year's nut crop. The greenish male and female flowers blossom on the same twig. The male flowers developed during the preceding year's growing season and overwintered as small cones; in May the cones expand to become dangling 2- to 5-inch catkins. The female flowers, shaped like spikes, bloom in groups of two to five at

The nuts of black walnut (above) are rounded; those of butternut (below) are oblong and covered with a sticky husk.

the twig tips. The wind takes care of pollination. Female flowers usually blossom before male flowers on the same tree; this increases the likelihood of cross-pollination, in which another, separate tree provides the male pollen.

The rounded or slightly oblong fruit of *J. nigra* is 1 to 2 inches in diameter. Walnuts are heavy, and they hang onto their twigs long after the tree's leaves have fallen. A walnut consists of a fleshy outer husk; a woody, rough-coated nut; and an oily, edible kernel. Technically, a walnut is a drupe, like the fruit of the plum—although in the case of the walnut, we discard the flesh, open the seed, and eat the contents. The fruit is a pale yellow-green that grows darker in October and November; as the nuts ripen, their outer husks become dry and brittle on the surface, black and mushy underneath. In the past, people used walnut husks to dye cloth brown. They also put the bruised husks in streams and ponds to stun fish for food, a practice that is now illegal.

Trees growing in full sunlight produce more fruit than those in forest stands. Good nut crops occur about twice every five years. Walnuts cling to the twigs singly, in pairs, and occasionally in trios. In autumn the nuts drop off the twigs (you don't want to park your car beneath a loaded tree) or are cut down by squirrels.

To separate the nuts from their gooey wrappers, grind the fruit underfoot, then pick out the nuts using fireplace tongs or while wearing rubber gloves. If you get the black muck on your skin, the resulting dark stain can take weeks to wear off. After removing their husks, let the nuts dry for a week or two. Drying causes the nutmeat to shrink slightly, making it easier to extract from the hull. The woody nut is dark brown to almost black. Although thick and hard, the hull is not difficult to crack. Hold the nut edge-up, and tap the seam with a hammer. The twin-lobed kernel, or nutmeat, must then be teased out of its convoluted inner chamber using a nutpick. Black walnuts have a hearty flavor. They can be eaten raw or baked into cakes, cookies, and nut bread. The nutmeats, crushed and boiled, yield a rich oil.

Squirrels and other rodents avidly forage for walnuts. Gray squirrels use their large incisors to chip through the hull from both sides. Red squirrels tend to gnaw from one end, and flying squirrels cut out four circular side openings. Chipmunks and mice also chew their way into the nuts to get at the energy-rich kernels. Gray squirrels hoard walnuts by burying them in the ground; after a year or two, unrecovered nuts may sprout and become new trees. Walnut trees in fencerows generally have been planted by squirrels using the fencerows as corridors to move between wooded areas.

Black walnut wood is hard, strong, and durable. Dried, it weighs thirty-eight pounds per cubic foot. It splits easily and makes a good firewood; the smoke from burning walnut has a pleasant tea-leaf fragrance. The sapwood of *J. nigra* is pale brown, sometimes almost white. The heartwood is what attracts human attention: a rich chocolate or purplish brown, sometimes with ample figuring, patterns of pale and dark wood that ripple through a board. Trees grown in the open tend to have more highly figured wood than forest-grown specimens. Because of its beauty, strength, stability after drying, and the fact that it is easy to shape, craftsmen have long employed black walnut for fine products, including furniture, paneling, cabinetry, and gunstocks. Colonists in Virginia began exporting the wood to England as early as 1610. Settlers also split black walnut for rail fences, fashioned it into waterwheels, and turned it into charcoal for making gunpowder. Cradles traditionally were made from valuable black walnut wood because they held something wondrously valuable within.

Black walnut is one of the most highly sought-after lumber trees in North America; it is now rarer than in times past because so many trees have been cut for the market. In the early 1800s the Springfield Armory in Massachusetts used large quantities of black walnut for rifle stocks, quickly exhausting the local supply. Today most commercial walnut comes from the Midwest. The best wood goes for veneer: A machine rotates the log while a fixed blade slices off a thin scroll, which is later glued onto furniture, plywood, and other products. The United States exports black walnut to many countries in Europe and Asia. Top-grade walnut sawlogs fetch thousands of dollars, leading thieves to cut down and steal trees.

The larvae of several moth species feed on black walnut foliage, including the caterpillars that later become luna moths, night-flying insects with beautiful pale green wings. Fall webworms often infest *J. nigra,* their messy silk nests cluttering the ends of the branches. Walnut trees attract yellow-bellied sapsuckers, which cut feeding wells into the bark in late winter and early spring; some trees are ringed with the birds' peck holes.

Scientists have isolated a chemical called juglone from the buds, nuts, roots, leaves, and stems of black walnut. Under some conditions, juglone can build up in the soil beneath walnut trees, where it may inhibit the growth of competing plants, including black walnut seedlings. Horses are very susceptible to juglone: Even the sawdust of black walnut, when used for bedding, can sicken them.

Willow

Black Willow *(Salix nigra).* Rugged, ragged black willow slouches on the banks of streams in farming country, on the edges of swamps, and in wet meadows, floodplains, and bottomlands. Conspicuous and common once you start looking for it, black willow is also easy to overlook or dismiss because it often appears straggling or in ill health, with a leaning trunk or several trunks splaying out from the same rootstock, its branches quilled with shoots, and sprouts issuing from crooks and knots, sometimes with a large limb or a split-away trunk moldering below, lying half in the water and half out.

Many willow species grow in New England, including several introduced from Europe and Asia. They range in size from creeping shrubs to big trees, with black willow our largest native. Black willow gets its common name, and also the taxonomic name *nigra,* from its dark, almost black bark. The species ranges from Maine and southern Canada south to Florida, and west to South Dakota and Texas; in the South black willow is sometimes called swamp willow. Pockets of black willows also show up in well-watered habitats in the Desert Southwest, California, and northern

Mexico. Black willow occurs throughout New England except for northern Maine.

In New England mature black willows usually stand about 30 feet tall, with a trunk diameter of 10 to 20 or more inches. Some trees reach a height of 60 to 80 feet, with a trunk 2 to 3 feet thick. The trunk or trunks are usually crooked and slanting; often they lean out over the water from the bank of a stream or pond. The crown tends to be wide, open, and round-topped. Black willow sometimes takes on a shrub form, and many streambank bushes are classified as *S. nigra.* In even-aged forest stands, particularly in the lower Mississippi Valley, *S. nigra* can reach 100 to 140 feet tall and 4 feet in diameter, ascending in a single, straight trunk free of limbs for a considerable height.

The bark is rough and deeply furrowed, with wide ridges covered by thick scales. The leaves are 3 to 5 inches long and very narrow, only ⅜ to ¾ inch in width. They stand off from the twigs on short stems; lanceolate in shape, they have round bases and taper to long points, with fine teeth on the margins. Sometimes they curve slightly to one side. Their surfaces are smooth, and they have a paler shade of green on the undersides than on the upper surfaces. Twigs and branch ends—visible after the trees shed their foliage in autumn—are long, smooth, drooping, and reddish brown, orangish, olive, gray, gold, or yellow in color. These branchlets are brittle at the base, and high winds and ice storms often snap them off.

The branch ends are viable and probably are more important in the spread and the reproduction of *S. nigra* than its seeds. If you take a fresh twig and put it in water, the underwater end will produce roots, and the exposed end will send out leaves. When twigs fall from a tree, they often land in the water and are carried downstream. Lodged against a bank in silt or mud, they become new trees—no doubt the genesis of the great numbers of large riverbank specimens. Black willows also sprout freely from the stump and root system.

Willows are some of the earliest trees to flower in spring. Blossoms emerge in March and April, before the leaves expand. Male and female flowers appear on separate trees, clustered on drooping catkins 1 to 3 inches long. Bumblebees, honeybees, and wild solitary bees gather willow pollen for their own sustenance; moving between male and female flowers, they effect pollination. Willow pollen is quite fine, and wind also shifts it between flowers. Wind-aided dispersal often leads to cross-pollination, and it can also result in hybridization between closely related species.

The conical fruit capsules split open in late spring or early summer, releasing thousands of seeds. The seeds are tiny and tufted with fine, long hairs. Windblown seeds dry out quickly, and unless they land on damp, exposed ground, they become defunct within about twenty-four hours. Seeds dispersed by water last longer, but only a few of them end up in places where they can germinate successfully. Young seedlings need full sunlight to survive and grow.

The roots of *S. nigra* require a constant supply of water during the growing season. The trees do best in wet areas that are not permanently flooded, at or slightly above the normal water level. Black willows shoot up

Black willow grows along streams and rivers and in other damp settings. It develops a wide, open, round-topped crown.

quickly: A seedling may be 5 to 7 feet tall after its first growing season. Trees begin producing seeds at around age ten, with the optimum seed-bearing age spanning twenty-five to seventy-five years. Full-size and mature by fifty-five, black willows begin senescing soon after that, usually dying before they reach eighty-five. Most large specimens have limbs broken off, which causes breaches through which wood-decay fungi enter.

Black willow root systems are shallow and branch extensively. They strengthen stream banks by binding the soil, helping to prevent erosion and flood damage. They elevate the land by trapping silt; sometimes up to 20 feet of the lower part of a tree's trunk will end up buried in sediment. Black willows grow in pure stands or occupy their damp habitats in company with river birch, red and silver maples, box-elder, sycamore, eastern cottonwood, and other trees.

Several species of wildlife eat willow twigs, buds, and leaves, including grouse, deer, moose, muskrats, and porcupines. Black willow is a favorite fodder for beavers, which cut down young specimens and dine on the bark, twigs, and foliage. A host of insects feed on the leaves. Willow bark is rich in salicin, the pain-relieving ingredient in aspirin; Native Americans used this bitter substance to treat a variety of ills. They also fashioned the inner bark into ropes, bags, and fishnets. Twigs of willow, known as osiers, can be woven into baskets and wicker furniture.

The reddish brown wood weighs twenty-seven pounds per cubic foot. Although soft and too weak for structural framing, the wood resists splitting; at one time, it was a top choice for artificial limbs. Early settlers turned willow wood into charcoal, which they ground fine and used as a component in gunpowder. Black willow makes a poor fuelwood, burning quickly and yielding little heat. The wood from larger trees has gone into millwork, furniture, doors, cabinetry, boxes, barrels, toys, and paper pulp. Black willow is sometimes planted as a shade tree.

George Petrides, in *A Field Guide to Eastern Trees,* admits that "identifying willows is often a difficult task even for the professional botanist." This confusion is caused by the way willows—both tree and shrub forms— cross-pollinate and produce hybrids whose leaves, colors, catkins, bundle scars, and bud scales vary from those of their parents and fail to conform to published descriptions. Other willows native to New England include meadow willow *(S. petiolaris)*, sandbar willow *(S. exigua)*, silky willow *(S. sericea)*, satiny or Ontario willow *(S. pellita)*, shining willow *(S. lucida)*, broadleaf willow *(S. glaucophylloides)*, Bebb willow *(S. bebbiana)*, and balsam willow *(S. pyrifolia)*.

A familiar shrubby species is pussy willow, *S. discolor*, common in swamps and moist to wet woods regionwide. All children should know of its catkins, whose coating of fine hairs feels like a kitten's soft fur. It is the immature male catkins that have this silken quality; as they mature, they send forth golden yellow, pollen-producing stamens.

Witch-Hazel

Common Witch-Hazel *(Hamamelis vir-giniana).* Witch-hazel is a common, well-known shrub that sometimes grows large enough to be considered a small tree—albeit a straggling, many-trunked one. A specimen recently found in Hartford, Connecticut, had a trunk 18 inches in circumference and stood 20 feet tall; its crown spread out 25 feet horizontally. Another, reported from the Virginia Appalachians, had a trunk circumference of 52 inches (one suspects that several stems had somehow grown together) and a 30-foot crown spread.

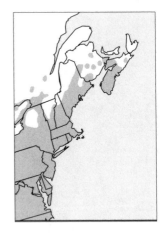

Witch-hazel ranges throughout the East, from Nova Scotia west across southern Quebec and Ontario to Wisconsin and Minnesota, and south to Florida and Texas. It is found in most of New England and is absent from northern Maine. It grows along streams, in swamps, and on the banks of lakes and ponds. It prefers moist, rich soil but will also take root on drier, less fertile sites, including rocky slopes. A shade-tolerant plant, witch-hazel grows slowly in the understory of oak-hickory and mixed hardwood forests.

The trunk of witch-hazel is short or nonexistent, generally splitting into many spreading, crooked stems at or slightly above ground level, creating a clump of small trunks emanating from a shared root system. The smooth or scaly bark is light brown, sometimes mottled with pale blotches. The crown is open and broad.

The leaf is oval, rounded or pointed at the tip, and has a blunt base that is divided into two unequal-size portions by the stem. The leaves alternate along the twigs. They measure 3 to 5 inches long and 2 to 3 inches wide and have five to seven veins on each side of the midrib; their wavy edges are decorated with rounded teeth. The leaves are dark green above and pale green beneath, and in autumn they turn a green-tinged yellow. Witch-hazel has an intriguing "naked" leaf bud: The bud is brown, and in it you can actually see the leaf that will emerge the following spring.

An excellent time to look for witch-hazel is right after the deciduous trees drop their leaves. Then, particularly on sunny days, the shrubs stand out dazzlingly beneath the hardwoods, their bare outer branches spreading a haze of spidery yellow flowers. *H. virginiana* is the only northeastern tree or shrub to blossom in autumn. It is also our only woody, deciduous plant to bear flowers and mature fruits at the same time.

Rounded flower buds begin forming in late summer. The flowers start to bloom in October, just before the shrubs drop their leaves. About an inch in diameter, the blossoms contain both male and female parts. Each blossom has four thin, ribbonlike petals that twist and flare outward from a central cup. The flowers usually cluster in groups of three, their commingled petals creating a busy, snarled-thread appearance. The flowering witch-hazel delighted Henry David Thoreau, who wrote on October 9, 1851, "I lie on my back with joy under its boughs. While its leaves fall its blossoms spring." The flowers' faint fragrance and bright colors attract pollinating insects.

On balmy Indian summer days, I have watched tiny gnats and larger wasps landing on witch-hazel flowers. John Eastman, in *The Book of Forest and Thicket,* suggests that these are likely to be fungus gnats and small parasitic wasps; Eastman also observed hover flies and tachinid flies visiting witch-hazel flowers. Since a witch-hazel holds its flowers for several weeks, it can usually count on a spell of warm autumn weather allowing insect pollinators to fly. If not, the flowers are capable of self-pollination.

Pollen grains do not actually fertilize the flowers' ovules until the following spring, and seeds begin developing at that time.

By early autumn, when a new wave of blossoms bursts forth, last year's flowers have become seed capsules: woody, rounded, yellowish brown vessels about ½ inch long. As they ripen, the capsules forcibly eject their seeds. The naturalist and wildlife artist Ned Smith writes in his book *Gone for the Day* of walking in the woods and hearing "the almost constant patter of [witch-hazel] seeds striking the ground or glancing off branches and trees." He explains the process: "The bony capsules split as they ripen, each exposing a pair of hard, slippery black seeds. While opening wider they shrink in diameter, exerting tremendous pressure upon their occupants, until the latter suddenly squirt from their chambers like apple seeds from between the fingers." Smith set up a group of ripe seed capsules at one end of a room, aiming them at the opposite wall. Overnight, all the seeds were expelled, and many of them bounced off the wall—a distance of 19 feet.

Witch-hazel bears both flowers and fruits at the same time; the small seed capsules and ribbonlike yellow flowers decorate the branches in early autumn.

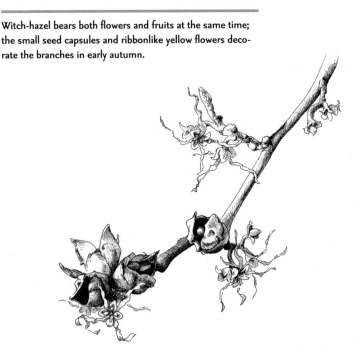

Some sources report that witch-hazel can shoot its seeds 30 feet. The empty pods, with their flaring lips, cling to the branches throughout the year and are a good identifying mark in winter.

A witch-hazel in full sunlight will bear a heavier seed crop than one growing in the shade. The seeds look like ¼-inch footballs; botanists believe that most of them remain dormant on the ground for two winters before germinating. Ruffed grouse scratch through the leaves beneath witch-hazels in search of the seeds and also sometimes stuff their crops with the plants' flowers; wild turkeys, bobwhite quail, and squirrels eat the seeds as well. I see no reason why small rodents such as chipmunks and mice would turn up their noses at such fare. White-tailed deer browse the foliage and twigs of witch-hazel.

Winter-bloom and snapping-alder are two other names for *H. virginiana,* both pointing out distinctive characteristics of the plant. Why the tree is called witch-hazel is less certain. *Witch* may be a variant of the Anglo-Saxon *wych,* meaning "bending," or it may refer to the plant's weird habit of blooming in autumn, when all other deciduous trees and shrubs look dead. Hazel denotes a resemblance to the hazels, nut-producing shrubs of the genus *Corylus.* Some people claim they can find underground water by using a forked stick, preferably of witch-hazel, which dips in their hands when held above a subterranean flow. Siting a well using this technique is known as "water witching."

The twigs, leaves, and inner bark of witch-hazel possess mildly astringent properties; Native Americans made liniment and poultices from them. In 1866 an entrepreneur named Thomas Newton Dickinson built the first commercial witch-hazel distillery in North America, in Essex, Connecticut. The company is still in business today; the lotion, which combines witch-hazel extract and alcohol, relieves minor skin abrasions and irritations such as poison ivy.

The wood of witch-hazel is hard, close-grained, and, at forty-three pounds per cubic foot, rather heavy and dense. But since it exists mainly in spindling stems, it has not found practical applications.

Because their branches are so flexible, witch-hazels are not vulnerable to wind-throw caused by storms. *H. virginiana* hosts few insect pests and is not known to be susceptible to any deadly microorganism-caused diseases. Where the shrubs grow in thickets, they provide shelter and escape cover for wildlife.

Common Introduced Trees

The following trees have been widely planted in New England. Some are North American in origin; others were brought from Europe and Asia. Many of them have escaped from cultivation and become established in farming country and forests. Several of the species are quite familiar, and people may be surprised to learn that they are not native to the region.

Ailanthus *(Ailanthus altissima).* Ailanthus has been planted as an ornamental, a shelterbelt tree, and a source of paper pulp. Considered the starling of introduced trees, this fast-growing Asian import has crowded out many native plants. Also known as tree of heaven (some dub it "tree from hell"), ailanthus can reach a height of 80 feet, although more frequently it is a short, low-forking, several-stemmed plant with an open, rounded crown. The branches are few, since ailanthus relies on large compound leaves for deploying its foliage. Both the form and the leaves of *A. altissima* resemble those of the sumacs. Ailanthus leaves are 1 to 2 feet long and consist of a central stem with thirteen to twenty-five or more leaflets arranged in opposing pairs and with a single leaflet at the tip. Each leaflet is lance-shaped, with a few large teeth toward the base. The crushed foliage and the male flowers emit a funky, disagreeable odor.

Ailanthus produces copious winged seeds that travel on the wind. It colonizes old fields, forest clearings, roadsides, abandoned factory sites, and vacant lots. A seedling can send down roots through a crack in concrete or asphalt, or a fracture in the rock face of a highway roadcut. Individual trees also spread by sending up shoots from their root systems. In cities and suburbs ailanthus roots clog drains and get into wells. Botanists strongly discourage the planting of this species, and in some areas workers have begun cutting down ailanthus and applying herbicide to the stumps in an effort to stop the spread of this undesirable alien. The *Invasive Plant Atlas of New England,* or IPANE, reports ailanthus growing in Connecticut, Rhode Island, and Massachusetts.

Apple *(Malus sylvestris).* Scattered over our old farm in northeastern Vermont are scores of apple trees: young shoots coming up in brushy fields, old fruit-bearing trees sprawling on hillsides and in fencerows, thick-trunked specimens trying to elbow out growing space along forest edges. I'm in the process of cutting down competing trees that are casting their

Apples nourish many wild animals. The apple maggot, the larval form of a North American fly species, has become adapted to feed on the fruit of this introduced tree.

shade on the apples, whose growth and prosperity I wish to encourage because their fruits feed a range of wildlife.

A mature apple tree has a short, rugged trunk covered with scaly gray bark; the trunk divides into many stout branches holding up a rounded crown. The oval leaves are 2 to 3½ inches long with wavy, saw-toothed edges. The handsome pinkish white flowers have five rounded petals; they blossom in May, and their perfume attracts nectar-gathering bees that effect pollination. The red, yellow, or greenish fruits ripen in late summer and early fall. The fruits are plentiful in some years, scarce or absent in others. Deer, bears, coyotes, foxes, raccoons, opossums, skunks, woodchucks, ring-necked pheasants, crows, woodpeckers, blue jays, finches, sapsuckers, robins, thrushes—it is almost easier to list the wild creatures that do not feed on apples than the ones that do. In addition to dining on the fruits, ruffed grouse nip off the energy-packed buds. Cottontail rabbits gnaw the bark, and deer browse on twigs and foliage. In spring and summer songbirds nest in the dense greenery.

Apple trees came across the Atlantic with the first settlers and followed them west through North America. John Chapman, known as Johnny Appleseed, a native of Leominster, Massachusetts, was an itinerant preacher in the early 1800s. He gave out apple seeds to settlers in the frontier states of Ohio, Illinois, and Indiana; he also planted many seeds himself, creating small orchards wherever he went. In addition to eating the fruit, people have used the tough, dense wood of the apple tree for tool handles, spoons, machine parts (cogs, wheels, and gears), paneling, and fuel. Old trees sometimes resurrect themselves: The trunk, which can be 3 feet thick on a venerable specimen, splits apart, and the broken tree falls to the ground—where its branches, in contact with the soil, send down roots and give rise to a new trunk.

Austrian Pine (*Pinus nigra*). Austrian pine carries its stiff, 3- to 6-inch-long needles in bundles of two. The tree is characterized by a straight trunk, dark green foliage, and a conical shape. The bark is dark gray to yellowish, rough and broken into irregular scaly plates. At maturity, Austrian pine reaches 50 to 100 feet tall. The egg-shaped cones are yellow-brown and 2 to 3 inches long. A fast-growing species, *P. nigra* tolerates pollution and drought. People have planted it in cities, in shelterbelts, and to create visual screens. It occurs naturally in Europe, Asia Minor, and North Africa.

Black Locust *(Robinia pseudoacacia).* Black locust is usually a medium-size tree, 30 to 40 feet tall, with a trunk 1 to 1½ feet in diameter. On good sites, such as moist limestone soil, it can grow to be 80 feet tall with a trunk 2 to 4 feet across. The bark is pale grayish brown to reddish brown, deeply furrowed, often with high, rounded ridges. Black locust leafs out in late spring, several weeks after most other trees have sent forth their foliage. The leaves are alternate and compound, consisting of a central stem feather-edged with numerous small leaflets. The overall leaf is 6 to 12 inches long. Leaflets are ovate, 1 to 2 inches long, and stand opposite each other save for the single leaflet at the tip; thus their number, seven to nineteen, is invariably odd. The leaflets droop and fold up at night and expand again during the day. On the twig at the base of the leaf stem stand a pair of stout spines ¼ to ½ inch long.

Black locust has airy compound leaves. Often the foliage shows damage from leaf-mining insects.

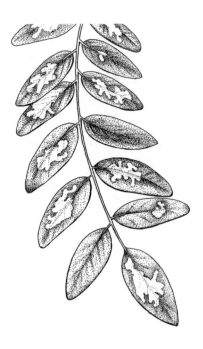

Black locust's natural range centers on the Appalachian Mountains, from Pennsylvania and Ohio south to Alabama; it also shows up in Missouri, Arkansas, and Oklahoma. New Englanders have planted it in farmyards and on lawns and town greens, and to create stock for fenceposts. In the wild locust establishes itself in abandoned fields, forest edges, fencerows, roadside thickets, and regenerating clear-cuts.

Locusts flower in late May or early June, after the leaves have emerged. The flowers hang down in drooping spikes 4 to 8 inches long. Each individual flower is five-petaled, creamy white, slightly less than an inch in length, and looks like a pea blossom. The flowers' nectar attracts pollinating insects, including honeybees. After they are pollinated, the flowers develop into flat pods 2 to 4 inches long and ½ inch wide; inside the papery walls of each pod are four to eight small seeds. The pods ripen by autumn and may hang in the trees through winter. Black locusts generally bear heavy seed crops yearly or at two-year intervals, with trees fifteen to forty years of age producing the greatest quantities of seeds. Black locusts propagate more frequently by sending up shoots from their root systems than through the dispersal of their seeds. The dense, broad-spreading roots produce sprouts that form thickets of genetically identical clones. Nitrogen-fixing bacteria in the root nodules help fertilize and enrich the soil.

Black locusts seldom live longer than a hundred years. Two of the trees' many insect pests are the locust leafminer and the locust borer, both beetle larvae. The leafminer defoliates trees, which can cause death during times of drought. Locust borers chew feeding tunnels in the wood, which let in heart rot fungi.

Black locust wood is very heavy, at fifty-two pounds per cubic foot. Hard and strong, it is stiffer than hickory and more durable than white oak. Its fuel value is among the highest of any American tree. Because it lasts for many years in contact with the soil, black locust is the top choice for a fence-post. People have fashioned the wood into trunnels ("tree-nails") for holding together the wooden frames of ships (the wood, when wet, expands and becomes leakproof), insulator pins on telegraph and telephone poles, ladder rungs, buggy hubs, mine timbers, railroad ties, boxes, crates, and stakes.

Blue Spruce *(Picea pungens)*. This slow-growing conifer of the Rocky Mountains has been planted in yards, campuses, towns, cemeteries, and woodlots, and on watershed lands. Blue spruces are also grown on commercial Christmas tree farms. Mature specimens typically become 50 to 80 feet tall, with some climbing to more than 100 feet. Individuals can live 600 years or longer. The tree is conical in form, with stout branches pushing out horizontally from ground level to the topmost growing whorl. The stiff, spiny needles are about 1¼ inches long. They range in color from a frosty blue-green to a pale yellowish green and persist on the twigs for as long as ten years. The chestnut brown cones are about 4 inches long (longer than the cones of our native spruces). They are borne in the top 10 to 25 percent of the tree, mainly at the ends of the branches. Blue spruces provide nesting habitat for songbirds, and many birds find winter shelter in the dense foliage.

European or Black Alder *(Alnus glutinosa).* This small tree is a native of Europe, North Africa, and Asia. It has been widely planted in the northeastern United States and Canada. The scientific species name refers to the glutinous, or gummy, feel of the young twigs. European alders thrive along streams and in wetlands. *A. glutinosa* is more upright and treelike than our native alder species, growing to 30 feet tall. The serrated, usually doubletoothed leaves are blunt-ended; the female cones are ⅜ to ⅞ inch long, twice as large as those of our native alders. (A shrub, common winterberry holly, *Ilex verticillata,* is sometimes called black alder. It is not related to European alder or to our native alder species.)

Honey Locust *(Gleditsia triacanthos).* Also known as sweet locust and thorny locust, honey locust is primarily a Midwestern tree, with a range extending from Pennsylvania south and west to Alabama, Texas, and South Dakota. It has been widely planted and is now naturalized throughout the Northeast, in rural areas, towns, and cities. The largest honey locusts have been reported from stream valleys in southern Indiana and Illinois: trees up to 140 feet tall, with trunks 4 to 6 feet in diameter. Specimens in New England are smaller.

A mature honey locust has a short trunk, a broad, open crown, and spreading branches that droop at their ends. The roots divide abundantly and, in good soil, may penetrate 20 feet below ground. On young trees the bark is smooth, with many conspicuous lenticels; on older trees the bark is grayish brown to almost black, marked with a few vertical fissures dividing thick, slablike ridges with projecting edges. The trunk is studded with thorn clusters that resemble spiny sea urchins. The spines are 2 to 8 inches long and needle-sharp. Many of the thorns branch, with smaller thorns angling out to the side. Because the thorns arise from the tree's wood, they cannot easily be pulled off. In some cases the thorns bear leaves, demonstrating that they are modified branchlets.

The tree's real leaves are 6 to 15 inches long, compounded of twenty or so leaflets, each ⅜ to 1¼ inches long, often with a slightly wavy edge. Unlike that of black locust, the leaf of the honey locust has no terminal leaflet. Sometimes a leaf will compound a second time, with one or more additional compound leaves branching off partway along the shaft of the original leaf. Honey locust leaves turn yellow in autumn and drop off early in the season.

In spring, after leaf emergence in mid- to late May, the trees put out small, greenish flowers, with both male and female blossoms appearing on the same tree, generally on different branches. Insects pollinate the female flowers. The resulting fruits are flat, mahogany-colored pods 6 to 16 inches long, which may become twisted as they ripen in autumn. The pods fall off the trees unopened. They contain many oval, brownish seeds in a sweet pulp. Cattle and hogs eat the pods, as do squirrels, deer, opossums, birds, and other wildlife; the seeds are spread about in the animals' droppings. Honey locust seeds have tough, impermeable coats that can keep them viable for years. Individual seeds become permeable after varying amounts of time, so that a single autumn's crop can yield seedlings for several years. If a seed passes through an animal's digestive system, it is more apt to sprout than one remaining uneaten. Seedlings establish themselves in open terrain and beneath gaps in the forest canopy.

The wood is dense, hard, and durable, much like that of black locust. People use it for fenceposts, railroad ties, rough lumber, and fuel. The Cherokee Indians in Tennessee made bows out of honey locust. No doubt they found many things to do with the thorns, as did the European settlers, who used them for carding wool and pinning shut the mouths of sacks.

Horse-Chestnut *(Aesculus hippocastanum).* The Eurasian horse-chestnut has been planted as a shade tree in the northeastern United States for many years. Henry Wadsworth Longfellow was probably referring to this tree and not the American chestnut *(Castanea dentata),* a native forest species, when he wrote in his oft-declaimed poem: "Under the spreading chestnut tree/the village smithy stands." It is said that horsemen in Turkey used the seeds of this plant to brew a remedy given to horses afflicted with coughing, a practice commemorated in both the tree's common name and its scientific species name.

Horse-chestnuts grow 60 to 75 feet tall. The tree's large compound leaf consists of a whorl of seven to nine broad, wedge-shaped leaflets. White flowers appear in late May, grouped in candelabra-like clusters 6 to 12 inches long. The resulting seeds develop inside leathery, thorn-studded, walnut-size husks, one seed per husk. The seeds are attractive: smooth, mahogany brown, somewhat flattened, and with a tan eyespot. They contain a toxic glycoside and have fatally poisoned children who have eaten them. Symptoms include depression, vomiting, weakness, stupor, and paralysis.

Norway Maple *(Acer platanoides).* In the Old World, Norway maple ranges from Norway to northern Turkey. Introduced to America as a shade tree, it has spread far and wide, thanks to its winged seeds dispersing on the wind. Mature specimens are 50 to 60 feet tall with a 2-foot trunk diameter. The leaves are big and broad, up to 8 inches across. They have the classic maple shape, with five coarsely toothed lobes, and they turn bright yellow in autumn. The leafstalks, when broken, exude a milky sap. Because it tolerates pollution better than our native maples, *A. platanoides* has been planted extensively as a street tree in urban areas. In the wild, look for it along roadsides and on disturbed lands. Norway maple casts a full, deep shade that can inhibit native plant regeneration.

Norway Spruce *(Picea abies)*. With its long, pendulous branches cloaked with soft-looking needles, Norway spruce looks as if it is wearing a green robe. It grows 50 to 80 feet tall, with a trunk 2 feet in diameter; very old trees can reach 125 feet in height and 3 feet in diameter. The lower branches sweep down to near the ground. The evergreen needles are ½ to 1 inch long, stiff, and a shiny dark green. The 4- to 6-inch cones are the largest of any spruce. In winter red and white-winged crossbills extract and eat seeds from the cones. Many birds seek shelter in Norway spruces during harsh winter weather, including mourning doves, crows, blue jays, tufted titmice, dark-eyed juncos, ruffed grouse, northern goshawks, and barred owls. A native of northern Europe, *P. abies* is a key forest species in Germany, Switzerland, Austria, and Russia. It has been planted as an ornamental and a forest and watershed tree throughout the United States.

Osage-Orange *(Maclura pomifera)*. From a limited range in Texas, Oklahoma, and Arkansas, osage-orange has been transplanted throughout North America east of the Rocky Mountains. Its common name stems from its place of origin, the area where the Osage Indians dwelt, and from its fruit, a yellow-green sphere like a lumpy, oversize orange. Osage-oranges thrive in fertile soils along streams but will also grow on drier upland sites. The tree becomes 30 feet tall, with a trunk 1 to 2 feet in diameter. The leaves are about 4 inches long, oval, and have a pointed tip; their upper surfaces are glossy green. In the past, farmers planted osage-orange hedgerows: The trees' inch-long thorns helped create barriers to keep livestock in fields. Some authorities estimate that more than a quarter million miles of osage-orange hedgerows were in place during the 1800s, before the invention of barbed wire.

Osage-oranges are either male or female. Inconspicuous greenish flowers blossom around June. The wind-pollinated female flowers become the wrinkly oranges, 4 or 5 inches in diameter and with a faint citrus smell. The hard, stippled surface of an osage-orange is made up of many small drupes (a drupe is any fruit with a fleshy part surrounding a single seed) compacted together. Too heavy to be distributed by the wind, and with seeds that are not especially attractive as wildlife food, the fruits are perhaps scattered by periodic flooding of the rivers along which the trees often grow in their native habitat. One wonders whether large, now-extinct mammals—Pleistocene-era mastodons, for example—may have distributed the seeds in their droppings. The wood of the osage-orange is hard, dense, and flexible. Native Americans used it for bows and war clubs. People have fashioned it into fenceposts, railroad ties, duck calls, harps, policemen's nightsticks, and wagon wheels. Osage-orange hedgerows offer escape cover to many birds and mammals.

Scots Pine *(Pinus sylvestris)*. A native of Eurasia, including the Scottish Highlands, Scots pine has been planted widely in North America by Christmas tree growers, farmers, city parks, conservation agencies, and water companies and other entities wanting to reforest watersheds or restore damaged lands. If Scots pine gets the ample sunlight it requires, it will thrive under a wide range of soil and moisture conditions. Trees can become 70 feet tall or taller, although most do not exceed 50 feet. The needles are 2 to 3 inches long, stout, sharp-pointed, and twisted. They come two to a bundle. From a distance, Scots pine can look like pitch pine; a good way to distinguish *P. sylvestris* is from its upper trunk and adjacent branches, whose bark is an eye-catching orange. The egg-shaped cones are 1¼ to 2½ inches long. The wood, relatively hard for a pine, is used for lumber and paper pulp. Ice storms and heavy, wet snow often break the top and limbs of this tree.

Sweet Cherry *(Prunus avium)*. The domestic sweet cherry is a native of Eurasia. Having escaped cultivation in North America, it now grows in forests, woods edges, and fencerows. The species name, *avium,* means "of birds" and refers to the fruit's attractiveness as a food for birds. Many sweet cherries have been planted by bird droppings. The mature tree can become 70 feet tall with a wide-spreading crown. The oval leaves are 3 to 6 inches long and end in a pointed tip; coarse teeth line their margins. The red to purplish cherries are ¾ to 1 inch in diameter, or about twice the size of the native black cherry. The handsomest paneling I have ever seen—a rich, fiery red, with orange and mahogany highlights and a swirling grain pattern—came from the wood of sweet cherry.

Weeping Willow *(Salix babylonica).* Weeping willow ranges from Canada to Georgia; it also grows west of the Mississippi River. Despite its scientific species name, China is the country of origin for this handsome tree. (When taxonomists first classified this species, they confused it with a poplar from the Euphrates River region of the Middle East.) The mature tree stands about 70 feet tall. The short trunk divides into many branches that arch upward, then cascade gracefully down. The finely saw-toothed, blade-shaped leaves are 2 to 5 inches long and ¼ to ½ inch broad. They are attached to thin, flexible yellowish or brown branches and twigs that, in drooping, seem to "weep" toward the ground. Weeping willow is one of the first deciduous trees to put forth foliage in spring and one of the last to shed its leaves in autumn. Greenish female flowers light up the tree in early spring. Weeping willows have been planted on farmsteads, in meadows, cemeteries, and parks, and on the banks of lakes and ponds.

Other naturalized willows include white willow *(S. alba),* a wetlands species from Europe brought to North America as early as the colonial period; and crack willow *(S. fragilis),* so named because its brittle twigs break off readily at the base. Settlers introduced crack willow to produce charcoal for the manufacturing of gunpowder. It escaped from cultivation and is now common along streams in parts of the Northeast.

White Mulberry *(Morus alba).* White mulberry is a Chinese tree originally imported to provide food for silkworms. The silk industry never got off the ground in the United States, but white mulberry escaped from cultivation and is now a fairly common tree, growing in fencerows, old fields, and disturbed areas. White mulberry is slightly smaller than the native red mulberry *(M. rubra).* It has yellow-brown bark, as opposed to the reddish brown bark of *M. rubra.* Its toothed leaves are hairless and smooth, not sandpapery like those of red mulberry. The leaves of both species are variable in shape. The fruits of white mulberry are whitish to pink, occasionally purple. Ripening in June, they make good preserves and are excellent dried and added to bread and muffins. Like red mulberries, they feed many wild birds and mammals. The unripe fruits and raw shoots contain hallucinogenic compounds that can make people extremely ill.

Glossary

Achene. A small, hard, dry, often seedlike fruit.

Ament. A spike-shaped reproductive structure supporting flowers that are all of the same sex; also called a catkin.

Bisexual. A flower that has both male and female sexual organs; also referred to as perfect.

Blade. The green, light-gathering part of a leaf, apart from the stalk.

Cambium. A layer of tissue, one cell thick, between the bark and the wood; through cell division, it produces phloem to the outside and xylem to the inside, annually increasing a tree's trunk diameter.

Catkin. A spike-shaped reproductive structure supporting flowers that are all of the same sex. (See also Ament.)

Clone. A group of genetically identical trees sprouting from a common root system.

Compound leaf. A leaf made up of two or more similar leaflets attached to a stalk.

Crown. The upper mass of limbs and branches in a tree.

Deciduous. Falling off, usually at the close of a season.

Drupe. A fruit whose flesh covers a hard pit or stone, which in turn houses a seed.

Habitat. The home of an animal or plant.

Heartwood. Woody tissue of the interior of the trunk, dead and no longer involved in transferring water; it is usually darker than the sapwood.

Lanceolate. Shaped like the head of a lance, tapering from a rounded base toward a pointed tip.

Leaflet. One of the small blades that makes up a compound leaf.

Lenticel. A pore in the bark of trunk or limb that allows an exchange of gases between interior wood tissues and the atmosphere.

Lobe. A segment of a leaf separated from other similar parts by a notch or cleft.

Midrib. The central, main rib or vein of a leaf or leaflet.

Nut. A hard, dry, single-seeded fruit with a stiff, sometimes thick covering.

Ovate. Egg-shaped.

Panicle. A compound flower cluster.

Petiole. The leafstalk.

Phloem. Food-conducting tissue; carries sugars throughout the tree. As it ages, it becomes part of the bark.

Pith. The soft, spongy tissue inside a twig.

Pollen. Dustlike substance released by a male flower, carrying genetic material and capable of fertilizing a female flower.

Pome. A fleshy fruit with an inner, seed-bearing core; for example, an apple.

Raceme. A collection of stalked flowers arranged singly on a stem.

Rachis. The elongated central stem of a compound leaf.

Radicle. The part of a plant embryo that develops into a root.

Ramet. A trunk that springs up from and belongs to a clone.

Samara. A winged fruit; also called a key.

Sapwood. The newly formed, light-colored wood lying to the outside of the heartwood; it carries water up from the roots to the leaves. Also called xylem.

Simple leaf. A leaf that is not compound and has a central midrib integral with the blade.

Sinus. The cleft or notch between two lobes of a leaf.

Stamen. The pollen-bearing part of a flower.

Sterigmata. Projections from twigs that bear the leaves or needles.

Strobile. A fruit sheathed with overlapping scales, such as the cones and conelets produced by pines, hemlocks, birches, and other trees.

Taproot. A strong, vertical, central root that anchors a tree in the ground.

Umbel. A flower cluster in which all the stalks arise from the same point.

Xylem. Sapwood.

Additional Reading

OVER THE YEARS, TWO FIELD guides have stood me in good stead. One is *A Field Guide to Eastern Trees,* by George A. Petrides, published in 1998 by Houghton Mifflin. The second is *The Audubon Society Field Guide to North American Trees,* by Elbert L. Little, published by Alfred A. Knopf; I have the first edition of 1980. As well as written descriptions, the Petrides book presents illustrations, while the Little volume relies on photographs. Using the combination of illustrations and photographs helps me identify trees more easily.

For detailed scientific information on trees, I rely on *Silvics of North America,* a two-volume compendium published by the U.S.D.A. Forest Service. It is available in book form and online at www.na.fs.fed.us/spfo/pubs/silvics_manual/table_of_contents.htm.

Reading the Forested Landscape: A Natural History of New England, by Tom Wessels, examines the evolution of the woodlands of central New England (southern Maine, New Hampshire, and Vermont, and northern and western Massachusetts). The book includes etchings and illustrations by Brian Cohen. The Countryman Press published this handsome work in 1997. Each chapter discusses a type of forest disturbance and teaches the reader to recognize its lasting evidence on the face of the land. Wessels is an ecologist at Antioch New England Graduate School.

One of my favorite books is *The Trees in My Forest*, by Bernd Heinrich. A University of Vermont ecologist, Heinrich has a marvelous grasp of how different aspects of nature fit together—weather, soils, physical forces, mammals, birds, insects, microbes—along with the ability to present scientific information in an engaging, readable prose. The book, published by HarperCollins in 1997, is illustrated with the author's own watercolors and pencil drawings.

New England Natives: A Celebration of People and Trees, by Sheila Connor, contains history, biological information, and lore. The book emphasizes how New Englanders have used trees, from the earliest Native Americans up until today. Harvard University Press published this large-format volume in 1994. It presents numerous photographs (both historical and botanically descriptive ones), etchings, portraits (of people and trees), maps, and diagrams, plus an exhaustive bibliography. Connor is an archivist at Harvard's Arnold Arboretum.

The following books also give insight into eastern trees and forests:

Borland, Hal. *A Countryman's Woods*. New York: Alfred A. Knopf, 1986.

Davis, Mary Bird, Ed. *Eastern Old-Growth Forests*. Washington, D.C.: Island Press, 1996.

Eastman, John. *The Book of Forest and Thicket*. Mechanicsburg, PA: Stackpole Books, 1992.

———. *The Book of Swamp and Bog*. Mechanicsburg, PA: Stackpole Books, 1995.

———. *The Book of Field and Roadside*. Mechanicsburg, PA: Stackpole Books, 2003.

Kershner, Bruce, and Robert T. Leverett. *The Sierra Club Guide to the Ancient Forests of the Northeast*. San Francisco: Sierra Club Books, 2004.

Kricher, John C. *A Field Guide to Eastern Forests of North America*. Boston: Houghton Mifflin, 1998.

Lillard, Richard G. *The Great Forest.* New York: Alfred A. Knopf, 1947.

Little, Charles. *The Dying of the Trees.* New York: Viking Penguin, 1995.

Little, Elbert L. Jr. *Atlas of United States Trees.* Washington, D.C.: U.S. Department of Agriculture, 1971.

Peattie, Donald Culross. *A Natural History of Trees of Eastern and Central North America.* Boston: Houghton Mifflin, 1966.

Pielou, E. C. *The World of Northern Evergreens.* Ithaca, N.Y.: Cornell University Press, 1988.

Platt, Rutherford H. *Discover American Trees.* New York: Dodd Mead, 1968.

Sloan, Eric. *A Reverence for Wood.* New York: Funk and Wagnalls, 1965.

Yahner, Richard H. *Eastern Deciduous Forest.* Minneapolis: University of Minnesota Press, 2000.

Index

Page numbers in *italics* indicate illustrations.

mountain-ash, American,
182–84, *183*
mulberry, black. *See* mulberry, red
mulberry, red, 185–86
mulberry, white, 299–300
musclewood. *See* ironwood

nettletree. *See* hackberry, northern

oak, bear. *See* oak, scrub
oak, black, 193–95
oak, bur, 215–16
oak, chestnut, 210–14, *211*
oak, chinkapin, 216
oak, iron. *See* oak, post
oak, mossycup. *See* oak, bur
oak, mountain. *See* oak, chestnut
oak, northern red, 187–93, *189*
oak, pin, 198–201, *200*
oak, post, 214–15
oak, red. *See* oak, northern red
oak, rock. *See* oak, chestnut
oak, scarlet, 195–98, *196*
oak, scrub, 201–2
oak, swamp, 208–9
oak, swamp white. *See* oak,
swamp
oak, water. *See* oak, pin
oak, white, *196*, 202–8, *205*
oak, yellow. *See* oak, black; oak,
chinkapin
oak, yellowbark. *See* oak, black
osage-orange, 297–98

pepperidge. *See* black-gum
pigeonberry. *See* dogwood,
alternate-leaf
pine, Austrian, 291–92
pine, black. *See* pine, pitch
pine, black jack. *See* pine, jack
pine, eastern white, 217–24,
219, 223
pine, gray. *See* pine, jack
pine, jack, *223,* 231–35, *232*
pine, Norway. *See* pine, red
pine, scrub. *See* pine, jack
pine, pitch, *223,* 224–28
pine, red, *223,* 228–31
pine, Scots, 298
pine, spruce. *See* hemlock, eastern
pine, torch. *See* pine, pitch
pine, white. *See* pine, eastern
white
planetree, American. *See* sycamore
poplar. *See* aspen, bigtooth; aspen,
quaking
poplar, balsam. *See* balsam poplar
poplar, tulip. *See* tuliptree
poplar, yellow. *See* tuliptree
popple. *See* aspen, bigtooth;
aspen, quaking

redcedar, eastern, 81–85, *82*
rowan, American. *See* mountain-
ash, American

sassafras, 236–40, *238*

Index of Scientific Names

About the Author

CHARLES FERGUS LIVES WITH HIS wife and son in the Northeast Kingdom of Vermont, in an old farmhouse on 108 acres of land, 80 of which are forested. He has written about nature and the outdoors for many magazines and newspapers, including *Audubon, Country Journal, Northern Woodlands, Science, Pennsylvania Game News,* and the *New York Times.* He is the author of fifteen books, including *Thornapples: The Comings, Goings, and Outdoor Doings of a Naturalist; Swamp Screamer: At Large with the Florida Panther; Summer at Little Lava,* named by Library Journal as one of the Best Sci-Tech Books of 1998; *Wildlife of Pennsylvania and the Northeast;* and *A Hunter's Book of Days.*